GANGS, PSEUDO-MILITARIES, AND OTHER MODERN MERCENARIES

International and Security Affairs Series
Edwin G. Corr, General Editor

Also by Max G. Manwaring

(ed. with Court Prisk) *El Salvador at War: An Oral History of Conflict from the 1979 Insurrection to the Present* (Washington, D.C., 1988)

(ed.) *Uncomfortable Wars: Toward a New Paradigm of Low Intensity Conflict* (Boulder, 1991)

(ed.) *Gray Area Phenomena: Confronting the New World Disorder* (Boulder, 1993)

(ed. with Wm. J. Olsen) *Managing Contemporary Conflict: Pillars of Success* (Boulder, 1996)

Spain and the Defense of European Security Interests: A Military Capability Analysis (Boulder, 1997)

(ed. with John T. Fishel) *Toward Responsibility in the New World Disorder: Challenges and Lessons of Peace Operations* (Portland, 1998)

(ed. with Anthony James Joes) *Beyond Declaring Victory and Coming Home: The Challenges of Peace and Stability Operations* (Westport, Conn., 2000)

(ed.) *Deterrence in the Twenty-first Century* (Portland, 2001)

(ed.) *Environmental Security and Global Stability: Problems and Responses* (Lanham, Md., 2002)

(ed. with Edwin G. Corr and Robert H. Dorff) *The Search for Security: A U.S. Grand Strategy for the Twenty-first Century* (Westport, Conn., 2003)

(with John T. Fishel) *Uncomfortable Wars Revisited* (Norman, Okla., 2006)

Insurgency, Terrorism, and Crime: Shadows from the Past and Portents for the Future (Norman, Okla., 2008)

GANGS, PSEUDO-MILITARIES, AND OTHER MODERN MERCENARIES

New Dynamics in Uncomfortable Wars

Max G. Manwaring

Foreword by Edwin G. Corr
Afterword by John T. Fishel

University of Oklahoma Press : Norman

Publication of this book is made possible through the generosity of Edith Kinney Gaylord.

Library of Congress Cataloging-in-Publication Data

Manwaring, Max G.
    Gangs, pseudo-militaries, and other modern mercenaries : new dynamics in uncomfortable wars / Max G. Manwaring ; foreword by Edwin G. Corr ; afterword by John T. Fishel.
        p. cm. — (International and security affairs series ; v. 6)
    Includes bibliographical references and index.
    ISBN 978-0-8061-4146-6 (cloth)
    ISBN 978-0-8061-6577-6 (paper)
    1. Gangs—Latin America.   2. Gangs—Europe, Western.   3. Asymmetric warfare—Latin America.   4. Asymmetric warfare—Europe, Western.
5. Mercenary troops—Latin America.   6. Mercenary troops—Europe, Western.   7. Counterinsurgency.   8. Political stability.   9. Sovereignty.
I. Title.
    HV6439.L29M36 2010
    322.4'2—dc22

                                                                2010008314

Gangs, Pseudo-militaries, and Other Modern Mercenaries: New Dynamics in Uncomfortable Wars is Volume 6 in the International and Security Affairs Series.

The paper in this book meets the guidelines for permanence and durability of the Committee on Production Guidelines for Book Longevity of the Council on Library Resources, Inc. ∞

Contents

FOREWORD

EDWIN G. CORR

Professor Max G. Manwaring in this book expands and elevates in sophistication his insightful, prescriptive, two-decades-old paradigm of and strategy for our country's successful political/informational/ military campaigns and operations in what he and John Fishel have called *uncomfortable wars*. These uncomfortable wars include what is again being referred to as counterinsurgency (COIN) in describing the United States' current involvement and actions in Iraq and Afghanistan. Manwaring focuses on, describes, and analyzes a range of state- and nonstate-related "gangs, agitators, armed propagandists, popular militias, youth leagues, and other mercenary organizations" and the effective and lethal roles such "gangs" play as midwives to social violence, insurgencies, revolutions, and civil wars.

Dr. Manwaring combines theoretical foundation (he quotes highly relevant contributions from Sun Tzu to Lenin to contemporary political-military thinkers) with the political case studies approach. He examines the current threat to international society and its system of nation-states that comes from asymmetric, irregular groups of nonstate actors whose purpose is to challenge and break down the existing social order and establish a new order—even though (in contrast to the bygone challenge of revolutionary communism) the emerging new social orders and forms of government are not always well defined. Manwaring shows us that the tactics of the nonstate actors and their supporters today have been used in the past and were well described by V. I. Lenin and others. Tying nonstate actors and state-supported gangs' activities and tactics to the teachings of Lenin is a brilliant and useful insight. At the same time, the case studies illustrate the "ad hoc, negative and reactive crisis management" responses of states instead of sound, proactive engagements based on well-conceived policy and strategy. The lessons learned from Manwaring's case studies provide principles and guidance for coping with the nonstate gangs employed by both states and nonstate challengers.

This book is grounded in Manwaring's more than thirty years of thinking about, studying, researching, and teaching warfare and strategy. It is a logical progression from John Fishel and Max Manwaring's *Uncomfortable Wars Revisited* (2006) and Manwaring's *Insurgency, Terrorism, and Crime* (2008).[1] I began my foreword to the Fishel and Manwaring book saying it was

> a synthesis of the most important body of thought and literature on national security strategy, policy, and implementation that has emerged over the past two decades to guide the United States in its conduct of foreign policy and war in an increasingly dangerous and changed world. The Manwaring Paradigm, or the SWORD Model, . . . has gained acceptance among leading thinkers on national security—both practitioners and academics—in the United States. The paradigm is the basis for a number of scholarly books and articles. It has become a part of the core curriculum at military universities, schools, and training institutions of the U.S. armed forces and national security community. The paradigm and the suppositions derived from it have been incorporated into U.S. Army and U.S. Air Force doctrine in field manuals and texts. In a very real sense this paradigm—originally set forth by Max Manwaring and subsequently elaborated and refined by him, John Fishel, a core group of intellectually close colleagues and practitioners, and a number of other contributors—is increasingly assuming the role in national security thinking and action today that George Kennan's policy of containment did throughout the half-century of the cold war.[2]

I stand by that statement. The analytical power of the Manwaring Paradigm and the validity of its emphasis on the primacy of politics and legitimacy (achieved by protecting and gaining acceptance by the civilian population) have received heightened and broadened attention since I wrote the above-cited foreword. Ironically, though the ideas pioneered and long championed by Manwaring (and Fishel) are in vogue in current writings and discussions about counterinsurgency, Manwaring and Fishel have received only limited recognition for them. The U.S. Army Field Manual (FM) 3-24 and Marine Corps Warfighting Publication No. 3-335, entitled *Counterinsurgency* (2006), builds greatly on the Manwaring concepts. The doctrine was belatedly applied and tested in Iraq: first by the United States Marine Corps and the U.S. Army in Al Anbar Province in 2005–2007 and subsequently at the national level in Iraq during the Multi-National Force–Iraq "surge," designed and led by General David H. Petraeus, beginning in 2008. The approach is credited for the United States' delayed but recognized relative military (but in 2009 not yet political) success in Iraq.

The improvements in the Iraqi security and political environment resulted, says Linda Robinson (in *Tell Me How All This Ends: General David Petraeus and the Search for a Way Out of Iraq* [2008]), because "Petraeus' willingness to grapple with Iraqi politics made all the difference." Robinson adds, "Petraeus waded deeper into the political mire than most other U.S. Generals would have."[3] I note that an unsung hero in the emphasis on the political and the success of the surge was U.S. Ambassador Ryan Crocker, a career Foreign Service Officer, who is an Arabist, at home in the Arabic language; knows Middle East culture and politics and how things are achieved there; and was a partner to Petraeus in making the surge a military success.

Field Manual 3-24 was published by the University of Chicago Press in 2007 with a foreword by Army General David H. Petraeus and Marine Corps Lieutenant General James F. Amos; another foreword by U.S. Army Lieutenant Colonel John A. Nagl; and an introduction by Sarah Sewall. An allegation in the two generals' foreword was that COIN doctrine had been ignored for the twenty to twenty-five years preceding the Second Iraq War, while Nagl asserted in his foreword that only "lonely voices" argued for an army focus on COIN in the

wake of the cold war, which left the army unprepared in this area of
conflict, and for which coalition forces in Iraq did not expect or plan in
the intervention to depose Saddam Hussein.[4]

The "lonely voices" and the incorporation of the lessons they had
learned into field manuals through their analysis and research of the
correlates for success in COIN were, I believe, more prominent and
widespread within the armed forces than is depicted in these forewords. I say this as a person who was involved as midlevel Foreign
Service officer in the insurgencies and the war in Southeast Asia, as
the U.S. ambassador to Peru during the Shining Path guerrilla insurgency, and as U.S. ambassador to El Salvador during the insurgency
and civil war there—and as someone who lectured at a number of U.S.
armed forces universities and schools throughout the 1990s and, as a
university administrator, was involved in the management in Iraq of a
program with Iraqi universities and ministries during 2003–2007. Even
though there was a turning of the U.S. military from counterinsurgency
immediately after the Vietnam War (American troops left in December 1971 and Saigon fell in 1975), U.S. involvement in insurgencies in
the 1970s and 1980s forced a return to the matter. The end of the 1970s
and the 1980s were particularly notable when the Soviets invaded
Afghanistan, the Sandinistas took power in Nicaragua, the Iranians
held Americans hostage in Tehran, and U.S. interests were jeopardized
by insurgencies in Colombia, Peru, Guatemala, El Salvador, Ethiopia,
Angola, and other states.

Fishel in the "Small Wars Council," part of the *Small Wars Journal,*
notes as a sign of revival of importance of counterinsurgency the 1981
publication of FM 100-20, *Low-Intensity Conflict.* This was followed by
Deputy Chief of Staff of the Army General Max Thurman's charge in
1984 to the Strategic Studies Institute of the U.S. Army to study the
correlates of success in counterinsurgency, which resulted in the Manwaring Paradigm (known as the SWORD Model) in 1986. This research
subsequently produced a joint U.S. Army–U.S. Air Force publication
that was adopted 1990 as FM 100-20, *Military Operations in Low Intensity Conflict.* This manual introduced the term "Operations Other than
War" (OTWA), which was later replaced in 1995 by "Military Operations Other than War" (MOOTWA) in a joint publication, these terms

perhaps revealing an effort to distance the armed forces from the essential concept of joint military-civilian campaigns.[5]

There was exposure to and teaching about COIN, especially to mid-level U.S. military officers, but these teachings were unappreciated if not ignored by many general officers and by colonels on the fast track to the general officer level. This situation derived from Weberian bureaucratic imperatives in large part caused by the "hangover" from the cold war that still permeated the Department of Defense and the U.S. armed forces and, not inconsequently, pressure from U.S. defense contractors who advocated to congresspersons who had defense jobs in their districts. This combination was enough to maintain a highly technical, expensively equipped, large-unit-oriented, Star Wars–type fighting force (which could be argued to be necessary for protection against emerging great powers), but the Department of Defense and the armed forces gave insufficient priority to COIN. Bigness, the commitment of large numbers of troops, and the use of costly sophisticated equipment was definitely better from these groups' points of view.

This situation was reinforced by a bias within the military personnel system that favored promotion and recognition of officers who commanded large units or oversaw costly equipment versus officers involved in COIN situations and foreign area specialists, who on the whole had a better appreciation of the value of counterinsurgency capabilities and for advisory and training roles by our armed forces personnel as opposed to direct military interventions. The continued dominance and concentration on exclusive, large, ever more expensively equipped armed forces rather than a military also focusing on asymmetric warfare and counterinsurgency is understandable up to the end of the cold war. It is less so after the cold war ended, because the United States has been intermittently engaged directly and indirectly in COIN and small wars from the end of World War II to the present: Korea, Cuba, the Philippines, Bolivia, Lebanon, Vietnam, Angola, Ethiopia, Peru, El Salvador, Nicaragua, Grenada, Panama, Haiti, Afghanistan (1979), Somalia, Kosovo, Bosnia.

The Manwaring Paradigm for COIN, or the SWORD Model (the U.S. Army's acronym), was part of the curriculum of U.S. armed forces universities and schools from the 1980s until the Second Iraqi War. It was incorporated into U.S armed forces field manuals and publications, and during this period a fairly large body of literature on the Manwaring Paradigm was produced,[6] as well as writings on counterinsurgency by other military analysts and academics. Worth noting is an article in *Military Review* (March–April 2006) titled "Principles, Imperatives and Paradoxes of Counterinsurgency," by Eliot Cohen, Lt. Col. Conrad Crane, Lt. Col. Jon Horvath, and Lt. Col. John Nagl. Crane, who was a classmate of General Petraeus's, has a doctorate in history from Stanford University; Nagl, a Rhodes Scholar, earned a doctorate from Oxford University. Both had major roles in drafting the U.S. Army FM 3-24 (also issued as Marine Corps Publication No. 3-335), *Counterinsurgency.* Their principles of COIN were similar to the tenets of counterinsurgency that Manwaring, Fishel, and other professors at U.S. armed forces colleges had been teaching. In fact, these four authors in an endnote to their article expressed thanks to Manwaring for their understanding of legitimacy as a main objective of counterinsurgency campaigns.[7]

Because of the United States' experience for almost a decade of engagement in Afghanistan and Iraq, current thought about how to do counterinsurgency has, I think, been overly affected by these experiences. The Petraeus and Amos FM 3-24 (2006) reflects this. The U.S. Army's new FM 3-07, *Stability Operations and Support Operations* (2008), attempts to rectify this bias by predicting that conflicts for the next twenty to twenty-five years will not be like Afghanistan and Iraq but will consist of U.S. indirect support of foreign governments battling against their own insurgencies. However, in my conversations with U.S. military officers, they find it difficult to think of themselves as supporters, trainers, and advisers rather than as engaged warriors. They discuss accurately their school-taught principles of counterinsurgency but seem not to have internalized these principles and still are prone to think in terms of the employment of U.S. combat units and large numbers of troops.

No two insurgencies are alike, but there are generalized principles that are valid for all of them. I am convinced that Todd Greenlee in his book title appropriately called the U.S. counterinsurgency effort in Central America (El Salvador and Nicaragua) the *Crossroads of Intervention*

(2008), that is, a crossroads between the Vietnam War and our twenty-first-century intervention in Iraq. By this he suggests that we got it right in El Salvador but not in Vietnam or Iraq. U.S. involvement in Central America was successful, in part, because the geographical scope was smaller but also because the direction and organization of U.S. strategy and counterinsurgency campaigns remained largely under civilian authority in cooperation with and with the full support of the U.S. armed forces regional commander. The stakes in terms of our national interest arguably were greater than those in Vietnam or Iraq or Afghanistan, because of the proximity of the region to the United States and the involvement of the USSR superpower in the conflict. The civilian leadership forced the primacy of politics, and our national interests predominated over winning military battles, even though winning battles was a vital part of success.[8] The counterinsurgency there was conducted in accord with the Manwaring Paradigm variables, which simultaneously grew to a fairly large degree out of the Central American conflict (while being verified by case and statistical studies of other insurgencies), and at the same time the paradigm's development within the U.S. Southern Command was helping to shape the role of the U.S. armed forces in the El Salvador conflict. (That role was also influenced greatly by the American public's strong opposition to U.S. direct military intervention in the wake of the U.S. failure in the Vietnam War.)

The approach taken by Professor Manwaring and his colleagues is more abstract and thereby more applicable to the range of insurgency types that exist and that the United States is likely to face in the twenty-first century. His concepts and variables are also more useful at the global, policy, and strategic levels than are the recent armed forces field manuals, which are most applicable at the campaign implementation level and for commanders at the battalion level and below.

In the same explorative and innovative manner as Professor Manwaring's previous work on warfare, this current book examines critically and prescriptively the phenomena of gangs and nonstate actors and the very significant role they perform both in carrying out successful insurgencies and in governments' dealings with them—not only countering and defeating them but also in governments themselves using such groups to defeat insurgents. Though the El Salvadoran civil war is not among the case studies employed by Manwaring in this book, my experience in that conflict fully validates the necessity of understanding and having proven tactics for coping with such gangs and popular organizations. The impact and violence of gangs and "peoples' fronts" employed by the Farabundo Martí National Liberation Front (FMLN)—especially by one of its five guerrilla armies/political fronts, the Popular Liberation Front (FPL), which followed the Vietnam communist pattern of revolution by "fight fight, talk talk"—was extremely effective. I know even better now how the FPL manipulated and effectively employed these groups, because of my recent talks with Salvador Sanchez Ceren (nom de guerre, Leonel Gonzalez), an FPL *comandante* and the 2009-elected vice president of El Salvador.[9]

Once more, Dr. Manwaring—drawing on history, citing great strategic and political thinkers, and extracting lessons from case studies—contributes richly to the literature of counterinsurgency and warfare. This time he introduces much-needed new thinking (blended with related writings of Vladimir Ilyich Lenin) about and provides answers to the threats of gangs and nonstate actors that are allied with and used by insurgents (and by counterinsurgents) to accomplish their objectives. Enjoy and remember the truths of another intriguing, valuable, and good read by Max G. Manwaring! Our national leaders need to internalize and be guided by his knowledge and wisdom.

PREFACE

This is another book in a series aimed at revitalizing strategic thinking on "uncomfortable wars," that is, conflicts that involve nonstate actors. In the past, policy makers and academics have tended to dismiss nonstate political actors as nothing more than inconsequential bit players in the global security arena. To add insult to injury, journalists are giving most of their headlines and sound bites to the conflicts in Afghanistan and Iraq. Yet there are over one hundred small, irregular, asymmetric, and uncomfortable wars ongoing around the world today. In these wars, there is much to be learned by anyone who has the responsibility of dealing with, analyzing, or reporting on threats generated by political actors who do not rely on highly structured organizations, large numbers of military forces, or costly weaponry.

These actors include a complex, protean, and enigmatic mix of transnational criminal organizations, small private (mercenary) military organizations, "street gangs" that control more than streets, small paramilitary or vigilante organizations, popular militias, youth leagues, and ordinary criminal triggermen. Additionally, many state- and nonstate-associated gangs—popular militias, youth leagues, criminal gangs *(bandas criminales)*, and other loosely organized networks of "propaganda-agitator" (political-criminal) gangs—are operating as state and nonstate surrogates in the contemporary asymmetric and irregular security arena. These kinds of actors have been operating for hundreds of years as "unofficial henchmen" that can be put to use in virtually any given contingency. Vladimir Ilyich Lenin articulated the political vision within which many nonstate and nation-state political actors now operate. Lenin argued that anyone wishing to force radical political-economic-social change or compel an adversary to accede to one's will must organize, train, and employ a body of political agitator groups. His intent was straightforward: if these instruments of statecraft succeed in helping to tear apart the fabric on which a targeted society rests, the instability and violence they create can serve as the "midwife of a new social order." In any event, in any phase of a revolutionary process, political-agitator gangs play substantial roles in helping their political patrons prepare to take control of a targeted political entity. This defines war, as well as insurgency, and shifts the asymmetric global challenge from abstract to real.

The relevance of this book, beyond serving as an attempt to address a major gap in the international relations and hegemonic war literature, is in its transmission of hard-learned lessons of the past and present to current and future decision, policy, and opinion makers. Accordingly, in the introduction I examine a few premier cases that illustrate how populists and neopopulists, New Left and New Socialists, criminal nonstate actors, and other state and nonstate actors use political-criminal (propaganda-agitator) gangs, people's militias, or youth leagues for national, regional, and global hegemonic purposes. After exploring Lenin's theoretical reality, chapter 1 presents vignettes that illustrate the diversity, complexity, and ambiguity of the contemporary gang phenomenon. Then follows an examination of five specific cases: first, the state versus parts of its own society (Argentine Piqueteros); second, nonstate actors versus other nonstate actors and the state (Colombian criminal gangs); third, a nation-state versus other states through proxies (Venezuelan popular militias); fourth, nonstate hegemonic actors versus nation-states (Al Qaeda in Europe); and, last, nonstate actors (private armies) versus other nonstate actors and the Mexican state. In these terms, this book provides a different and essential perspective regarding the omnipresent unconventional war situation. It also, one hopes, might be an instrument in generating success against persistent "unofficial" state and nonstate threats and eventually turning that success into sustainable internal and external peace and well-being.

With this brief review of the scope of the project as background, I would like to thank some of the people whose influence, knowledge, experience, wisdom, support, and patience made this book possible. Acknowledging and thanking every person who has helped somewhere along the way would be impossible. However, a few of the "usual suspects" must be given some credit for their contributory efforts. They include Ambassador Edwin G. Corr, Lieutenant Colonel (Dr.) John T. Fishel (U.S. Army, ret.), and Colonel Robert M. Herrick (U.S. Army, ret.). These individuals have been constant colleagues, friends, and mentors for over thirty years. The suspects also include, in alphabetical order, Dr. Robert J. Bunker, Colonel Arturo Contreras (Chilean Army, ret.), Ambassador David C. Jordan, Dr. Gabriel Marcella, Ambassador Ambler H. Moss, Jr., Dr. William J. Olson, and Colonel John Waghelstein (U.S. Army, ret.). They all have made me seem more knowledgeable and articulate than I really am. Finally, this book is the direct result of a U.S. Army War College Sabbatical Leave, in 2008, that allowed me to carefully examine the cases noted above and illustrate the wide possibilities of state- and nonstate-associated gangs in a new era of asymmetric war. For that I must thank Professor Douglas C. Lovelace, Jr., director of the Strategic Studies Institute of the Army War College; and Dr. William T. Johnson, dean of academics at the Army War College.

Finally, this book should not be construed as reflecting the official position of the U.S. Army War College, the Department of the Army, the Department of Defense, or the U.S. government. I alone am responsible for any errors of fact or judgment.

Gangs, Pseudo-militaries, and Other Modern Mercenaries

INTRODUCTION

A poorly understood aspect of "wars amongst the people" deals with the complex protean character and hegemonic role of gangs, agitators, armed propagandists, popular militias, youth leagues, and other mercenary organizations operating as state and nonstate surrogates in the murky shallows of the contemporary asymmetric, irregular, and political global security arena.[1] These are not tattooed teenage brigands but ordinary-looking men and women who are politically and commercially dexterous.

The problem of these types of political actors goes back at least to the sixteenth century, as observed by Niccolò Machiavelli: "Some have made themselves masters of [city-states] by holding private correspondence with, and corrupting one part of the inhabitants. They have used several methods to do this."[2] Machiavelli must have thought that everyone clearly understood what he was saying, because he did not elaborate. Everyone knew that political leaders, regardless of title, employed "unofficial henchmen" whom they could put to good use in a contingency. However, V. I. Lenin, in the early twentieth century, was the one who articulated the strategic asymmetric-irregular-political vision within which many contemporary nonstate and nation-state actors now operate.[3] Others, including Mao Zedong, have since elaborated and refined Lenin's basic political-revolutionary model, but the original tenets remain as useful today as in the past.[4] Lenin argued that anyone wishing to compel an adversary to accede to his will "must create [organize, train, and employ] a body of experienced agitators."[5]

Working within and among peoples, these nonstate actors appear to be formless and do not often present a coherent structure that can be attacked militarily. As a result, the main protagonist (state or nonstate hegemon) avoids making a direct attack on an opponent and eludes being cited in international parlance as an aggressor. At the same time, the targeted state or other nonstate entity is forced to operate in accordance with its adversary's logic—not its own. The ultimate objective of the principal protagonist (aggressor or hegemon) is, of course, to capture the will of a people, bend that will to its own ends, and achieve some form of effective political control.[6] This reality is not merely a singular social problem, a law enforcement issue, or even a military matter. It is a type of contemporary irregular internal and/or external conflict that is playing an increasingly sophisticated role in creating multidimensional indirect threats to stability, security, and effective national sovereignty all around the world today.[7]

Lenin argued strenuously that a successful revolution (radical political-social change) is a process, not an outcome. As a consequence, he identified four general phases (steps or stages) in that process as the only roads to power. The phases provide the primary bases for the operationalization of indirect but total war. After an organizational stage, in which a solid and secure base understructure is established, they require the application of "voluntary-coercive" methods, followed by less subtle "repression and terror" measures, and, fourth, if necessary, the obvious threat or direct use of military or paramilitary power to complete the process. The first three general phases also provide the bases for understanding how a militarily weaker political actor might deal effectively with threats to the achievement of its hegemonic internal and external objectives.[8]

Thus, Lenin's classic strategic vision is relevant to modern political discussions regarding "new" socialism, populism and neopopulism, and hegemonic challenges to stronger opponents. Lenin's democratic socialism was the dictatorship of the proletariat. In these terms, only a Leninist social democracy can represent the democratic will of a people (the proletarian or working class). His methodology was, therefore, simultaneously populist and neopopulist: he was a populist in the sense of opposing liberal democracy and a neopopulist in terms of opposing a bourgeois-capitalist political-economic system.[9] He was hegemonic in terms of the Leninist dictum that only with the "defensive" extinction of all opposition can a new social order (as well as true sovereignty) come about.[10] In addition, only when Leninist surrogates are in place all around the world will social democracy be safe and peace possible.[11] During every phase of the revolutionary process, agitator-gangs (popular militias) play significant roles that support their political patrons' efforts in taking control of a targeted political-economic-social system. As a result, state-supported and state-associated gangs and nonstate hegemonic challengers are important components of a highly complex political-psychological-military act known as contemporary irregular asymmetric political war.[12]

The logic of the situation argues that the conscious choice made by strategic leaders in the international community and individual nation-states about how to respond to the gang phenomenon will define the processes of national, regional, and global security, stability, and well-being far into the future. Carl von Clausewitz reminds us, "The first, the supreme, the most far-reaching act of judgment that the statesman and commander have to make is to establish ... the kind of war on which they are embarking; neither mistaking it for, nor trying to turn it into, something that is alien to its nature."[13] This requires a new insurgency/counterinsurgency paradigm in which the traditional state military and police security organizations continue to play major roles—but closely coordinated with all the other instruments of national power under the control of the civil authority. Thus, the strategic relevance and imperative of this book is the transmission of hard-learned lessons of the past and present to current and future civilian and military leaders. These leaders will be solving this set of security problems in the twenty-first century, and they must think about these problems from multiple angles, at multiple levels, and in varying degrees of complexity. Accordingly, this book examines a few premier cases that illustrate how populists and neopopulists, the New Left, New Socialists, or twenty-first-century socialists, criminal nonstate actors, and other nonstate and state actors use agitators, gangs or "super gangs," and popular militias for national, regional, or global hegemonic purposes.

GENERAL METHOD

Case study methodology does not require the testing or demonstration of hypotheses. Thus, there is no need for sophisticated statistical computations, testing, and analysis. What is needed more than anything else is ingenuity, flexibility, and sensitivity to the need to collect relevant evidence with minimal expenditure of time, effort, and money. The purposive sample of cases was chosen for the above-stated general purposes and, more specifically, to familiarize readers with the diversity and complexity of the state-supported gang phenomenon, to articulate the patterns (models) that states and their surrogates apply to achieve explicit or implicit strategic political objectives, and to clarify the types of linkages between mercenary gangs and their employers. Each case is analogous to the conduct of an experiment on related topics.[14] If all cases turn out as expected, they provide compelling support for this set of specific purposes. Then, with this information, strategic-level analytical commonalties and recommendations can be determined that are relevant to each specific type of gang-state relationship explored—and the larger, general global security problem.[15] This takes us to the theoretical linear-analytic approach of this book.

Robert K. Yin defines the linear-analytic approach as the traditional or standard case study approach to case studies. That is, the major components include "the issue, the context, the findings, and conclusions and implications." The issue and context answer the "what and why" questions, the findings examine the "who, how, and so-what?" questions, and conclusions and implications address key points, recommendations, and countermeasure issues.[16] Consequently, the primary components of each case study are the following:

- The issue;
- The context (theoretical, historical, economic, sociopolitical, organizational);

- The findings or outcome (where the protagonist's program leads, or has led); and
- Key points and lessons.

These elements are closely related and overlapping, in that they are mutually influencing and constitute the "cause and effect" dynamics of a given situation. Without a fundamental understanding of the answers to these questions, the various types of state-supported or state-associated gang activity are not likely to be clearly perceived, and the response to such activity may turn it into something that it originally was not.[17] The cause and effects related to the components of the linear-analytic approach, as discussed in the following chapters, demonstrate that associated threats are not abstract—they are real. The primary intent of this methodology, then, is to help political, military, and opinion leaders, as well as concerned citizens, think strategically about explanations of many of the "wars amongst the people" that have emerged out of the cold war and are taking us kicking and screaming into the twenty-first century.

THE CASES

The cases discussed in the following chapters help explain highly complex political war and make clear why Lenin insists that politics is war carried out by "other means."[18] The foundation for the later case studies places the state-supported gang issue in the context of Lenin's theoretical reality. Lenin reminds us that the use of relatively small propaganda-agitator gangs is an indirect approach to power that is an integral part of the process of radical political change and "creates its own legitimacy."[19] Two examples illustrate the diversity, complexity, and ambiguity of the contemporary gang phenomenon. At one end of the continuum, the Jamaican gangs (known as posses) have become a special set of social actors. With the unacknowledged acquiescence of the Jamaican government, the posses are performing some of the health, education, and welfare functions of the state in the neighborhoods they control. In contrast, Hezbollah, a major "super gang," has become a premier nonstate hegemonic challenger in Lebanon, a feat accomplished with support from the Iranian and Syrian governments. Despite these differences, Hezbollah and the Jamaican posses share a common denominator: the ultimate objective of both organizations is to compel radical political change to achieve some form of effective political control. The following cases fall somewhere between the Jamaican and Hezbollah extremes.

The first, and perhaps the simplest to comprehend, consists of "old-fashioned" state-supported gangs (the Piqueteros) that appear to be propelling contemporary Argentina toward populist antidemocratic and antisystem solutions to chronic political and socioeconomic problems. The relatively one-dimensional populism of Argentina contrasts with the ongoing multidimensional conflict in Colombia, where several types of illegal nonstate groups (pseudo-militaries, gangs, or *bandas criminales*) are devolving out of President Álvaro Uribe's AUC (the paramilitary-vigilante United Self-Defense Groups of Colombia) demobilization and reintegration program; there is also an uncomfortable association between the gangs and the Colombian elites that see the power to control narcotraffickers, insurgents, paramilitaries, and their associated gangs as the same power that would control them. A more subtle program, operating at the regional rather than nation-state level, is Hugo Chavez's populist and neopopulist/antidemocratic and antisystem agenda, which is intended to liberate Latin America from economic dependency on and the political imperialism of the North American "Colossus" (the United States). This program relies on a Leninist combination of political, economic, social, informational, and military/paramilitary-popular militia activities through which a traditional nation-state (Venezuela) can subvert targeted governments and coerce radical political-economic change, all the while maintaining plausible deniability. Still another case explores and assesses Al Qaeda's strategic and sophisticated use of small Leninist-type political-criminal (propaganda-agitator) gangs in coercing substantive change in Spanish foreign and defense policy. This is an important and instructive example in which a nonstate actor—not a traditional nation-state—plays an unconventional role as a regional or global hegemon. The last case brings us close to home and back to Machiavelli's warning regarding mercenaries making themselves masters of (city-)states. In this instance, the Mexican Zetas are taking control of parts of the country that are not controlled by the State, and imposing their own rule of law on targeted societies.

All of these case studies, and the many more examples of asymmetric warfare occurring throughout the world at any one time, provide inescapable evidence that war (conflict) is changing. That requires a sea change in the conceptualization of warfare, which, in turn, demands fundamental change in how conflict is managed. That will require the astute political-psychological use of "brain power" rather than the traditional application of technology and "brute force."

What we find in this broad array of cases is that the global struggle for power, influence, and resources continues with different actors, different names, different rhetoric, and different instruments of power. Lenin's strategic vision for the achievement of political power and social change is no longer the property of Leninists. All people are free to study it, adapt it, and implement it for their own purposes. The most salient reality of this situation is that many state-supported or state-associated actors all around the world are deeply involved in indirect struggles to coerce radical political change—and achieve power. These actors are being ignored or, alternatively, are considered too hard to deal with. Yet they have the capability to seriously threaten the interests and well-being of the global community. However, understanding and learning how to deal with irregular actors is as important as understanding and dealing with opponents that are more conventional.

CHAPTER 1

WHERE LENIN LEADS

Beginning Lessons for the Wars in Our Midst

Armed nonstate groups all over the world are directly challenging targeted governments' physical and moral right and ability to govern. This almost chronic political chaos is exacerbated by state actors using gangs, popular militias, youth leagues, or their equivalents to indirectly threaten the stability and security of other state and nonstate entities. This can be seen propagating its respective forms of instability, violence, and state failure in large parts of the Middle East, Asia, Africa, Latin America, and Europe. In many of these cases, governments are either waging war on their citizens or have become mere factions among other competing political organizations contesting the right to govern all or part of a destabilizing national or subnational territory. Agitator gangs play significant roles in helping their political patrons prepare to take control of a targeted political-social entity. Accordingly, in all the instances of the approximately one hundred insurgencies, irregular wars, or whatever else they may be called that have been instigated since the ending of the cold war, the gang phenomenon (gangs and their possible allies) has been heavily involved in over half of them.[1]

In this connection, there appears to be virtually no recognition of the fact that the lessons of the Vietnam War, the Persian Gulf War, the Iraq War, the Afghanistan War, and the many smaller conflicts that have taken place over the past several years are not being lost on the new political actors emerging into the contemporary multipolar global security arena. Ironically, strategies being developed to protect or further the interests of many state and nonstate players on the international scene are inspired by the dual idea of evading and frustrating superior conventional military force.[2] The better a power such as the United States becomes at the operational level of conventional war, the more a potential opponent turns to irregular asymmetrical solutions.[3] Ralph Peters warns us that in current and future conflict, "[w]ise competitors . . . will seek to shift the playing field away from conventional military confrontations toward unconventional forms of assault. . . . Only the foolish will fight fair."[4] And Colonel Thomas X. Hammes of the U.S. Marine Corps reminds us that irregular asymmetric wars against state and nonstate actors are the only kinds of wars the United States has ever lost.[5]

Vladimir Ilyich Lenin taught the broad strategic vision within which many contemporary weak political actors operate against stronger adversaries.[6] An explanation of that model begins with the notion that gangs or their equivalents are integral psychological-political instruments to coerce radical political change and accommodate their own interests.[7] That explanation of state-supported and state-associated gangs, and their place in the contemporary asymmetric global security environment, begins with two salient contextual realities. The first, long overshadowed by Mao Zedong and other revolutionary practitioners who are more recent, is the theoretical-political context. The second, well remembered in Eastern Europe if nowhere else, is the political-operational reality. Representing extremes of the state-associated and state-supported gang spectrum are two vignettes that demonstrate the diversity of the Leninist model: the Jamaican posses' contemporary "social work" and the Hezbollah "super gang" confrontation with Israel in Lebanon in 2006. This will provide a place from which to begin to understand the diversity, complexity, and ambiguity of the gang phenomenon.

CONTEXT

The political reality centers on the fact that the ultimate objective of any international protagonist (aggressor or hegemon) is to capture the will of a targeted society and its decision makers, bend that will to the protagonist's own ends, and achieve some form of effective political control over the opponent. This reality is not merely a social problem, a law enforcement issue, or even a military matter. It is a holistic approach to contemporary irregular internal and external conflict that is playing an increasingly sophisticated role in creating indirect multidimensional threats to security, stability, well-being, and effective national sovereignty all around the world today. A principal instrument within the idea of coordinating all instruments of power to attain the ultimate objective is the propaganda-agitator gang (frequently called cells, groups, popular militias, or youth leagues). These gangs are the entities that quietly take propaganda, corruption, subversion, and coercion into a targeted society.

An understanding of the historical reality begins with Lenin reminding us that the use of propaganda, corruption, subversion, and coercion (soft power) is an indirect approach to power. He further reminds us that power achieved indirectly "creates its own legitimacy." These methods do not directly threaten other nation-states or territories. Indirect methods do, however, threaten the security and well-being of peoples and leaders and are designed to persuade or coerce a change of public and governmental perceptions in favor of the "indirect aggressor." That model has proven effective—especially when backed by serious coercive power.[8] In general terms, then, the historical reality can be seen in the Soviet-Russian application of Lenin's strategic vision in Eastern Europe between 1946 and 2007.

This political-theoretical-historical context begins the process of explaining the "who," "what," "why," "how," and "so what" questions regarding indirect irregular asymmetrical challenges to the contemporary Western world. This context also provides an understanding of the fact that the Leninist model is not a hard and unalterable architecture for compelling fundamental political change. Rather, it is a valuable guide to those who wish to better understand and deal with the contemporary "art of war."[9]

The Theoretical Reality: Lenin's Strategic Vision for the Achievement of Political Control or Power

All his life, Lenin studied, thought, wrote, spoke, and observed individual, local, national, and international economics and politics. He came to understand the dialectics of Georg Hegel and Karl Marx, the notion of correlation of forces, and the fact that politics at any level can be a war carried on by "all means."[10] At a relatively early age, Lenin felt that he could understand everything and could explain everything. He had developed a paradigm (conceptual framework or architecture) into which he could put facts and data and generate meaning. Lenin's paradigm provided the basis for understanding the realities of politics, economics, and war. All this provided a workable explanation for how a militarily and industrially weaker political actor might deal effectively with the threats of a stronger actor to achieve hegemonic internal and external objectives.[11]

The Primary Assumption. Lenin's primary assumption is straightforward: any socialist state (a social democracy) is at considerable risk as long as even one bourgeois state (a liberal democracy) continues to exist. He argued, "It can only be with the extinction of all [bourgeois states] that Socialism comes about, as well as true sovereignty. . . . Then you will be able to start building the edifice of communist society, and bring it to completion."[12] This assumption became a blanket justification for Soviet intervention abroad from 1917 to 1989. In these terms, only a social democracy, or its clients, can represent the democratic will of the people (the proletarian working class of a society). And only when social-democratic surrogates are in place all around the world will social democracy be safe and peace possible.[13]

Nevertheless, neither this assumption nor any other Leninist dictum can be considered the intellectual property of Marxists, Leninists, or Maoists only. The idea of being surrounded by enemies is not one confined to Soviet paranoids. Every state and nonstate actor must eventually seize as much political power as possible to guarantee the political, commercial, ideological, or religious environment it desires. Thus, any government, insurgent or terrorist group, criminal or gang organization, warlord, drug cartel, or even political reformer can adapt Lenin's revolutionary model to the group's or the individual's requirements and capabilities.[14]

The Ultimate Political Objective. According to Lenin's primary assumption and real-life experience, the ultimate political objective of any state or nonstate actor must be to achieve as much freedom of movement and action as possible—as quickly as possible. This freedom facilitates the achievement of the power to compel fundamental radical political-social-economic change.[15] Given the dialectic, that political end can only be attained as a result of what Lenin called a defensive war, or a set of civil wars between "democratic" and bourgeois elements at the local, regional, national, and global levels. Yet the "axial point of the struggle to unhinge the entire capitalist international order is the nation state," and (as noted above) a war to protect the homeland or its external interests is a defensive war and a civil war—even if there is only one opponent left alive in the world.[16]

Clearly, terminology has become confusing and words take on meanings that Lenin—or any other protagonist—wants them to mean. Words such as "democratic," "defense," "liberal," bourgeois," and "war" become major weapons in the revolutionary struggle. They render traditional Western concepts and terminology regarding politics, war, morality, victory, national security, and sovereignty irrelevant. A major consequence of the drastic change in rhetoric and meanings is that the targeted state or nonstate actor is forced to operate in accordance with his adversary's logic—not his own. Another consequence is that words, perceptions, ideas, and dreams have become primary tools of statecraft. At the same time, the idea of the "enemy" and the conventional military center of gravity are drastically changed, and the ways and means of attacking an opponent are infinitely broadened.[17]

The New Enemy and Center of Gravity. Lenin argued that "democratic" political leaders must seek to radicalize peoples' thinking and values. The first step in that direction is for leaders to begin to understand that the enemy cannot be merely a traditional nation-state (although the state is the axis for unhinging the international system); rather, the enemy is the social class that traditionally has controlled the state for its own greedy purposes. The second step in that direction is for leaders to understand that the enemy cannot be only the military formations the state might be able to put into the field; rather, the enemy is now everyone and anyone who supports the "bourgeois class" in any way. Thus, the enemy can be a nation-state, a nonstate actor, an internal or external institution, or an individual who might conceivably be able to threaten the social-democratic order.[18]

As a consequence, the conventional state-centric center of gravity (the source of all power on which everything depends) can no longer be the state or easily identified state-supported military formations. Rather, the center of gravity is the bourgeois government's and the people's morale and will—more specifically, the opponent's decision-making leadership and public opinion.[19] The basic reality of this new center of gravity is that information (propaganda)—not military technology or firepower—is the primary currency by which modern "war amongst the people" is run.[20] Contemporary war, therefore, takes place in an environment shaped by words, ideas, beliefs, expectations, deceptions, and political will—and the unifying political, intelligence, and information (communications) organizations that can culturally challenge any given enemy of the "people."[21]

Ways and Means of Conducting Defensive War against a Bourgeois Enemy. The Marxist (scientific) name used by Lenin for the effort that breaks up and finally defeats an opposing state and its bourgeois internal and external accomplices is "dictatorship of the proletariat." The erosion of the enemy state is accomplished by the systematic (dictatorial) application of indirect and direct, state and nonstate, military and nonmilitary, lethal and nonlethal, and a mix of some or all of these kinds of actions. That is, "Any war is merely the continuation of peace time politics by other means."[22] In short, *all* ways and means (political-economic, social-psychological, and military-paramilitary) are used to destabilize the bourgeois state and generate the erosion and ultimate defeat of liberal democracy and market capitalism.[23] Thus, Lenin applies the notion of total war to defensive war on two different levels: first, one must achieve total political objectives (radical change); and second, one must use a totality of ways and means to compel fundamental political change and new values (or restore old systems and values).[24]

Most important, however, is Lenin's insistence that before beginning a revolutionary process, one must know precisely what he wants to achieve, that is, the positive political outcome desired. Such knowledge will lead directly to effectively compelling an adversary to do one's will and generate the political change required. Also, before beginning a revolutionary process, one must understand the political-psychological-socioeconomic and military situations; "the correlation of forces" must be in favor of making a successful revolution. Otherwise, to begin the process "would be wrong, absurd."[25] Finally, before beginning a revolutionary process, the leadership must be prepared to conduct a coherent, holistic, multidimensional conflict. Still more important is that the leadership must be prepared in advance to lead the masses once the conflict begins to end. There is more than one example of a political actor losing his revolution (or civil war) as a result of the lack of appropriate leadership preparation and education.[26]

What, More Specifically, Is to Be Done? As noted above, the operationalization of Lenin's scheme for conducting defensive war against enemies and compelling radical change begins with the organization, training, and utilization of a body of experienced agitators and propagandists (propaganda-agitator gangs). The tasks of this organization include, first, "[s]preading, by propaganda, among the workers a proper understanding of the present social and economic system . . . and an understanding of the struggle between classes." Second, and "[i]nseparably connected with propaganda," in Lenin's model, "is agitation. . . . Agitation means taking part in all manifestations of the working-class struggle. . . . There is NO issue affecting the life of workers . . . that can be left unused for the purpose of agitation."[27] Lenin further argued that if this instrument of statecraft succeeds in tearing apart the fabric on which a targeted society rests, then the resulting violence and instability can serve as "the midwife of a new social order."[28]

In this situation, the principal tools (means) of the propaganda-agitator gangs include public diplomacy at home and abroad; intelligence, information and disinformation, and propaganda operations; cultural and political manipulation measures (such as bribery, corruption, coercion, repression, terror, and subversion); and specifically prescribed covert and overt violence (such as instigating demonstrations, strikes, riots, and other civic violence, in addition to mutilation, murder, kidnapping, arson, and other persuasive intimidation actions).[29] The intent is for the propaganda-agitator gangs (or cells or groups) to act in such a manner as to would evade foreign and internal notice and commentary—and the supporting state would always be able to claim plausible deniability for their actions.[30] But if all these indirect soft-power efforts fail, Lenin insisted that there is another—a final, decisive, and direct hard-power—instrument of statecraft: the armed forces and their "internationalist and liberating mission."[31]

The Old and the New. In *Dragonwars,* J. Bowyer Bell warns us that "much of the world is ripe for those who wish to change history, [a]venge grievance, find security in a new structure, or protect old ways . . . [and] those who are apt to destabilize order are not easily swayed for they seek not tangibles, are not the Marxist man, but seek the realization of a dream, the rewards of history. These aspirations are not easily accommodated. [Thus], the next century, as [with] the last, offers the prospect of wars—old wars, but also new wars that deploy assassins, plague, and the unconventional."[32] Thus, little has changed over the years in terms of the basic essentials of irregular/asymmetric war. Historian Ian Beckett reminds us, "The past is not another country. Indeed . . . the past represents both the shadow of things that have been, and of those that will be."[33]

Some Political-Historical Reality: Operationalization of Lenin's Strategic Vision

Lenin's argument (discussed previously) that a successful revolution is a process rather than an event requires defining the desired outcome and having a thorough, multidimensional understanding of the situation, or the correlation of forces.[34] Lenin identified four general phases (steps or stages) in the revolutionary process. They are intended as guidelines rather than any kind of absolute formula for success. But these phases are not options among others: they are the only road to power. They must be implemented at the "right times," in the "right combinations," and by trained, patient, calculating, and iron-willed leaders.[35] These phases provide the primary bases for the operationalization of indirect but total war. They require (1) a preparatory organizational period preceding (2) the application of voluntary-coercive methods, which are to be followed by (3) less-subtle repression and terror and, if necessary to complete the process (4), the obvious threat and/or direct use of military power. A brief outline of the organizational period and the subsequent phases and methods used in various insurgencies and other asymmetric conflict from 1917 to the present follows.

Phase One—The Preparatory Organizational Period. The key component of Lenin's four-stage revolutionary process is the foundational preparatory organizational effort. It is at this point that a small elite political-military command (strategic directorate) begins to motivate, recruit, train, and educate intelligent and disciplined young men and women. There should be no rush to action. The intent is to generate conscience (motivation, enlightenment, and discipline), develop a flexible political and military structure out of small cells consisting of five to seven people, and build support mechanisms for an expanding and ever-more-active organization. All of this is done with a vision of preparing individual men and women who can plan and implement an effective set of programs for taking effective political control of societies and states. Lenin's premise is logical and clear: power is generated by intelligent, enlightened, motivated, well-educated, and disciplined individuals. Until an adequate leadership base is developed that can lead and implement radical political-economic-social change, "it would be absurd" to move into the subsequent stages of the revolutionary process.[36] There is little point in taking down one despotism only to create another in its place.

Phase Two—The Application of "Voluntary-Coercive" Methods. Examples of these methods include but are not limited to donating money, personnel, and other assets to cooperative officials, candidates, trade unions, political parties, and parliaments; withdrawing assets from uncooperative individuals, unions, parties, and so forth; establishing control of key businesses to influence or manipulate a given economy; sending "fraternal letters" and making personal visits and phone calls to people one wants to influence or manipulate; publicly questioning officials, policies, and practices through statements, interviews, and articles in official and semiofficial or accommodating media outlets; publicly and officially denouncing and perhaps criminalizing individuals, factions, parties, and other uncooperative entities; initiating sanctions against, or interfering with, the intrastate and interstate flow of trade, transportation, energy, and other commerce; rigging or buying elections at local and national levels; disseminating derisive information, disinformation, and propaganda against uncooperative or hostile individuals, parties, and institutions; mobilizing demonstrations, strikes, civil violence, riots, and other types of agitation in targeted localities, regions, and countries; and conducting carefully targeted mutilations, kidnappings, assassinations, and other persuasive-coercive activities.[37]

There is nothing new or surprising in the above list of voluntary-coercive methods; they are well known and commonly used in national and international statecraft. What might make these methods more than usually "persuasive" is that these kinds of actions are often accompanied by covert violence and disinformation efforts conducted by official state security forces and/or unofficial state-supported gangs (popular militias) with specific orders to be "especially persuasive."

Phase Three—The Application of "Repression and Terror" Methods. Again, examples include but are not limited to the following:

- Internal as well as external opponents are openly and viciously maligned, intimidated, threatened, maimed, or assassinated. For example, against Soviet advice, Jan Masaryk, Czechoslovakia's noncommunist foreign minister in 1947–48, accepted an invitation for Czechoslovakia to take part in the newly proposed Western-sponsored Marshall Plan. Shortly thereafter, he was reported to have fallen from his office window into the courtyard of the Foreign Ministry. Czechoslovakia did not take part in the Marshall Plan and remained within the Soviet sphere of influence. The exact circumstances of this fatal fall have never been made public.[38]
- "Popular militias" (gangs) are mobilized to agitate and create a climate of fear and insecurity among the general population. The demonstrations, strikes, riots, and other violence generated by these gangs may or may not be acknowledged by official state security institutions but are certainly not spontaneous. Whatever

the case, officials blame such gang actions on their political enemies or on circumstances that the state claims are beyond its power to deal with. For example, in 1946–47, popular militias helped create a climate of fear and insecurity that Communist Party spokesmen blamed on political critics. Thus, in Bulgaria, seven out of twenty-two members of the Presidium of the Agrarian Union and thirty-five out of the eighty members of its governing council were in prison. Typical of the charges was one against a journalist accused of having, "in a truly criminal manner, called the Bulgarian government political and economic dreamers."[39]

- The above types of repression and terror methods, if not entirely successful, are likely to give way to subversion and open state violence. As one example, popular militias (gangs), nationalities, communities, parties, tribes, and factions of any or all of the above may be mobilized to divide or destroy opponents. For example, in Albania in 1948, Enver Hodxa mobilized the southern Tosk communities against the northern Ghegs.[40]

- Subversion and state violence can also progress to the planning, organizing, and implementing of political or military coups—or the more blatant military occupation of a country or part of a country. For example, the Soviet Union occupied Bulgaria from the end of World War II until 1947; Hungary until the mid-1950s (and again after 1956); Romania until 1958. In addition, Russian forces remained in Estonia until 1994, and the German Democratic Republic remained under Soviet military occupation throughout its entire forty-five-year existence.[41]

- Subversion and a more contemporary type of unconventional state violence can been seen in Russian efforts to influence "fascistic" political decision making in Estonia in 2007. For example, the Estonian government defied Russian threats and removed the so-called "Bronze Soldier" (the monument to the Russian Army that memorializes the Soviet liberation of Estonia in World War II). Reportedly, in retaliation, Russia organized and implemented cyber attacks against Estonian electronic infrastructure, banks, telecommunications, and media outlets. The Russians also overtly cut off the critical natural gas flow to

Estonia. In addition to the electronic cyber and computer attacks, the Russians organized violent demonstrations in the capital city of Tallinn (some have claimed that the organizers were Russian special forces personnel dressed in civilian clothes), and the Russians used their own Nashi youth organization (a type of popular militia in the form of a youth league) to "spontaneously" demonstrate against the Estonian embassy in Moscow. These kinds of actions, even though nonlethal, impaired the security and well-being of Estonia as seriously as a conventional bombing campaign would have done.[42]

- All these kinds of coercion, repression, subversion, and terrorism noted in phases two and three do not preclude holding "peace talks" or overtly working with possible opponents, while simultaneously conducting various covert coercive actions against them. As long as the class struggle continues, all interests are subordinated to that struggle, as is morality: as Lenin stated, "Morality is what serves to [help] destroy the old exploiting society and . . . build up a new communist society."[43]

When Lenin said that all means must be employed against an opponent to attain success in the revolutionary process, he meant *all* means. As a consequence, if the various indirect measures outlined above fail, then the threat of direct overt violence is always implicit in the rhetoric of socialist democracy.

Phase Four—One Example of Military Invasion. Perhaps the best example of the application of the Leninist revolutionary model can be seen in a review of the events that led up to the Soviet–Warsaw Pact invasion of Czechoslovakia (coup or countercoup, depending on one's position) in October 1968. On October 31, 1967, a group of students from Prague's Technical University organized street demonstrations to protest electricity cuts in their dormitories. Calls then and subsequently for "More Light" triggered a broader political notion of more light in the minds of the Czech citizenry that extended well beyond local university housekeeping difficulties. That notion was given more impetus as a result of the violent suppression of those demonstrations. General public discontent and unrest were obvious, and the government concluded that it had to respond to calls for "More (Political) Light." The impasse and the accompanying indecision finally gave way two months later, at the beginning of 1968.[44]

On January 5, 1968, the Central Committee of the Czech Communist Party elected as its new first secretary a "reform" candidate: Alexander Dubcek. He was thought to be a credible *apparatchik* who could appease popular resentments but who would be faithful to the party, and to democratic socialism. Shortly after his election, Dubcek called for a relaxation of press and media censorship and initiated a purge of "hard liners" from the party and the army. On 27 March, the Central Committee adopted an "Action Program" calling for (1) a federal state that included the Czech Republic and Slovakia as equals; (2) other political parties to begin to compete in free elections; and (3) relaxation of formal controls on the expression of public opinion. This experiment with reform was to take place over a ten-year period. The so-called Prague Spring (with more light) had begun—with strong public consent.[45]

Concern on the part of the Soviet Union regarding the Czech reforms was formally expressed as early as March 21, 1968. At a meeting of the Soviet Politburo in Moscow, it was argued that contamination from the Prague Spring was having an antisocial effect on young Ukrainians. Soon thereafter, similar allegations were reported by Polish and East German leaders regarding the youth in their countries. As a consequence, the Soviet defense minister was authorized to prepare a contingency plan for military operations in Czechoslovakia. Not until July 1968, however, did the Soviet and other Warsaw Pact leaders agree that the Czech reforms were beginning to move out of party control.[46] As a result, a series of voluntary-coercive, repressive, subversive, and violent actions were initiated and implemented in quick succession.

On July 14, Soviet, Polish, East German, Bulgarian, and Hungarian party leaders agreed to send a fraternal letter to the Czech Communist Party warning it of the risk of counterrevolution, along with a list of measures that were expected to be taken. Two weeks later, Czech and Soviet leaders met in a face-to-face discussion in which Alexander Dubcek tried to convince Leonid Brezhnev that the Communist Party was not jeopardizing its position by enacting reforms; rather, it was actually strengthening its popular support. Brezhnev was not convinced.

The Warsaw Pact then announced forthcoming military maneuvers to take place near the Czech borders. On August 3, Brezhnev announced that communist parties were free to apply the principles of Marxism-Leninism and socialism in their own countries but were not free to deviate from those principles. The same day, five members of the Czech Presidium sent a secret letter to the Soviet leadership describing the reformist threat to the Communist Party and requesting Warsaw Pact military intervention in Czechoslovakia, in a clear example of subversion. On August 13, in a telephone conversation with Brezhnev, Dubcek tried to reassure the Soviet leader that his reforms were no threat to the social-democratic system. Brezhnev remained unconvinced. Five days later, the decision was made to invade Czechoslovakia. On August 21, five hundred thousand Soviet, Polish, Hungarian, Bulgarian, and East German troops moved unopposed into Czechoslovakia.[47]

Alexander Dubcek and his "reformist" colleagues were arrested, flown to Moscow, and obligated to sign documents renouncing their "Action Program" and agreeing to Warsaw Pact occupation of their country. Thus began the restoration of order and the *status quo ante* in Czechoslovakia. This violent repression became known in the political rhetoric as "normalization."[48] Under these conditions, Dubcek was allowed to stay in office until formally removed in April 1969. In the meantime, the previously scheduled Czech Communist Party Congress was canceled; the idea of free elections was shelved; censorship was reestablished and other reforms ended; the party was purged of all "unreliable" elements; leaders who had been prominent in even simply involved with the Prague Spring reform movement were asked to sign statements for public consumption renouncing their actions and rejecting the Dubcek reforms; Czechoslovakia was occupied by Soviet-led Warsaw Pact forces; and never again would it be possible to maintain that social democracy rested on popular consent.[49] Again, Lenin would remind us that power provides its own legitimacy.[50]

Eroding Legitimacy. As one analyzes the phase one, two, three, and four methods of Lenin's revolutionary process (political-psychological war), one can readily imagine why and how state-supported and state-associated gangs can be used to help erode the effective sovereignty and legitimacy of targeted states. Thus, we come back to where we began. In studying insurgency or counterinsurgency, guerrilla war, terror war, irregular war, asymmetric war, conflicts short of conventional war, national liberation movements, or any other term for revolutionary war, we find that these expressions mischaracterize the activities of state-supported or state-associated gangs. These gangs in fact play major roles in helping their political masters prepare to take control of a targeted state, part of a targeted state, or a nonstate political actor. As a result, they are engaged in a highly complex political-psychological act, known as political war. That is why Lenin insists that politics is war carried out by "other means."[51]

SOME CONTEMPORARY REALITY: TWO VIGNETTES

Threats involving the gang phenomenon come in many forms and in a matrix of different kinds of challenges that vary in scope and scale. If these threats have a single feature in common, it is that they are well-calculated, multidimensional, and systematic attempts to coerce radical political change. The activities of two very different organizations—the Jamaican posses and Hezbollah—represent the extremes of the state-associated and state-supported gang spectrum. At one end of the continuum are the Jamaican posses (gangs), which have become a special set of social actors. With the completely unacknowledged acquiescence of the Jamaican government, the posses are making a social investment in the neighborhoods they control: that is, they are performing some of the functions of the failing Jamaican welfare state.[52] At the other end of the spectrum is Hezbollah, one of the largest and most powerful "super gangs" in the world, which has become a premier nonstate hegemonic challenger with the virtually explicit support of the Iranian and Syrian governments.[53]

Jamaican Posses (Gangs)

Similar to gangs in other countries in the circum-Caribbean region and elsewhere in the Western Hemisphere, Jamaican posses are relatively homogeneous, violent, and ubiquitous. There are estimated to be at least eighty-five different posses operating on the island, with anywhere between 2,500 and 20,000 members.[54] The posses are the by-products of high levels of poverty and unemployment and lack of upward social mobility. Moreover, the posses represent the consequences of U.S. deportation of convicted criminals back to their countries of origin as well as the regressive politics of democracy in the region.[55] Unemployment and criminal deportation speak for themselves, but the political situation in Jamaica requires some elaboration.

The Political Situation in Jamaica. Given the shift from the production of commodities toward knowledge-based products and services and reduction of the costs of transport, goods, and labor under economic globalization, the Jamaican government has experienced a loosening of control over its traditional resource bases. As a result, the government no longer has the income to provide an array of public services in a welfare-type state. When the Jamaican government provides public assistance, it has tended to outsource delivery of services to private and semiprivate organizations. Under these conditions, local posses have taken on a social investment in the areas they control. An important part of the posses' programs of action is called "shared government, with a welfare aspect."[56]

As a result, gang-controlled communities in Jamaica are considered to be among the safest in the country, and the posses are helping the people in their "jurisdictions" with education, public health, and employment problems. Thus, as the state has reduced its traditional security and service functions, the gangs have stepped in to fill the vacuum and have become—among other types of social actors—social workers.[57] Nevertheless, the Jamaican posses remain deeply involved in serious intergang rivalry and violence. Their actions reflect on Jamaica not as a "failed state" but as a failing state in the process of reconfiguration. Jamaica appears to be slowly moving toward something like a "criminal state," a "narco-state," or a "criminal-narco-state."[58]

The Jamaican Posses' Reputation and Operations within the Political System. Jamaican posses are credited with being self-reliant and self-contained. They have their own aircraft, watercraft, and crews for "pick up and delivery." They also use their own personnel to run legitimate businesses and conduct money-laundering tasks. In that connection, posses have expanded their operations throughout the Caribbean Basin as well as into the United States, Canada, and Europe. The general reputation of Jamaican posses is one of high efficiency and absolute ruthlessness in pursuit of their territorial and commercial interests. Examples of swift and brutal violence include but are not limited to fire bombing, throat slashing, and dismemberment of victims and their families. As such, Jamaican posses are credited with the highest level of violence in the English-speaking Caribbean and 60 percent of the crime in the region.[59]

The posses use the level of violence they consider necessary to protect their markets and control their competition. Violence is their political interface to negate law-enforcement efforts directed against them by police and other security organizations. As they seek to control or incapacitate national and international security institutions, they dominate community life, territory, and politics. In this environment, posses are forced to link with and provide services to other posses and to other illicit transnational organizations from time to time. Domination of posses' respective turf in Jamaica's confined area makes constant cooperation and negotiation with other gangs, TCOs, and the government into required conditions for generating the degree of stability necessary to conduct profitable business. That kind of cooperation was demonstrated in May 2006 with a month-long series of civic activities called a "Safe Communities Campaign." The purpose of this government initiative was to assist selected communities—and the posses in them—to think and act in terms of reggae icon Bob Marley's message of "love, peace, and unity."[60] When these kinds of efforts fail, however, the results are a level of violence commensurate with the level of importance of the issues involved. In that context, one can see the rise of private, gang-controlled enclaves that coexist in delicate, often symbiotic, relationships with the Jamaican government and its security institutions.

Thus, as one kind of authority has withdrawn from a given turf, another has moved in to fill the vacuum. That, in turn, blurs the line between criminal and political violence and gives the posses increasing immunity to state intervention and control. The shift in authority also exacerbates the confusion regarding traditional distinctions between police law enforcement functions and military national security functions. As a consequence, very little that is effective or lasting has been done to control or eliminate the Jamaican posses.[61] As other consequences, the effective sovereignty of the state and the personal security of citizens are being challenged every day. Posses' commercial motives for controlling people and territory are, in fact, an implicit political agenda.[62]

The Effectiveness of the Jamaican Posses. The democratically elected governments in the Caribbean argue that criminal gangs, such as the Jamaican posses, have been able to profit from their globalized operations to the point of placing themselves beyond the capability of most of the mini-countries in the region to eliminate them or even seriously disrupt their operations. Today, it is estimated that any given gang-cartel combination earns more money in a year from its illicit activities than any Caribbean country generates in legitimate revenues. Thus, individual state governments in the circum-Caribbean region are simply overmatched by the gang phenomenon. The gangs and their various allies have more money, better arms, and more effective organizations than do the small nation-states. And gangs are gradually supplementing the brute violence of previous generations with the brainpower of a new generation of members who are computer savvy and business-school trained with MBAs. Additionally, many of this younger generation of gang members, like the older generations, are recipients of "graduate educations" from North American and other prison systems.[63]

In all, increasing posse effectiveness, violence, and impunity have fueled doubts in the Jamaican citizenry about the problem-solving ability of their elected leaders. Given the reality of the posses' combination of power and beneficial social welfare activities, citizen support and allegiance tend to go to the posses that deliver consistent services and security, rather than to the government that appears to be unable or unwilling to honor the social contract.[64]

The "Hezbollah Surprise" of 2006

The Israeli military force that invaded southern Lebanon in the summer of 2006 was considered to be a world-class entity. The force had its own "shock and awe" strategy, and it—and its civilian and military leaders—expected a quick and easy conventional war of attrition. The intent (objective) was to completely incapacitate the Hezbollah movement in Lebanon. Instead of a quick and easy victory, however, the Israeli military force was surprised and thwarted on a least four levels.[65]

The First Level. On this level, the Israelis discovered that success in contemporary irregular conflict cannot be reduced to buying more and better, and heavier, equipment than the enemy has; fielding more troops than the enemy possesses; utilizing better conventionally trained and experienced leadership than Hezbollah could possibly develop; developing a far more sophisticated logistical system than Hezbollah could contemplate; and utilizing superior photo, electronic, and signal intelligence technology.[66]

The Second Level. The Israelis, at this level, were surprised and frustrated by Hezbollah's Katyusha and Al-Fajr rockets, Zelzal missiles, and antitank missiles; the remarkable power of a small "death army" with low technology and high religious motivation, combined with the associated operational skill and effectiveness of the Hezbollah antitank squads; the astonishing initiative, determination, and vision of Hezbollah unconventional leadership; the ability of the Hezbollah military force to move freely among the Lebanese population and easily secure the relatively meager provisions they required; the uncanny knowledge (human intelligence) that the Hezbollah force had at its disposal concerning Israeli formations, strengths, tactics, and predispositions; and the decisive power and effectiveness of the Hezbollah political-psychological (media) campaign in Lebanon and the rest of the world.[67]

The Third Level. At the third level, it was found that perceived moral legitimacy of purpose and behavior was the most important strategic principle operating in the conflict. In addition, military force is still a key element in determining the final outcome of a conflict, but that force must be supplemented by other dimensions of power, as well as the organization, equipment, training, and education to deal with the reality of existential asymmetric warfare. Also, the need to isolate enemies politically and physically from external and internal sources of support cannot be ignored—the political risk of not doing so is greater than the risk of making an effective effort. Human intelligence and culturally effective political-psychological information and propaganda campaigns are vital to success, as is unity of civil-military effort at all levels—not just a unity of military command.

The Next Level. At a more holistic level, the lessons from the first three levels of analysis equal a sum greater than its parts. Regardless of whether a conflict took place 2,500 years ago or last year, the evidence indicates that all victories display one common denominator: the winner is the hegemonic power or power bloc that best combined the diverse dimensions of the entire (global) "battlefield." The major characteristics (dimensions) of a given conflict are defined as military, economic, political-diplomatic, information media, psychological-cultural, technological, and electronic. Each dimension can be further divided into subparts. For example, the economic dimension of contemporary war may be broken down into trade war, financial war, sanctions war, and cyber-economic war (such as shutting down an adversary's banking system or natural gas or oil supplies).[68]

At the same time, each of the subparts (supporting elements) of a given dimension can be combined with as many others as a protagonist's organizational capability can accommodate. The combining of dimensions and their subparts provides considerably greater strength (power) than one, or perhaps two, operating alone. And the interaction among dimensions and subparts of conflict prevents the military, technological, or any other dimension from serving as the automatic dominant factor that might define any given conflict situation. This gives new and greater meaning to the notion of a political actor using *all* available instruments of national and international power to protect and achieve its objectives and interests. As only one example, military war should probably always be supported by media war and a combination of intelligence war, cyber war, and diplomatic war.[69]

All of this requires an understanding of "warfare as a whole."[70] This type of war is not a test of expertise in conducting legal or illegal violence or terrorism, creating instability, or achieving commercial, ideological, or moral satisfaction. Over the long term, it is an exercise in survival.

The Effectiveness of Hezbollah. Israel unleashed escalating levels of military force upon and among the civilian populations in which Hezbollah had taken shelter. This singular military effort generated a double negative. First, the Israeli armed forces, more or less indiscriminately, inflicted casualties on civilians as they attacked Hezbollah forces. That kind of action was seen as disproportional and unnecessary in the eyes of the Lebanese population and the international media. Second, because of negative popular opinion and the surprising capabilities of the Hezbollah forces, the Israelis could not achieve their objective to militarily incapacitate the Hezbollah organization in Lebanon.

The Israelis were fighting a limited military war of attrition against an opponent they did not take seriously. Israeli intelligence was good but not adequate to the task; Israeli military equipment and other technology was good but not appropriate to the task; and the Israeli local and international media effort was good but totally outclassed. Additionally, the strategic environment within which the war was taking place was misunderstood or ignored, and the various multidimensional centers of gravity were not assessed or considered in holistic terms. As a consequence, the Israeli invasion of Lebanon and confrontation against Hezbollah in 2006 was labeled an "absolute folly."[71]

Hezbollah was seen by all parties to the conflict as the winner. Primarily, this was because Hezbollah was perceived as the unequal victim of the world-class Israeli armed forces. Hezbollah was portrayed to the world as representing Arab pride and legitimate Arab socio-economic-political hopes and wishes for the future. As long as Hezbollah did not abandon the field, it would be the winner; moreover, for each Hezbollah fighter killed in the 2006 war of attrition, a minimum of ten new supporters are estimated to have emerged out of the various global Muslim communities.[72] While the Israelis were busy fighting a conventional military war of attrition, Hezbollah was subtly making unconventional long-term political-psychological preparations to take indirect control of the Lebanese state.

Strategic Realities

In addition to common political objectives and the diversity of ambiguous actions, these two vignettes reflect some hard strategic realities: (1) the traditional fundamentals of power, and the instruments of the state that exercise it, are still necessary but not sufficient to deal with the irregular asymmetric task at hand; (2) contemporary use of repression, coercion, terror, and even relatively conventional military action is more political-psychological than the common wisdom tends to allow; (3) the Leninist model allows an almost infinite range of variations on the revolutionary theme; and (4) an adequate response to the gang phenomenon requires profound changes in thinking and actions.

FINAL OUTCOME

The strategic multidimensional paradigm outlined above acknowledges the fact that the final outcome of any irregular or counter–irregular war effort is not primarily determined by the skillful manipulation of violence in the many military battles that take place once a conflict of this nature is recognized to have begun. Rather, control of the situation is determined by the level of perceived moral legitimacy; organization for unity of effort; intelligence and information; the ability to reduce or enhance internal and external aid to one side or the other; and the discipline, motivation, and capabilities of the security organizations involved in the shooting part of the war. To the extent that all these factors are strongly present in a balanced strategy, they favor success. To the extent that any one component of the model is absent, or present only in a weak form, the probability of success is minimal.[73] Underlying this paradigm is the concept that the new center of gravity is public opinion and the resultant political decision making.[74] Qiao Liang and Wang Xiangsui warn us that the contemporary battlefield is everywhere and includes everyone. People and soldiers may evade conventional weapons, but they cannot evade words, ideas, and perceptions that strike directly into one's mind and heart.[75]

KEY POINTS AND LESSONS

The cases outlined above—and subsequently in this book—represent a diverse array of contemporary conflict situations that focus on state-associated and state-supported gangs and hegemonic nonstate actors (such as Al Qaeda). The differences in the ambiguous, irregular, and asymmetric conflicts are illustrated by a range of modes of operation. Yet despite the uniqueness of each case, there are important strategic commonalities. Some of the most salient are as follows:

- Regardless of ideology or mode of operation, the ultimate political objective of any state or nonstate actor must be to achieve as much freedom of action and movement as possible. That, in turn, leads to the necessity of taking control of, incapacitating, or deposing or replacing a targeted government. This kind of war, thus, is not limited in any way; it is total.
- The erosion of an adversary's will and ability to be proactive is accomplished by systemic application of a multidimensional combination of direct and indirect, state and nonstate, military and nonmilitary, and lethal and nonlethal actions. In short, all ways and means are used to destabilize a targeted state or nonstate actor and contribute to its ultimate defeat.
- Because all instruments of soft and hard power (political, psychological, economic, and military/paramilitary) come into play, the center of gravity (the source of all power, upon which everything depends) can no longer be only military. As Carl von Clausewitz noted, in this type of war, the center of gravity must be public opinion and political decision-making leadership.[76] The battlefield has, thus, expanded to include everything and everybody.
- The principal tools of statecraft have changed from reactive military confrontation to the proactive and coercive use of words, images, symbols (to include actions), perceptions, and ideas.
- As a consequence, "[w]arfare is no longer an exclusive Imperial garden where professional soldiers alone can mingle."[77] Nonprofessional warriors who can conduct media war, financial

war, trade war, psychological war, network (virus) war, guerrilla war, and chemical-biological-radiological war (to include drug war), as only a few examples, must now be included in an organizational architecture for conducting contemporary irregular, asymmetric, political-psychological war.

Contemporary irregular war requires a sea change in the paradigm of warfare—a broadening and transforming of the notion of conflict. It is surprising and dismaying that most world political and military leaders do not yet understand some of the most fundamental principles that Sun Tzu taught 2,500 years ago: "[W]ar is to be preceded by measures designed to make it easy to win. The master conqueror frustrated his enemy's plans and broke up his alliances. He created cleavages between sovereign and ministers, superiors and subordinates, commanders and soldiers. His spies and agents were active everywhere, gathering information, sowing dissension, and nurturing subversion. The enemy was isolated and demoralized, his will to resist broken. Thus, without battle his army was conquered, his cities taken, and his state overthrown. . . . [But the] indispensable preliminary to battle is to attack the mind of the enemy."[78]

CHAPTER 2

THE ARGENTINE PIQUETEROS

"Rent-a-Mobs" or Agents for Radical Political Change?

A popular cultural myth in Argentina has it that an Argentine coup d'etat *(golpe de estado)* is no more violent than a Mexican wedding party. That may be close to true, but Argentina's political history has been marked by considerable violence as well as periods of wedding-party stability and prosperity. Violent conflict between those advocating a strong unitary state and those demanding a weaker federal government prevailed in the early decades after independence from Spain was achieved in 1816. In 1852, the federalists under General Justo José de Urquiza took control of the country and adopted a liberal-democratic constitution (in 1853) that promulgated a federal and presidential republic with a bicameral congress. Nevertheless, the federalists governed with a strong hand *(mano dura)* for more than twenty years. By the 1930s and 1940s, Argentina had become one of the richest countries in the world. Millions of relatively well educated Europeans immigrated, and large amounts of capital flowed into the country. Argentines had good reason to agree with their European cousins that Argentina was "the country of the future."[1]

Democracy, peace, and prosperity were disrupted by a military coup in 1930. The coup initiated a long period of political, economic, and social instability in Argentina, with subsequent coups in 1943, 1955, 1962, 1966, and 1976. Over the years, Argentina moved back and forth from civilian to military governments, from liberal-democratic to authoritarian-conservative political politics, and from economic stability to economic stagflation and political chaos. In the middle of this period of instability and decline, Colonel (later, General) Juan Domingo Peron took control of the country. In the context of political chaos and socioeconomic decline, Peron and Peronism encouraged Argentines to pursue a confrontational, populist, and nationalistic agenda in which the sovereign nation and socioeconomic justice *(justicialismo)* were identified with poor Argentine workers (the shirtless ones; *descamisados*). At the same time, economic "dependency" and political "imperialism" were identified with the U.S.-European-oriented oligarchy. The policies associated with justicialismo produced a long, continuing, and growing discontinuity among different social-economic-political groups; a specific part of the Argentine population arbitrarily defined as poor; asymmetry in donor (government) and donee (the poor) relationships; arbitrary donor discretion in distributions to the poor (clientelism); and the entrenchment of dependent donees. Within that context, inflation, unemployment, corruption, stifling bureaucracy, banking crashes, and civil violence have become the norm. Over the years, Argentina gradually devolved from an affluent democracy to the status of a failing state.[2]

What followed the military coup that deposed Peron in 1955 was political deadlock, terroristic insurgency, and the resultant "dirty war." Peronist resistance to subsequent governments made sure that governmental rule would be impossible without Peron. Peron's opponents in government and society unsuccessfully did all they could to outlaw Peron and Peronism and prevent his return to power. Thus, with this gridlock, the only way for either side to attempt any kind of political action or governance was through either popular or state violence. In that connection, Argentina experienced three failed attempts at rural guerrilla warfare between 1959 and 1969 and had two new Peronist governments between 1973 and 1976. In 1969, the insurgents decided in favor of urban warfare. Over the period of time between the ouster of Peron in 1955 and his return from exile in 1973, numerous urban insurgent organizations emerged. Six major groups—two Marxist-Maoist-Guevarist oriented and four populist-nationalist-Peronist oriented—eventually dispersed or joined with the Revolutionary People's Army (ERP) or the Peronist Montoneros. The Montoneros became the largest and most active of the two revolutionary movements. By

1975, the Montoneros had over five thousand combat troops operating throughout Argentina—primarily in the Buenos Aires metropolitan area. At the same time, the Montoneros organized over eight thousand political activists (mass front groups) capable of mobilizing hundreds or thousands of demonstrators for any given mass event.[3] Within that cohort, a new social movement emerged out of the liberation theology movement—the Piqueteros (unemployed workers, "pickets").[4]

Toward the end of the revolutionary period in 1979, Montonero leadership tended to ignore the sociopolitical side of the conflict and primarily used the mass front groups overtly in support of its military activities. As a consequence, these "noncombatant" political activists acquired considerable visibility and became easy prey for the Argentine security forces. As the Montoneros increased the intensity of their unrealistic war of attrition against the much larger Argentine military forces, the security forces were killing and imprisoning suspected Peronist activists—literally—by the truckload. Additionally, there were those, including some Piqueteros, who did not appreciate being used as "cannon fodder" and moved back into the "urban jungle." Thus, over the last year of the insurgency and dirty war, the Montonero leadership found that there was "no one and nothing" to lead.[5]

In 1981, General Roberto E. Viola succeeded General Jorge R. Videla as president, but before the year ended, General Leopoldo Galtieri replaced Viola. These changes were decided unilaterally by members of the sitting military junta—no elections were held. In 1982, however, the humiliating defeat of the Argentine forces in the Malvinas–Falkland Islands War forced General Galtieri's resignation. General Reynaldo Bignone then succeeded Galtieri in office and quickly called for elections, leading to the victory of a civilian Peronist political leader, Raul Alfonsin, in October 1983.[6]

Despite the many difficulties perpetrated by the still-entrenched advocates of populist justicialismo, presidential elections held since Argentina's return to democracy in 1983 have fulfilled minimum democratic standards. Yet the sluggish performance of the Argentine economy explains why about 30 percent of the population lives below the poverty level and why, after twenty-five years of democratic governance, regional surveys illustrate both a profound popular dissatisfaction with liberal democracy and the presence of corrupted, insensitive, or misguided political parties.[7] As a consequence, large numbers of Argentines reject the liberal-democratic tradition, espouse strong state control of the economy, are more than wary of institutional relationships with the "imperialist" United States and Europe, and question the foundations of their political-economic system. Many of these people declare that they have espoused the doctrines of neo-populist New Socialism.[8]

This revelation brings us back to the revolutionary groups or movements that do not recognize themselves as part of the liberal-democratic tradition but instead support the methods and solutions of failed predecessors. As such, they provide a new model for now and the future that takes us beyond the use of armed violence to a more benign approach to revolutionary change.

ADDITIONAL CONTEXT

Over the past 150 years or more, Argentine politics moved from democratically elected and relatively responsible executives and legislatures to various military juntas and then into the streets. Even with the current minimum level of democracy (elected civilian officials) in place after 1983, there is still a general popular sense of exclusion from the decision-making process and an associated sense of governmental corruption and insensitivity to the legitimate needs and desires of the Argentine populace. Neither the government nor the people are comfortable with the present political situation, and the government and its opposition tend to combine any kind of lawful or illicit political action with some form of state or popular violence.[9]

As a consequence, the Piqueteros fit into the context of two realities: preexisting Peronist ties and the contemporary Argentine political system. Theoretically, the historical-ideological linkages of nonstate actors such as the Piqueteros to institutionalized political forces such as Peronism determine the specific development of organization, motive, and action, which in turn explain the group's identity and place in the current political system.[10]

Origins of the Piquetero Movement

Professor Guillermo Gini, of the Catholic University of Argentina, tells us that the "seeds of the Piquetero movement were sown in the 1960s by Catholic priests involved in the Liberation Theology Movement. At that time, the very small and loosely organized groups were concerned with the problems of equitable income, and land and property distribution. Main efforts centered on helping squatters gain legal title to occupied properties, advocating extensive public works projects for job creation, and campaigning for new social values—that is, the values of Liberation Theology."[11]

Later, in the 1970s, the relatively inconsequential organizations that would come to be known as "Piqueteros" were assimilated primarily into the Peronist Montonero and secondarily into the communist EPL (People's Liberation Army) insurgency organizations. At the outset, even though small, the organizations representing unemployed workers were allowed a voice in the political-military decision-making processes of the insurgency and with the (Peronist) Justicialist Party and the Revolutionary Communist Party. During that violent and polarized insurgency and associated dirty war, strong Peronist identities were forged—to the point where even those Piqueteros currently associated with the Communist Party still claim to vote Peronist. In any event, most of the various Argentine labor organizations are still dominated by leaders whose formative experiences were gained with Peronist political-military tutelage.[12]

The Peronist Experience, 1955–79

During his eighteen years of exile, General Peron used the Montonero insurgents as a clandestine, violent, and primary means of breaking the Peronist–anti-Peronist political impasse. He also used small groups within the insurgent organization to act as political bridges to worker-based mass movements and to rebellious youth and other compatible movements. This tactic ultimately proved successful. The military was nudged out of government, and democratic elections were called that put a Peronist, Hector Campora, into the Argentine presidency in 1973. Those elections paved the way for the general to return to Argentina.[13] During Peron's exile—and shortly after his return to power—Montonero actions centered on a Peronist-populist-nationalist political-psychological war to "liberate" Argentina from foreign economic domination and dependency. The Montoneros focused their early efforts against the oligarchy, members of which were perceived to be acting in behalf of foreign interests—and against those of Peron.[14]

On Peron's return to Argentina and to political power, a general political amnesty was proclaimed. Accordingly, Montoneros were given important posts in the government and in the national universities. As a consequence, there was a major political opportunity to abandon the armed struggle and cooperate peacefully to establish a stable and new government. Some Peronists took advantage of this situation. Others, however, never abandoned their vision of taking control of the state and imposing radical political change. They conducted several covert operations and, after Peron's death in 1974, openly renewed hostilities. At that point, the insurgents began to argue that they were liberating Argentina from the military and security forces that were acting on behalf of the oligarchy. In those terms, the Montonero vision of a "New Argentina" and a "New Motherland" could be achieved only by building an insurgent force capable of defeating the Argentine military and security institutions.[15]

Thus, the insurgents were no longer "the proletariat in arms." The people who were supposed to bring national and social liberation to Argentina developed into an ideology-bound, bureaucratized, isolated, cynical, mirror image of their enemy. The Argentine government's ultimate counterinsurgency response came in the form of a "dirty war" and an unprincipled repression of the part of society that supported the Peronist-populist-nationalist vision of the future. Accordingly, in December 1976, the Montonero leadership quietly followed the group's erstwhile Marxist-Guevarist allies (ERP) into exile. However, they continued to direct limited military operations from abroad until the final "Popular Counteroffensive" of 1979. The state response went far beyond neutralizing the remaining insurgents. The Argentine state response was total (not in any way limited) and could accurately be described as state terrorism.[16] These heartrending memories are still vivid in the minds of the Argentine citizens—and former insurgents—who witnessed and experienced the actions of the state from 1976 through 1983. And there is still a great deal of sympathy for the idea of a New Argentina—among Piqueteros as well.[17]

The Organizational Development of the Piqueteros

During periods of political-economic crises in the 1980s and through the early 2000s, unemployed workers organized into militant neighborhood unions (groups or gangs). Neighborhood political brokers *(punteros)* employed these "rowdy and fractious" picket groups to exercise a combination of persuasion and coercion (propaganda and agitation) to organize or to defuse given projects (depending on the "rent-a-mob" requirements of the moment). These projects ranged from general protests, marches, and riots to occupations of public buildings, factories, and businesses to blocking specific streets, roads, and highways.[18] At the same time, Piqueteros were used to participate in larger mass protests, mobilizing several thousand militants. As an example, a combination of center and left-of-center groups and Piqueteros joined together in December 2001 to bring about the "popular impeachment" of two presidents of the republic (Fernando de la Rua and Adolfo Rodriguez Saa) within a period of ten days.[19] Additionally, during the Nester Kirshner administration, half the members of the Supreme Court were forced from office, with a little help from his Piquetero friends.[20]

These diverse forms of civil disobedience and disruption are not regarded as simple collective resistance against grievances, insensitive or misguided governance, or any kind of insurrection. The operative word is "disruption." Even though the participants shout invective, carry heavy sticks, wear masks or paint their faces *(carapintadas)*, break windows, throw rocks and other projectiles, and look and act very fierce, they stay just below the threshold of unacceptable violence. These kinds of populist demonstrations are regarded as a substantive step toward "real democracy." And after several years of growing unemployment, inflation, a questionable quality of governance, and weakened structures of representative democracy, a country that was once 80 percent middle class is increasingly receptive (or acquiescent) to populist calls for direct democracy.[21]

After regaining access to public office in 1983, Peronist politicians began to use state resources to secure alliances with neighborhood punteros and develop patronage-based support networks *(agrupaciones)* to strengthen their control of both party and government.[22] The availability of ample public money and more than enough unemployed workers generated some rapid and far-reaching effects. First, *puntero* leaders reportedly flocked to the emerging *agrupaciones* and converted themselves and their lieutenants into government employees. Second, the patronage networks began to replace labor unions as the primary source of party manpower. Third, the Peronistas built a powerful political machine, and clientelist networks replaced agrupaciones as "plausibly deniable" instruments of illicit government and party power. Fourth, unemployed Piqueteros proved to be ready, willing, and able to defuse potential protests and riots that could prove embarrassing to Peronist-controlled municipal, provincial, and national governments, and they supported other government-instigated socially disruptive actions. All of that proved crucial to Piquetero organizational growth and influence.[23]

Further Organizational-Financial Development

In 1996, President Carlos Menem reorganized the basis of the patron-client networks. Under Plan Trabajar (Work Plan), he decentralized the allocation of funds and transferred responsibility to political bosses (punteros) for the distribution of resources (subsidies, or plans, called *planes*) to unemployed workers. The plan provided a monthly subsidy (stipend) to the unemployed in exchange for some sort of service to the state. Menem and his successors, however, did not require the beneficiary to work. The current Kirshner variation on the plan allows Piquetero organizations to directly monitor and disburse funds by formally organizing as nongovernmental organizations. This decentralization encouraged the further expansion of clientelistic networks among political leaders, party brokers, and potential beneficiaries.[24] This further decentralization allowed Piquetero leaders additional control over their membership, as well as the use of the subsidies. Nevertheless, the *planes* come from the government, and the government has the leverage to ask for political compromise in return. Thus, Piqueteros are acting as government agents (mercenary gangs) for all kinds of populist political-economic-social "disruption," in exchange for political favors or economic advantages.[25]

As Piquetero organizations grew to an estimated total membership of 300,000 by the mid-2000s, the number of cash transfers to the unemployed likewise increased. As examples, during the Menem administration, approximately 100,000 *planes* were distributed; the Duhalde administration (2002–2003) increased subsidies to 2,000,000; and the subsequent Kirchner administration reportedly distributes about the same number of *planes*. In 2004, each subsidy *(plan)* translated to 180,000,000 Argentine pesos per year; 2,000,000 *planes* thus yield a substantial entitlement of 3,600,000,000 pesos a year.[26]

The decentralization of social subsidies generated at least two additional effects. First, it encouraged the organization of small groups of unemployed workers into larger groups that could qualify as nongovernment organizations to distribute the subsidies. Second, it promoted the expansion of corrupt networks that have been known to misuse these public funds for partisan and personal purposes. Another consequence related to the decentralization process is different from but related to the first two: the 300,000 Piqueteros are not united. They have divided themselves into two major coalitions that define themselves by their level of willingness or unwillingness to cooperate with government—the *oficialistas* and the *opositoras*. The oficialistas are closer to the Peronist government, whereas the opositoras are more reluctant to cooperate with the government.[27]

More about Organization, Linkages, and Motives

Organization and Decision Making. The Piqueteros are fractious groups with a long tradition of relative autonomy, freedom of discussion, and collective democratic decision making. As a consequence, Piquetero organizations are not vertical, hierarchical, or authoritarian structures; they are horizontal networks and only loosely tied together. The model of the open assembly *(asamblea)* has been defined as a prime feature of Piquetero decision making. Open debate among people who know each other, have perhaps fought side by side, have worked with each other over the years, and share common interests and background generally leads to a pragmatic and collective decision-making process.[28] In the Piquetero case, then, protests and physical opposition to public policy and specific politicians do not reflect a history of political exclusion as much as the fading memory and experience of former inclusion in legitimate or illegitimate political processes. However, as one Piquetero stated, "The discussions [among Piqueteros] are fierce, but with time people will accommodate to each other, because the person who doesn't accommodate will be left behind and will lose his subsidy."[29]

Internal Linkages. As a result of the collective decisions made among individuals whose personal and family relationships go back twenty to fifty years, two major coalitions of Piqueteros have emerged, as noted above. The strongest coalition is called Central de Trabajadores Argentinos (CTA). The organization that stands out in this coalition is the Federacion de Tierra y Vivienda (FTV), led by Luis D'Elia. This is the largest Piquetero organization, boasting more than 125,000 members. The FTV unites the oficialistas. This group tends to have close ties with the Peronist Judicialist Party, and members or their families may have been involved with the Peronist Montoneros in the insurgency and dirty war. This group also tends to enjoy a good relationship with the past and present Peronist Kirshner administrations.[30] An additional motive for this association might be that D'Elia has been the minister of housing in the Kirshner administrations and has access to the ministry's budget. Another large organization in the CTA coalition is the Barrios de Pie y Patria Libre (BPPL). This group has an estimated 60,000 members. Not surprisingly, the CTA coalition is credited with controlling the largest number of *planes* (subsidies), more than any other. As an example, CTA manages about seventy-five thousand subsidies; in contrast, the *opositora* Bloque Piquetero Nacional (BPN) has a membership of 70,000 to 90,000 but controls only ten thousand subsidies.[31]

The second coalition (the opositoras), thought to be the most dangerous of the Piquetero organizations, is the Corriente Classica y Combativa

(CCC). That group counts about 150,000 members and unites the more leftist-oriented branches of the Piquetero movement. It is closely associated with the Revolutionary Communist Party (CPR) of Argentina. Most of the *opositora* membership has personal or family links that go back to the communist EPL and the insurgency of the 1970s. Nevertheless, the CCC and the BPN maintain links with the Peronists. The principal organization within the CCC is the BPN, noted above.[32]

A Motive Issue: Contradiction or Distortion. Of the total 2,000,000 *planes* being allocated by the state, only about 200,000 are being controlled by the various Piquetero organizations. The difference of 1,800,000 subsidies is being administered by the municipalities; this puts control more directly into the hands of local politicians, giving the Peronist political apparatus considerable leverage with the entire Argentine underclass.[33] As noted above, those individuals who allocate those public resources enjoy considerable latitude in the mercenary distribution of the subsidies. These state subsidies to the "rent-a-mobs" pay for political and electoral support, attacks on opponents of government policy and actions, and acts of intimidation against personal enemies. This type of illicit clientelism is further defined by patronage, bribes, kickbacks, cronyism, and personal whim. This type of "disruption" is also a strategy or tactic intended to encourage or discourage public opinion in one direction or another. It has been proven to be effective in controlling, disciplining, co-opting, and mobilizing parts of Argentine society for one partisan or personal purpose or another.[34] For example, during the 1989–90 hyperinflation, punteros used small groups (gangs) of unemployed workers for the kinds of persuasion and coercion purposes mentioned above. This action also included the unlawful expulsion of antigovernment activists from their neighborhoods. As a result, the Menem administration was never embarrassed by widespread protests, riots, or looting.[35]

The close association of unemployed workers with the government, then, indicates a compromise of Piquetero objectives. The national, provincial, and municipal governments are major targets of Piquetero protests, but they also provide resources that allow Piquetero existence. This compromise, contradiction, or distortion of organizational objectives applies to both the oficialistas and the opositoras, regardless of their claims regarding allegiance to government. Both coalitions share similar objectives. Mid- to long-term objectives focus on the improvement of state-funded societal assistance, employment programs, and community works projects. Additionally, Piquetero objectives extend to the establishment of a government of popular unity (based on direct democracy) and ultimately to new values and a New Argentina. Nevertheless, over the past several years, the significance of the unemployed workers movement has been confined (and is likely to continue so) largely to a negative veto or impeachment power against specific government policies and party politicians.[36]

Underscoring the compromise of government objectives is that the Argentine government subsidizes unemployed workers within and outside of the various Piquetero organizations in an effort to maintain political-social-economic stability, even while, paradoxically, the government also pays unemployed workers to "destabilize" the system. As a consequence, there is a distortion in the government's agenda, as well as in that of the Piqueteros. Those distortions work on two levels: antiliberal democracy and an antistate political-economic-social system.

WHERE THE GOVERNMENT AND PIQUETERO CONTRADICTIONS LEAD

The contemporary decline of the traditional nation-state has been articulated most effectively in the idea of the "New Middle Ages." This notion has it that the state is only one of many political-social actors involved in internal conflicts, fragmented political authority, identity politics, political-economic-social instability, personal and collective insecurity, and chronic poverty in a large part of a given society. In this context, the inability of representative democracy to meet its social-contractual obligations to its citizens can lead to the decline of the state into a neomedieval condition.[37] As a corollary, Robert D. Kaplan makes the argument that "[o]nce the legal monopoly of the armed forces, long claimed by the state, is wrested out of the hands of the state, existing distinctions between war and crime will break down, and national security will be viewed as a local concept."[38] Historically, and in Argentina today, anti-democracy and antisystem objectives of competing internal actors act as catalysts to compel a process of radical political change. That process starts with populism and neopopulism and proceeds through an erosion of regime authority, legitimacy, and effectiveness. In the end, the state cannot control its national territory or the people in it. The result takes us to state failure and, possibly, the "New Middle Ages."[39]

Populism

Populism is not a new political phenomenon, and it is not confined to Argentina, Venezuela, or any other country in Latin America. Populism has been a political reality in any country, anywhere, and at any time when people are under great stress because of any kind of profound change. The whole dynamic supporting populism relies on the fact that a disaffected group within a political system does not consider the incumbent government as legitimately representing its interests in a given crisis situation. At some point in the dilemma, a charismatic leader emerges who is able to capture the imagination of the population and form a direct bond with "the people." Then, that leader finds legal and illegal ways and means to bypass incumbent political leadership and institutions that are perceived to be obstacles to solving the problems at hand.[40]

Argentina is a case in point. During the nineteenth century, that country went through a succession of seemingly endless internal wars (1816–53) led by regional *caudillos* (strongmen). After peace was established and prosperity came to the nation, a series of military coups and military dictatorships—beginning in the 1940s—severely weakened the structures of representative democracy that had been promulgated after 1853. The problem that brought on this instability is normally explained as the social unrest generated as a result of the mid-twentieth-century industrialization and unconscionable exploitation of workers.[41] As a consequence, populism in Argentina is a latent political problem with a legacy of deteriorated governance and a deeply divided society. That issue reemerges in crises of political representation and is profoundly antidemocratic.[42]

Populism is, thus, defined as a "political problem with entrenched disregard for democratic institutions."[43] Another important and closely related defining element of populism is the emergence of a "leader that is seen as a messianic figure in whose hands the fate of a nation will be carried."[44] Populist leaders also tend to be "outsiders," as opposed to being members of "foreign-dominated" ruling elites. They appeal to people as "uncontaminated" and as strongly nationalistic.[45] Shortly after taking political power, the leader has historically proceeded to bypass, dismantle, or erode those leaders and institutions that restrict the concentration of power in his hands. Channels for traditional popular participation—and especially dissent—are thereby systematically closed. The alternative to representative democracy is direct democracy, that is, the creation of a direct link from the leader to the people, and back again, without any intervening or opposing elements to contend with.[46]

Accordingly, populism is not necessarily ideological (left or right). Thomas Legler, a Canadian scholar, argues, "Populism is more a style or way of doing politics than an ideology."[47] More than anything else, populism is expedient. And because of the politically uninhibited direct relationship between the leader and the people of a given polity, populism has historically been totalitarian. That kind of direct democracy stems from the logic of the French Revolution of 1789: if the people want something, then constitutions, government institutions, and politicians must not get in the way. Thus, the question is, Who determines what the people want (the general will)? In case after case, in the past and almost universally, the answer is, The leader does (and don't you forget it!). Jean Jacques Rousseau wrote, "For whoever refuses to obey the general will and is unwilling to comply with the body politic, there is no other recourse than to force him to be free."[48]

Neopopulism

The term "neopopulism" has taken on some "new" populist meanings. The term was coined in an attempt to differentiate contemporary governments and movements from past populist entities and as a way of avoiding the erroneous left-right ideological dichotomy. Nevertheless, there are some authentically new populist characteristics that deserve serious attention. Neopopulism is not the traditional opposition to ruling oligarchies and unresponsive liberal-democratic institutions. Instead, it targets the entire political-economic-social system. Thus, it is not antiestablishment; it is not antidemocratic; it is antisystem (antieverything).[49]

Another defining characteristic of neopopulism involves the core constituency (supporters) of neopopulist movements. Traditionally, key populist support has come from the military, organized labor, or organized agricultural workers. Contemporary supporters tend to come from the "new working class" (proletariat). That would include radical student groups, new technological professionals, and newly unemployed workers who have appointed themselves as the "new" extraparliamentary opposition. In the case of Argentina, the new opposition exercises popular impeachment of leaders and popular vetoes of laws, decrees, policies, and programs.[50] Other players that might be included in the new opposition would include activist racial, ethnic, and religious groups.[51] These neopopulist constituents not only act as a new opposition to the traditional political-economic-social system but also tend to preempt state security and other public service institutions. They act as parallel state instruments for some social services (health, education, and welfare), as well as for social control and discipline. As such, in Marxist-Leninist terms, these new supporters define themselves as the antithesis of traditional politics. These are the "New Socialists." They consider themselves as the "new" midwifes of social systems and values for the twenty-first century.[52]

Behind the destabilizing populist and neopopulist actions that define the terms and subvert democracy and the state, there is an explicit political agenda. Generally, Piquetero organizations claim that they do not want governmental power. They state that they are not interested in inclusion in a system based on exploitation and repression. For them, the starting point for changing Argentina—or any other country in the liberal-democratic world—is the construction of something new from below. Their aim is to go beyond the struggle for equitable income distribution, jobs, and sociopolitical "inclusion"; the ultimate objective is to achieve "dignity," that is, to create a "New Argentina" that will discipline the government and the economy to the needs of the people.

That final objective requires a slow but sure, relatively nonviolent march to revolution. But, importantly, the final objective also requires the destruction of the state system to establish a "New Motherland."[53]

The Neopopulist Piquetero Road to Dignity

Despite their loose organization and differing political allegiances, Argentine Piqueteros share a common tactical methodology and a common set of long-term political objectives. The notion of the meta-phorical long march to achieve the revolution that will create a new political-economic-social system for a New Argentina explains both methodology and objectives.[54] The long march, however, cannot ignore the contemporary populist Argentine governments. The question becomes, Is the government a bump in the road, or is it a facilitator of Piquetero dignity?

Piquetero Methodology and Objectives. As a consequence of the experi-ence of devastating defeat of the violent Che Guevara–inspired insur-gency (1973–79), Piqueteros understand that they cannot attack the state and its security organizations directly. In his *Changing the World without Taking Power,* John Holloway (a revolutionary Argentine aca-demic) further explains the logic of that hard-learned lesson and pre-scribes a slow and not-too-violent diminishing of the power of the state. That strategic vision requires a strategy that will change Argentina by indirectly assaulting the foundations of the state, by creating a counter-power—a soft power that will almost imperceptibly dissolve what is left of Argentine liberal democracy, the capitalist economy, and, thus, the entire political-economic-social system. The complete destruction of the state, then, is achieved indirectly so that a new and better state and system can be created.[55]

Piqueteros call this antistate strategy "disruption." Disruption and its collateral (indirect) damage to the security, stability, development, and effective sovereignty of the Argentine state starts with roadblocks, marches, and sit-ins. It continues with popular impeachment of unac-ceptable leaders and popular vetoes of unpopular laws, policies, and other actions of government. These first steps toward diminishing the power of the state are the propaganda-agitation tasks of small groups of global social democrats that will lead to the generation of the "correlation of forces" that will enable the revolution. These are the kinds of efforts that will generate "dignity." Disruption ends with the establishment of a new system, controlled by direct democracy, that will "discipline the government and the economy to the needs of the people."[56] Dignity will thereby be achieved.[57] Interestingly, the resultant New Argentina would look something like the revolutionary state advocated by V. I. Lenin.[58]

Additional slow steps that might be taken along the revolutionary Piquetero road would include the propagation of direct democracy; the promotion of the people's ownership and control of the means of production and distribution; and the advocation of an egalitarian distribution of wealth. These efforts are expected to be helpful in reconciling the entire Argentine society to those ideals and speeding the correlation of forces toward the revolutionary threshold. At the same time, Piquetero political-economic-social disruptions will perpetuate a climate of crisis and instability that will preclude a return to liberal-democratic channels for popular political expression.[59]

The Role of the Argentine Government in the Long March. As noted above, the various populist Argentine governments over the years have used the Piqueteros and other unemployed workers for their own purposes. Piqueteros are not just passive recipients of government stipends. They have been used as grassroots political support organizations and as parallel structures for government social services and security in zones ceded to their control. They have also become appendages to the government for social control, acting as instruments to propagandize the population and to harass and intimidate any possible opposition. Argentine governments have, thus, found the Piqueteros to be useful, and helpful, in a manner by which governments—national, provincial, and local—can claim plausible deniability for instigating illicit and destabilizing partisan actions.[60]

At the same time, the Piqueteros have found government subsidies and mercenary destabilization tasks to be supportive of their antidemocratic and antisystem strategies. Apparently, either the government and its client Piquetero organizations are collaborating in the erosion of democracy and the state, or else there are those in Peronist governments who expect to control the evolution of that correlation of forces for their own populist and neopopulist purposes. Of course, there may be Piqueteros who expect that their increasing counterpower may eventually be capable of controlling diminishing governmental power.[61] It is probably too early to determine whether the various Argentine governments have acted as a bump in the Piquetero road or as a facilitator for radical populist change. However, if the government is a bump in the road, it would not be a significant obstacle in a long march. Additionally, the Peronists appear to be acting as facilitators of their own concept of neopopulist change.[62]

Public Opinion and Decision Making. A former prime minister of Spain, José Maria Aznar, warns us that disruption and its associated conflicts take place among and between individual people representing diverse segments of a society. These conflicts take place in the flesh and in the media: the media is where the real revolutionary struggle takes place. In using the media as a primary instrument to facilitate the metaphorical long march and establish a New Argentina, each neopopulist actor (government and nongovernment) constantly feeds the dream of a better future, hides the disasters it generates, puts off objective analysis of its actions, bends criticism, adulterates the truth, and numbs, corrupts, and degrades the public spirit. As a consequence, public opinion and governmental decision making are likely to be informed by disinformation that does not reflect sociopolitical reality. Yet the strategy of disruption does not directly attack national territory, people, or institutions. Rather, it indirectly undermines the democracy, security stability, development, peace, and prosperity (well-being) of people.[63] The assault on and the degradation of public opinion and governmental decision making take us directly to the problem of state failure.

The Path to the New Middle Ages: State Failure

Whatever the causes, instability within a nation-state leads to a crisis of governance and a downward spiral into violence, loss of de jure and de facto sovereignty, and failing and failed state status. In the novel *The Constant Gardener*, author John Le Carré vividly and succinctly captures that linkage. He answers the question "When is a state not a state?" from the point of view of a commonsense practitioner:

> I would suggest to you that these days, very roughly, the qualifications for being a civilized state amount to—electoral suffrage, ah—protection of life and property—um, justice, health, and educations for all, at least to a certain level—then the maintenance of sound administrative infrastructure—and roads, transport, drains, et cetera—and—what else is there? Ah yes, the equitable collection of taxes. If a state fails to deliver on at least a quorum of the above—then one has to say the contract between the state and citizens begins to look pretty shaky—and if it fails on all of the above, then it's a failed state, as we say these days.[64]

The Situation in Argentina. However, just because a state fails does not mean that it will go away. In fact, failing and failed states tend to linger and go from bad to worse. The longer they persist, the more they and their spillover problems endanger regional and global peace and security.[65] Ample evidence demonstrates that failing and failed states become, as examples, dysfunctional states, rogue states, criminal states, narco-states, military dictatorships, or new "peoples' democracies."

The long-term decline of the Argentine state is characterized by a reduced role in governance and security and by diminishing effective sovereignty. More specifically, the country is experiencing an unsettling diminution of its capability to manage political, economic, and social problems that are increasingly interconnected, intractable, and volatile. More specifically, Argentina is challenged by the emergence of alternative centers of power and authority—most notably the Piqueteros and other organizations emulating their tactics. The resultant decline of the state has thus far been relatively subtle and gradual. At some point, however, changes in degree can become a change in kind. A multitude of incremental shifts can sooner or later generate a major tipping point from which the state moves from high to low levels of performance and legitimacy; from civil disobedience to instability, to political-economic-social chaos; and from control of the national territory and the people in it to a loss of effective sovereignty. All these elements—and more—constitute a long-term "durable disorder" that leads to state failure. The kind of future that might be expected of a failed state has been articulated as the "New Middle Ages," "New Medievalism," or "neomedievalism"—or even the "New Dark Ages."[66]

In any event, Argentine politics is characterized by several highly interrelated, neopopulist elements that give it a neomedieval quality: competing institutions with overlapping jurisdictions between the state and internal nonstate actors (such as the Piqueteros); multiple or fragmented or compromised loyalties and identities; great inequality between and resultant marginalization of various segments of the society; fluid and porous boundaries within the country, the provinces, and the municipalities, controlled alternatively by the state and the parallel structures of the unemployed workers movement (Piqueteros); and contested property rights and legal statutes between formal property rights and the de facto property rights of squatters, as well as between laws and decrees and groups throughout the country contesting their legitimacy (such as "popular impeachment"). Each of these elements poses a formidable set of challenges to the state. They feed off one another in ways that are not only mutually reinforcing but also multiply the difficulties in developing an appropriate response. Thus, one can readily envisage the transformation of Argentine politics as a nonlinear move from the present to the New Middle Ages.

Instability and Democracy. The future of Argentina will depend on the approach taken to establish or reestablish democracy. Populist direct democracy has proven to lead to one form or another of totalitarianism. Liberal democracy's potential contribution—that political authority and the rule of law come from each and every member of society— can be eroded to the point of disappearing. Thus, the main lesson that comes out of an examination of the populist and Piquetero paths to a New Argentina is straightforward: the attack on Argentine democracy and system is not being conducted by a conventional military organization or another nation-state. At base, the real enemy is the individual internal political actor that plans and implements the kind of destabilizing political-economic-social disruption that exploits the root causes of instability and threatens the national well-being.

KEY POINTS AND LESSONS

- Argentina has experienced a long history of tumultuous destabilizing crises that have given rise to populist responses.
- The Piquetero unemployed worker's movement has flourished in that political environment. One example demonstrates that reality—in 1996, President Menem decentralized the allocation of funds to unemployed workers and transferred responsibility to neighborhood political bosses (punteros) for the distribution of those subsidies. Because the subsidies come from the government, government officials have the leverage to ask for political compromise in return. Thus, Piqueteros are acting as government agents (mercenary gangs) for all kinds of populist political-economic-social "disruption."
- The various Piquetero organizations are not united: they are divided into two major coalitions that define themselves by their relative level of willingness or unwillingness to cooperate with the government—oficialistas (officialists) and opositoras (oppositionists).
- The association of unemployed workers with the government indicates a compromise of both Piquetero and government objectives. The national, provincial, and municipal governments are major targets of Piquetero protests and disruption efforts, but the government provides resources that allow Piquetero existence. At the same time, the government subsidizes the unemployed workers in a supposed effort to maintain political-economic-social stability. Paradoxically, the government also pays "rent-a-mobs" to destabilize the system.
- These distortions work on two levels: antiliberal democracy and an antistate political-economic-social system. That dual-level process compels a move toward radical political change.

The change is led by antidemocratic populism and antisystem neopopulism and proceeds toward state failure.

- As a result of government and Piquetero antidemocratic and antisystem actions, the Argentine political-economic-social system is not being attacked by any kind of external enemy but is being attacked from within by those who use liberal-democratic freedoms and institutions to further their radical ambitions to create a New Argentina.
- Another result of these antidemocratic and antisystem actions is the strategy of disruption to achieve radical populist change. Disruption is a relatively nonviolent process through which groups of propaganda-agitators can destroy the state and change the world without taking government power. That is, they can destroy the state by using unconventional soft power as a counter to the traditional hard power of the state.

The great irony in the compromise, contradiction, or distortion of government and Piquetero objectives is that governments that maintain themselves through disrupting and destabilizing populist processes and uncertain mercenary support must be concerned with two innate weakness: first, questionable legitimacy and limited sovereignty; and second, the constant pending threat of being ousted in the same way it maintains itself. This irony is eloquent evidence of a serious assault on the democracy and effectiveness of the Argentine state.

Of great importance is that the "disrupters" of the Argentine system are mercenary groups working for the state, on one hand, and working toward their own revolutionary objectives, on the other hand. Machiavelli warns us, "The arms by which a prince defends his possessions are either his own, or else mercenaries, or auxiliaries, or mixed. . . . The mercenaries . . . are useless and dangerous, and if anyone supports his state by the arms of mercenaries, he will never stand firm or sure. They are disunited, ambitious, without discipline, faithless, bold amongst friends, cowardly against enemies. They have no fear of God, and they keep no faith with men."[67]

CHAPTER 3

FROM THE BARREL OF A GUN AND DEEP POCKETS

The Gang Role in Coercing Political Change in Colombia

Over the past forty to fifty years, Colombia's potential, its democracy, and its effective sovereignty have been slowly deteriorating as a consequence of three simultaneous ongoing and interrelated wars involving three major violent, internal nonstate groups: FARC (Revolutionary Armed Forces of Colombia), the paramilitary/vigilante AUC (United Self-Defense Groups of Colombia), and the illegal transnational drug industry. This unholy trinity (or nexus) of politically motivated and terroristic transnational criminal organizations (TCOs) and nonstate actors is perpetrating a level of human horror, violence, criminality, corruption, and internal instability that is threatening Colombia's survival as an organized democratic nation-state. Additionally, neopopulist (antisystem) activities of some of that country's elites further complicate the conflict picture. These elites have never supported the idea of strong national institutions and the development of a viable nation-state. The issue is, simply, that the power to control terroristic insurgents or criminal drug traffickers is also the power to control the virtually autonomous elites.[1]

At the same time, a new dynamic is being introduced into the ongoing multidimensional conflict in Colombia. Several types of illegal nonstate groups (gangs) are devolving out of President Álvaro Uribe's AUC demobilization and reintegration program.[2] An even greater potential threat to security and stability coming out of the emergence of these new *bandas criminales* (criminal gangs) is thought to be the possible formal establishment of a federation of splinter AUC groups, existing

56

drug trafficking organizations, currently faltering FARC units, and the much smaller ELN (National Liberation Army) insurgent group. Such a federation could become a significant terrorist-criminal-insurgent non-state actor in the Colombian malaise.[3]

These various actors, each challenging the state in its own way, are generating a triple threat to Colombia. First, through murder, kidnapping, intimidation, corruption, and other means of coercion and persuasion, violent internal insurgents and criminals undermine the ability of a government to perform its security, service, development, governance, and other legitimizing functions. Second, by taking control of large portions of the national territory, the narcos, FARC, ELN, paramilitaries, and the new criminal gangs associated primarily with AUC and FARC directly perform the tasks of government and act as sovereign entities within the state. Third, through impunity, corruption, and legal maneuvers, the nonviolent neopopulist elites compromise the ability of the state to perform its legitimizing functions. Yet legally, and ironically, this set of conflicts within the general insurgency war remains more of a law enforcement issue and a socioeconomic reform issue than a threat to Colombian national security and sovereignty.[4]

This case, then, is a point from which to examine the destabilizing actions of multiple political-criminal-terrorist gangs in an insurgency war and to explore the extent to which these nonstate actors, including the subtle elites, tend to erode the state and its democratic institutions to accomplish neopopulist antisystem objectives: that is, radical change toward either a utopian future or back to a better past, depending on the political sponsors.[5] That, in turn, brings us to the "What if?" questions: What if criminal and elite self-interest and insurgent ideological and commercial objectives come to a functional unity and to fruition? What if the Colombian political-economic system is destroyed? What then?

This case also provides a foundation for understanding that (1) counterinsurgency and insurgency both have pervasive and protean natures that need to be taken into account; (2) subnational (intrastate) conflict may involve multiple and diverse protagonists, including some elites; (3) motives are likely to be more commercial and self-serving than ideological; (4) objectives may be more populist-neopopulist or political-psychological than military; and, as a consequence, (5) human terrain is considered more important than physical terrain. Thus, this case yields lessons that might help strategic leaders understand how governments might ultimately control—or succumb to—the multiple threats inherent in contemporary intrastate political war.

THE ORGANIZATIONAL AND MOTIVATIONAL CONTEXT OF THE GENERAL COLOMBIAN CONFLICT

The unstable political-economic-social-security environment generated by *la violencia* (the violence) that began in 1948 has allowed insurgents, paramilitaries, and drug traffickers to grow in influence, expand their activities, and prosper. Most of the elites continue to make money as well. Accordingly, the Colombian central government has faced and continues to face three different wars, plus one, which gives Colombia the worst record of political violence in the Western Hemisphere. In turn, that multibelligerent internal war virtually guarantees uncontrolled violence, political disarray, and rural and urban poverty.[6] The organizational and motivational context of the situation focuses on the main protagonists—and did not change much over the past several years, until recently.

The Protagonists

The Narcos. The illegal transnational drug traffickers of Colombia—known as *narcóticos* or *narcotraficantes ilegales trasnacionales* and generally called *narcos* for short—operate as a consortium that functions in much the same way as virtually any multinational Fortune 500 company. Products are made, sold, and shipped; bankers and financial planners handle the monetary issues; and lawyers deal with the legal problems. The consortium is organized to achieve superefficiency and maximum profit. It has chief executive officers and boards of directors, councils, a system of justice, public affairs officers, negotiators, project managers—and enforcers. Plus, it operates in virtually every country in the Western Hemisphere and Europe.[7]

Additionally, the illegal drug industry has at its disposal a very efficient flat organizational structure, the latest in high-tech communications equipment and systems, and state-of-the-art weaponry. With these advantages, decisions are made quickly that can ignore or supersede laws, regulations, decisions, and actions of the governments of the nation-states in which the illegal drug industry operates. Narcos also have assassinated, bribed, corrupted, intimidated, and terrorized government leaders, members of the Colombian Congress, judges, law enforcement and military officers, journalists, and even soccer players. As such, the illegal narco-trafficking industry is a major agent for destabilizing and weakening the state governmental apparatus.[8]

At the same time, cosmetic narco patronage to the poor, narcos' creation of their own electoral machinery, open participation in traditional political parties, the financing of friendly election campaigns, and the assassination of "uncooperative" elected officials has facilitated even greater narco influence over the executive, legislative, and judicial branches of the Colombian government. All of this prevents responsible democratic governance and any allegiance to the notion of the public good and the general welfare. In that process, the illegal drug trafficking consortium is working toward a symbiotic relationship with the state and in a sense is becoming a virtual state-within-the-state.[9]

The Insurgents. The FARC insurgents are essentially a *foco*—an insurrectionary armed enclave—in search of a mass base. Because of their general lack of appeal to the majority of the Colombian population, the insurgents have developed a military organization designed to achieve the "armed colonization" of successive areas within the Colombian national territory. The intent is to "liberate" and mobilize the "disaffected and the dispossessed" population into an alternative society. That is, FARC responded to the lack of popular support, as did the communists in Vietnam, by attempting to take control of the human terrain. In this effort, FARC has proved every bit as ruthless as the Vietcong. Torture and assassination—to say nothing of kidnapping, extortion, intimidation, and other terrorist tactics—are so common as to go almost without comment except in the most extreme cases. Strategically, operationally, and tactically, the FARC approach to taking control of the state has been the Vietnamese approach.[10]

These terrorist-type activities, designed to dominate the human terrain more than the physical terrain, probably would have remained more or less out of sight and out of mind of mainstream Colombia had they been confined to underpopulated and underconsidered rural areas of the country—and had the insurgents not become involved in the illegal drug phenomenon. In 1982, a decision was taken by the Seventh Conference of FARC to develop links with the Colombian drug industry that would provide the money and manpower necessary for the creation of a "true Bolivarian democracy."[11]

As a result, it has been estimated that FARC expanded from approximately two thousand guerrilla fighters in 1982 to over seventy company-sized units with approximately eighteen thousand to twenty-two thousand fighters in 2005. FARC strength remained at about twenty thousand combatants until it began to diminish in 2007–2008. From the early 1990s to 2008, illicit drug money provided FARC with the capability of confronting regular Colombian military units up to battalion size and of overrunning police and military installations and smaller units. Accordingly, FARC presence spread from 173 municipalities in 1985 to 622 in 1995. In 2005, FARC was reported to maintain an armed presence in every department throughout Colombia and to control approximately 40 percent of the national territory.[12]

Since 2005, however, FARC has sustained serious military setbacks as a result of President Uribe's democratic stabilization policies and the creation of a Coordinating Center for Integrated Action (CCAI) to facilitate cooperation among civilian agencies, the military, and the police. In 2008, estimated FARC combatant strength was down to approximately eight thousand, and government statements claimed that the insurgency was in full retreat. Nevertheless, there is evidence that FARC still maintains an armed presence in every department of the country, and many analysts argue that rumors of its demise are greatly exaggerated.[13]

Even though there is evidence that FARC is militarily weaker now than it has been at any time in the past thirty years, it has organized an active international support network (the Coordinadora Continental Bolivariana [CCB]) and a secret political party structure (the Clandestine Colombian Communist Party, known as PC-3) that will allow it to survive—and prosper. The CCB is composed of governments in the

Latin American region (primarily Venezuela, Nicaragua, and Ecuador), nonstate regional actors, and European groups (including designated terrorist organizations such as the Basque Independence Movement [ETA] in Spain and the Provisional Irish Republican Army [PIRA] in Ireland). The support received from members and associates of the CCB is known to have led to knowledge, technology, financial, and personnel transfers that have greatly enhanced FARC's political-military-economic-informational capabilities.[14] The PC-3 is a parallel structure to the overt Colombian Communist (Bolivarian) Party. It is designed to (1) conduct strategic intelligence and propaganda and provocation (agitation) activities; (2) infiltrate and penetrate the state and its institutions and other political parties, social organizations, universities, and the media; and (3) conduct other subversion and destabilization actions as opportunity allows.[15] This is a classic Leninist response to a military setback, and it has serious implications for the ongoing internal war in Colombia, portending a move away from the direct confrontation of the armed forces through guerrilla war and toward the subtle continuation of the revolutionary struggle against the state through political-psychological coercion. In these terms, the gang phenomenon takes on preeminent importance.

As a consequence, a military victory over FARC is unlikely as long as it retains the international support network and clandestine political party apparatus that can provide international support and legitimacy and enhance the organization's ability to advance its internal political agenda. In that connection, FARC's myriad local bodies have access to a virtually inexhaustible pool of marginalized youth living at the seams of rural and urban society, and FARC's political apparatus is placed in positions throughout the country from which to move into or control the major population centers.[16] FARC's stated—and recently restated—political objective in all this is to eventually organize an army that can conduct a "final offensive against the government, and do away with the state as it now exists in Colombia."[17]

A new problem may be developing, however. With Colombian military successes and the death and defection of key leaders, FARC is experiencing some disarray and fragmentation. There is evidence that disaffected units and individuals are breaking away from the insurgent organization and merging with AUC groups or drug cartels for self-enrichment. Thus, some FARC units are expected to emerge as a variation on the existing bandas criminales.[18]

The Paramilitaries. The AUC groups (paramilitaries) began as vigilante self-defense organizations to protect family, property, and the law and order of a given political-geographical area. These groups were semi-autonomous regional alliances relatively independent of each other. Nevertheless, a central organization existed primarily to develop a national coordinated strategy against the FARC and ELN insurgents. That national front organization provided guidance, training, and other help to member paramilitary organizations as necessary. The strategy and tactics of AUC, interestingly, mirrored those of the insurgents. The paramilitary groups sought to expand their control of grassroots levels of government—municipalities or townships in rural and urban areas—and to exercise political influence through the terroristic control, intimidation, corruption, or replacement of local and national officials. Like the insurgents, the paramilitaries profited from drug trafficking.[19]

Because of AUC's willingness to fight the insurgents and its ability to provide elementary justice and personal security to those defined as noncollaborators (with FARC) who lived in areas where the state was absent or ineffective, the paramilitaries consistently improved their standing in Colombian society. As examples of their success, the number of AUC groups increased from 273 to more than 400, and the paramilitaries achieved an armed presence in about 40 percent of the municipalities of the country by 2005. Additionally, in the elections of 2006, thirty-three senators and fifty members of the House of Representatives were elected from areas under paramilitary control.[20] Interestingly and importantly, the national government's estimate of the strength of AUC during that period was only five thousand to ten thousand active combatants.[21]

In 2005, the Colombian government publicly disavowed AUC. Since then, President Uribe has made a considerable effort to demobilize AUC and is claiming success. An estimated thirty-two thousand AUC fighters (note the disparity between this figure and those in the previous paragraph) have reportedly been disbanded, but one must temper this reduction in membership numbers with the following realities: the government has been known to tamper with statistics for political purposes; hard-core AUC members are not giving up and continue to fight; the various AUC units have become increasingly autonomous; and demobilized AUC members are operating in an outsourcing mode as "subsidiaries," "pseudo-paramilitaries," or "gangs" (bandas criminales)—renting their services to the highest bidder.[22] As such, the paramilitaries remain a third set of competing nonstate actors—along with the various insurgent organizations and the illegal drug consortium—challenging the authority of the state and claiming the right to control all or a part of the national territory.[23]

The Social-Political Elites. Each one of the three sets of armed nonstate players involved in the Colombian crisis generates formidable problems, challenges, and threats to the state and the region in its own right. What are we to make of the more subtle but still dissident actions of the "elites" that further complicate the intranational conflict mosaic of mutual and conflicting interests?

Colombia's elites have traditionally shown very little interest in the military and have never supported the idea of a strong central government or strong state institutions. As a result, the burden of fighting Colombia's internal wars falls primarily to the relatively poorly supported military and to the hapless peasantry. As one example of elite lack of cooperation with or involvement in the general conflict, the Constitutional Court has ruled that only professional (that is, volunteer) soldiers—not conscripts—can be ordered into combat. Subsequent attempts to introduce a lottery system of conscription in 2004, which could have drafted children of the elites and brought them into the war, failed to get a final reading in the Congress.[24]

Additionally, in the 1960s and the 1970s, when military victory was thought to be within the grasp of the armed forces, politicians asserted to be acting as elite surrogates essentially "pulled the rug out from under" the armed forces and did not allow the successful conclusion of the war. At the same time, there was also a common and strong belief that the Colombian armed forces overused the FARC threat as a means to support expansion of the military budget. The same feelings are being expressed at this time. In sum, the military leadership generally argues that the controlling elites fundamentally distrust and historically under-resource the armed forces.[25] This takes us back to the broader assertion that the Colombian elites have not historically supported (and do not now support) strong government or strong national institutions. This lack of support can be attributed to the fact with which this discussion began: the power to control insurgents, narco-traffickers, and transnational criminal organizations is the same power that can control internal elites and transnational corporations. As a consequence, "[s]tate institutions do not work. Impunity and corruption are rife. The legal system does not work; so, major criminals are extradited to the United States for trial and incarceration and some people take the law into their own hands and have virtually no fear of legal consequences."[26] In those terms, "[t]he political structure and elites simply accommodate the continuing violence, absorb it, while the population makes the necessary psychological adjustments, as if it were a normal condition, like rain."[27]

Sovereignty-Free Actors. The critical point of this argument is that the substance or essence of the long-continuing Colombian crisis centers on the general organization, activities, and threats of what James Rosenau calls the major violent stateless "sovereignty free" (nonstate) actors at work in that country today.[28]

Motives and Linkages

The motives for the establishment of an informal narco-insurgent-paramilitary alliance are straightforward: to accumulate wealth, to control territory and people, to establish and maintain freedom of movement and action, and to attain a certain level of legitimacy. Together, these elements represent usable power—power to allocate values and resources in a society.[29]

The equation that links illegal narcotics trafficking to insurgency and to the paramilitaries in Colombia and elsewhere turns on a combination of need, organizational infrastructure development, ability, and the availability of sophisticated communications and weaponry. For example, the drug industry possesses cash and lines of transportation and communication. Insurgent and paramilitary organizations have followers, organization, and discipline. Traffickers need these to help protect their assets and project their power within and among nation-states. Insurgents and paramilitaries are in constant need of logistical and communications support—and money.[30]

Together, a possible formal federation of the main protagonists would have the economic and military power equal to or better than that of many nation-states in the world today. If this possibility were to come to fruition, this alliance would also have another advantage. As indicated above, all three groups possess relatively flat organizational structures and sophisticated communications systems that, when combined, create a mechanism that is considerably more effective and efficient than any slow-moving bureaucratic, hierarchical governmental system. The organizational advantage of the nexus is a major source of power in itself.[31]

Internal Objectives. The narco-insurgent-paramilitary nexus is not simply individual or institutional intimidation for financial or criminal gain. Nor is it just the use of insurgents and AUC groups as "hired guns" to protect illegal drug cultivation, production, and trafficking; these are only business transactions. Rather, the long-term common objective of each party to the alliance is to—one way or another—control or radically change the Colombian political system.[32]

Narcos may not seek the overthrow of government as long as the government is weak and can be controlled to allow maximum freedom of movement and action.[33] The insurgents, in contrast, seek the eventual destruction of the state as it exists. Whether the insurgents are reformers or criminals is irrelevant, for their avowed objective is to take direct control of the government and state.[34] Likewise, the paramilitaries want fundamental change; apparently they are interested in creating a strong state that is capable of unquestioned enforcement of law and order. Whether the vigilante groups are "democratic" or authoritarian is also irrelevant. For their own self-preservation, they have little choice but to try to take direct or indirect political control of the state.[35] The potential narco-insurgent-paramilitary government change or overthrow effort, therefore, would be directed at the political community and its institutions. In this sense, the nexus is not simply criminal in nature. It is much more; it is a major political-psychological-moral-military entity. At the same time, the countryside ceases to be a simple theater for combat and becomes instead a foco, or base, from which to build or destroy (depending on what side of the equation one is on) substantive political power.

To be sure, the present informal narco-insurgent-paramilitary alliance is a loose and protean merger subject to many vicissitudes. Nevertheless, this "marriage of convenience" has lasted and appears to be getting more dangerous. The logic is simple: if all else fails, one or more parties may be able to out-politic the Colombian government and—through political persuasion, corruption, bribery, and impunity—buy and intimidate its way to victory.[36]

External Objectives. The narco-insurgent-paramilitary alliance appears to have developed a political agenda for exerting leverage in the international as well as the Colombian national arena. The perceived goal of a given national agenda would be to promote an "egalitarian social revolution" that will open up economic opportunities for everybody—and give the organization the legitimate basis for acting as some sort of nationalistic "narcocracy." The objectives of the international political agenda are to establish acceptance, credibility, and de facto legitimacy among the sovereign (perhaps criminal or rogue) states with which parts of the organization may negotiate.[37]

In that connection, the spillover effects of the Colombian illegal drug and arms trafficking industry have inspired criminal violence, corruption, and instability throughout Latin America in general and Caribbean transit countries in particular. For some time, the illegal drug industry has operated back and forth across Colombia's borders and adjacent seas and oceans. Colombian insurgents and paramilitary groups have also insinuated themselves into the neighboring countries of Brazil, Ecuador, Panama, Peru, and Venezuela. The resulting destabilization is acknowledged to undermine the security, well-being, and effective sovereignty of these countries as well.[38] Throughout Latin America, the situation in Colombia has led to the addition of a new term to the

Spanish lexicon—the cognate is "Colombianización"—that defines a political-social situation generated by narco-trafficking and insurgency. "Colombianization" refers to the disintegration of national institutions, a massive decay of civil society, and a permanent state of violence.[39]

The State-within-the-State. Clearly, all of the nonstate criminal-terrorist organizations that constitute the Colombian narco-insurgent-paramilitary nexus are significant political actors with the ability to compromise the integrity and sovereignty of individual nation-states.[40] This takes us back to the idea that this unholy trinity is effectively creating a virtual state-within-the-state and a phantom state among states. As early as 1994, Robert Kaplan warned that the alternative to the creation of a new state-within-the-state was criminal anarchy.[41] Even so, criminal anarchy provides a type of governance for the people under its control. That governance may be based on leader whim, feudal characteristics, and political inconsistency—but it is governance. The Colombian narco-insurgent-paramilitary alliance is not simply a criminal violence or socioeconomic issue, however. This alliance is developing a sophisticated political agenda, and it poses a clear and present danger to the existence of Colombia, as we now know it.[42]

A NEW DIMENSION IN THE COLOMBIAN CONFLICT: AUC AND OTHER GANGS

A new force inserting itself into the Colombian conflict is a large number of criminal gangs that have come into being as a result of the formal demobilization of AUC and the disintegration of some FARC units. These gangs are altering the configuration of the insurgency and the illegal drug industry, as well as complicating the already crowded conflict arena. Because of that new set of actors, the generally autonomous nature of AUC and its new creations, and the lack of certainty regarding FARC, understanding and predicting what the gangs may or may not be doing—and what they may or may not mean—are increasingly difficult. Despite the general lack of certainty regarding the new gangs, however, there are a few things that are becoming clearer as the bandas criminales become more involved in the general conflict.

First, we know that all the newly devolved gangs are more autonomous, less well understood, and more unpredictable than their parent organizations. We also know that the autonomous and ad hoc organization of the new gangs complicates the assessment of who they are, their numbers, why they do what they do, and their linkages with other organizations, both legal and illegal. Additionally, we know the following:

- As of the end of 2008, there were an estimated one hundred or more independent bandas criminales operating actively over at least 20 percent of the Colombian national territory. Membership estimates ranged from three thousand to over ten thousand.
- Like their parent, the new AUC gangs tend to be organized horizontally with no predetermined structure. The specific structure of a given gang is determined by its leadership, the tasks it must perform, and the requirements of the locale within which it operates.
- AUC organizational groups are established through a process of franchisement.
- Parent organizations generally allow subordinate groups considerable latitude in the ways and means chosen to accomplish a given suggested task.
- Particularly "dirty" operations are often conducted by "hired guns" from among aspirants, sympathizers, or unemployed "nobodies," rather than by regular members of an AUC or FARC organization.
- Gang organizations conduct four basic operations: (1) direct and sometimes lead specific military operations (such as "social cleansing") against selected insurgent or "uncooperative" groups; (2) perform the business-as-usual armed propaganda functions prescribed by V. I. Lenin for propaganda-agitator gangs;[43] (3) direct and sometimes lead relatively sophisticated political and psychological actions; and (4) collect, hold, and allocate money, weapons, and other resources.[44]

Second, the use of terror, fear, and other "barbaric" methods (mutilation, kidnapping, murder, rape, pillage) is considered to be a force multiplier and a rational psychological means of controlling a larger population. More specifically, these methods allow a small force to convince the people of a given area that the AUC paramilitaries are the real power in the country; exert authority over a population (even a population under the nominal control of a government or another nonstate actor); persuade or coerce public opinion, electoral conduct, and leader decision and policy making; and hold off a much larger force and fight another actor at the same time.[45]

Third, the relationship of the new gangs to elements of the Colombian government or to neopopulist elites is becoming more evident. Evidence of AUC association with the government and some of its major institutions—and resultant support—can be seen (if not proved in a court of law) in two different instances. In the first example, ties between paramilitary groups and Colombian legislators can be seen in the fact that more than forty current and former congressmen have been charged with one type or another of collaboration with AUC. It has been and continues to be asserted that "Congress is awash in AUC cash" to ensure that paramilitary influence remains strong in the highest levels of government.[46] The second instance involves the close, if informal, ties to the paramilitaries that the Colombian military has long been thought to have, from the time of the initial organization of AUC. As evidence of this, the army chief, General Mario Montoya, was recently implicated in collaboration charges initiated by the attorney general, and the intelligence chief, Jorge Noguera, was dismissed as a result of similar charges. Additionally, specific documents are now coming to light that indicate close ties between the army and the AUC.[47]

Fourth, several types of gangs are devolving from the AUC demobilization program. The common beliefs regarding motives and ties back to AUC are that the related groups are all involved in some sort of criminal activity and are controlled and led by hard-core paramilitary leaders who have not demobilized. Two groups in particular—the New Generation Organization (ONG) and the Black Eagles—operate in several Colombian departments (provinces) and provide good examples of the new gang phenomenon. A third set of groups, associated with the old AUC Northern Bloc, is also worth consideration.

The New Generation Organization is an example of a new group that has continued acting much as the old AUC did. ONG in the southern Department of Nariño is fighting the insurgents. ONG is also working to control (for its own purposes) drug crops, processing facilities, and trafficking routes into Ecuador and in the Pacific Ocean. Additionally, ONG has formed an ad hoc alliance with an armed wing of a drug cartel called the Rasrojos. Reportedly, the purpose of that alliance is to provide protection from other gangs, drug cartels, and insurgents operating in the region.[48]

In the north of Colombia—La Guajira, Norte de Santander, and Santa Marta, as examples—newly emerging gangs are involved in lucrative smuggling opportunities for commodities such as drugs, weapons, and oil. They compete with other illegal groups and the Colombian state for access to smuggling routes and oil pipelines that lead to key ports on the Caribbean Sea. Thus, the Black Eagles and their transnational criminal organization (TCO) and other gang allies are not operating like the old-style AUC: they are not deliberately targeting the FARC and ELN insurgents but are instead operating as ad hoc alliances with various drug, criminal, and insurgent groups. More often than not, they tend to fight any other group that might be in control of valuable commodities, strategic corridors, and seaports. Thus, the Black Eagles appear to have inserted themselves forcefully into an existing transnational criminal network. In that connection, and like some other Latin American gangs, some Black Eagle gangs are engaged in extortion and racketeering and have been known to rent themselves out as mercenary soldiers and *sicarios* (hired killers).[49]

Elsewhere along the Caribbean coast of Colombia and in the slums of some of the major cities, new AUC gangs are literally going from house to house and neighborhood to neighborhood conducting "social cleansing" operations against FARC and ELN insurgents. At the same time, these operations contribute to creation of the political space necessary to allow the gangs to achieve their commercial (self-enrichment) objectives. These new bandas criminales are thought to be connected with the old AUC Northern Bloc (BN) umbrella organization. That organization comprised a large network of gangs that operated independently until their co-option or subordination to AUC prior to 2002. The basic structure of the BN is still intact and is reportedly trying to reassert control of areas where the constituent gangs formerly operated.[50]

Fifth, the new AUC and FARC gangs seem to be more than bandas criminales: they are reshaping the narco-terrorist-insurgent-criminal world in Colombia and are exacerbating threats that are already eroding Colombian democracy and the Colombian state. In these terms, the new gangs are doing what gangs all over the world do best. As they evolve, they generate more and more socioeconomic-political instability and violence over wider and wider sections of the political map; they coercively neutralize, control, depose, or replace existing governmental service and security institutions; they create autonomous enclaves that are sometimes called criminal free-states, sovereignty free-states, para-states, or "ungoverned territories"; and thus, they change values in a given society to those of their criminal or ideological leaders and act as Leninist "midwives" that begin the process of radically changing the society and the state.[51]

CONSEQUENCES:
WHERE THE CRIMINAL TRINITY LEADS

Today's threats from the unholy trinity at work in Colombia and the rest of the Western Hemisphere come in many forms and in a matrix of different kinds of challenges, varying in scope and scale. If they have a single feature in common, it is that they are systematic, well-calculated attempts to coerce radical political change. In that connection, we shall explore briefly two of the many consequences the narco-insurgent-paramilitary union has generated: the erosion of Colombian democracy and the erosion of the state.

The Erosion of Colombian Democracy

In Colombia we observe important paradoxes. Elections are held on a regular basis, but leaders, candidates, and elected politicians are also regularly assassinated. Literally hundreds of governmental officials who are considered unacceptable by the nexus (unholy trinity) have been assassinated following their election. Additionally, intimidation, direct threats, and the use of relatively minor violence on a person and his or her family continue to play an important role *prior* to elections. As a corollary, although the media is free from state censorship, journalists and academicians who make their antinarco-insurgent-paramilitary opinions known through the press—or too publicly—are systematically compromised, intimidated, or assassinated.[52]

Consequently, it is hard to credit Colombian elections as democratic or free. Neither competition nor participation in elections can be complete in an environment where armed and unscrupulous nonstate actors compete violently with the government to control the government—before and after elections. Moreover, Colombia should not be considered as a democratic state as long as elected leaders are subject to control or vetoes imposed by vicious nonstate actors. As a consequence, Ambassador David Jordan argues, Colombia is an "anocratic" democracy, that is, a state that has the procedural features of democracy but retains the features of an autocracy in which the ruling elites face no scrutiny or accountability.[53] In any event, the intimidating and persuasive actions of the narco-insurgent-paramilitary alliance in the electoral processes have pernicious effects on Colombian democracy and tend to erode the ability of the state to carry out its legitimizing functions.

The Partial Collapse of the State

The Colombian state has undergone severe erosion on two general levels. First, despite government claims to the contrary, the state's presence and authority is questionable over large geographical portions of the country. Second, the idea of the partial collapse of the state is closely related to the nonphysical deterioration of democracy. Jordan argues that corruption is key in this regard and is a prime mover toward "narco-socialism."[54]

In the first instance, the notion of partial collapse of the state refers to the fact that there is an absence or only partial presence of state institutions in many of the rural areas and poorer urban parts of the country.

Also, even in those areas that are not under the direct control of narco, insurgent, or paramilitary organizations, institutions responsible for protecting citizens—notably, the police and judiciary—have been coerced to the point where they find it very difficult and dangerous to carry out their basic functions. Indicators of this problem can be seen in three sets of facts: first, the murder rate in Colombia is among the highest in the world; second, and perhaps most important, the proportion of homicides that end with a conviction is less than 4 percent;[55] and third, many of Colombia's worst criminal warlords and drug traffickers are extradited to the United States for trial, conviction, and incarceration.[56] These indicators of impunity strongly confirm that the state is not adequately exercising its social-contractual and constitutional-legal obligations to provide individual and collective security within the national territory.

In the second instance, nonphysical erosion of the state centers on the widespread, deeply entrenched issue of corruption. As one example, in 1993 and 1994, the U.S. government alluded to the fact that former president Ernesto Samper had received money from narcotics traffickers. Later, in 1996, based on that information, the United States withdrew Mr. Samper's visa and decertified Colombia for not cooperating in combating illegal drug trafficking. Subsequently, the Colombian Congress absolved Samper of all drug charges by a vote of 111 to 43.[57] Unsurprisingly, another indicator of government corruption at the highest levels is found in the Colombian Congress. The Colombian Senate—in a convoluted legal parliamentary maneuver—decriminalized the issue of "illicit enrichment" by making it a misdemeanor that could be prosecuted only after the commission of a felony.[58] Clearly, the reality of corruption at any level of government favoring the illegal drug industry, the paramilitaries, or other criminal elements militates against responsible governance and the public well-being. In these terms, the reality of corruption brings into question the reality of Colombian democracy and the reality of effective state sovereignty.

The Gang Challenge and the Threat

The gang challenge to Colombian national security, stability, and sovereignty and the attempt to neutralize, control, or depose incumbent governmental institutions take us to the strategic-level threat. In this context, crime, violence, and instability are only symptoms of the threat. The ultimate threat is either state failure or the violent imposition of a radical neopopulist socioeconomic-political restructuring of the state and its governance in accordance with criminal values. In either case, gangs contribute to the evolutionary state failure process, by which the state loses the capacity and/or the will to perform its fundamental governance, service, and security functions. Over time, the weaknesses inherent in its inability to perform the business of the state in various parts of the country lead to the erosion of state authority and legitimacy. In the end, the state controls neither its national territory nor the people in it.[59]

However, the fact that a state fails does not mean it will go away. (Haiti comes immediately to mind.) Unfortunately, particularly for their citizens, failing and failed states tend to linger and go from bad to worse. The lack of responsible governance and personal security generate greater poverty, violence, and instability—and a downward spiral in terms of development. A failing state becomes a zero-sum game in which gangs and other nonstate protagonists involved are the winners and the rest of the members of society are the losers. The longer failing and failed states persist, the more they and their regional spillover effects endanger regional and global peace and security. Failing and failed states become dysfunctional states, rogue states, criminal states, narco-states, new "people's democratic republics," or draconian states (for example, military or civilian dictatorships), or they reconfigure themselves into entirely new states.[60] In that connection, some close observers of the gang phenomenon assert that the coerced change toward criminal values in targeted societies leads to a "New Dark Age."[61]

Nevertheless, the foregoing possibilities do not delineate the end of the state failure problem. Sooner or later, the global community must pay the indirect social, economic, and political costs of state failure. The global community is increasingly expected to provide the military/police and financial leverage to ensure peace, security, and stability in an increasing number of postconflict and unstable situations. The consistency of these lessons derived from relatively recent experience—from Asia's Golden Triangle to the Middle East, from Mexico and Central America to Haiti, and from Colombia to the rest of Latin America—inspires confidence that these lessons and the associated threats are valid.[62]

Internal and External Responses to Armed Nonstate Threats

Colombia, the United States, and other countries that ultimately might be affected by the destabilizing consequences of the narco-insurgent-paramilitary alliance in Colombia have tended to deal with the problem in a piecemeal, ad hoc fashion or have ignored it. Significantly, in Colombia this has been done within an environment of mutual enmity between the civil government and the armed forces.[63] With the promulgation of the sociopolitical-military Plan Colombia in 2000, however, and subsequent policies such as Democratic Security in 2002, Libertad Uno in 2003, and Plan Patriota in 2004–2005, there is now the basis of a coherent political-military project—but not the kind of holistic "game plan" advocated by the former U.S. ambassador to Colombia, Myles Frechette.[64] Frechette calls for a holistic, long-term national capability-building "game plan" that would include taxing the upper elements of society that now pay few or no taxes.[65] Additionally, in Colombia there is no apparent quest for improved governmental legitimacy; no serious effort to implement a viable unity of civil-military effort; no coordinated, long-term plan to isolate the armed protagonists from their various sources of support; and no commitment to the country or to allies to "stay the course of the war." Moreover, the intelligence and information wars within the war leave much to be desired.[66] In all, Colombia appears to be simply "muddling through" and, after nearly fifty years, either adapting to the situation or still hoping for the problem to go away.

Externally, the United States has tended to ignore the insurgency and paramilitary problems in Colombia, except for making rhetorical statements regarding the peace process, terrorist activities, and human rights violations. Though the United States has focused its money, training, and attention almost entirely on the counterdrug campaign, its rapid but limited infusion of military hardware, a rigorous program designed to transform the Colombian military into a more aggressive combat force, and badly needed financial assistance have allowed the Colombian government under President Uribe to recover some the political ground and national territory ceded to FARC over the past several years. Nevertheless, the United States has tended to see the Colombian crisis in limited terms—the number of hectares of coca eradicated, the number of kilos of coca that have been detected and destroyed, and the number of narcotraffickers jailed. Thus, even though the United States and Colombia have achieved a series of tactical successes against the narco-terrorists, Colombia's violent nonstate actors remain relatively strong and wealthy. At the same time, Colombia becomes relatively more fragile.[67]

Externally, also, Venezuela has recently been implicated in a history of active collaboration with FARC that is now part of the Coordinadora Continental Bolivariana. In addition, documents authenticated by Interpol appear to show that President Hugo Chavez has offered FARC up to $300 million and also suggest that Venezuela has helped FARC obtain small arms and ammunition and has facilitated meetings with arms dealers. Traditionally, these kinds of nation-state activities are within the realm of "plausible deniability," and Mr. Chavez has denied these allegations.[68]

Finally, the other countries in the Western Hemisphere affected by the nefarious activities of the narco-insurgent-paramilitary nexus tend to do little more than watch, wait, and debate about what—if anything—to do regarding the seemingly new and unknown criminal-insurgent-paramilitary phenomenon. As a consequence, effective sovereignty, democracy, socioeconomic development, territory, infrastructure, stability, and security are quietly and slowly destroyed—and tens of thousands of innocents continue to be displaced or killed.

KEY POINTS AND LESSONS

- Colombia faces not one but a potent combination of three different armed threats to its democracy and its being. That "unholy (Hobbesian) trinity" of illegal drug traffickers, insurgents, and paramilitary organizations has created a situation in which life is indeed "nasty, brutish, and short."

- Each set of violent, stateless, sovereignty-free nonstate actors that constitute the loose trinity has its own specific—and different—motivations, but the common denominator is the political objective of effectively controlling or radically changing the Colombian government and state as we know it.
- The narco-insurgent-paramilitary alliance utilizes a mix of aggressive, widespread, and violent political-psychological, economic-commercial, and military-terrorist strategy and tactics to control the human and physical terrain in Colombia and other countries where it operates. The generalized result of the state-destabilization activities of this alliance is a steadily increasing level of nonstate wealth and power that many nation-states of the world can only envy.
- At the same time, the unholy trinity represents a triple threat to the effective sovereignty of the Colombian state and to its hemispheric neighbors. It undermines the vital institutional pillars of regime legitimacy and stability, challenges the central governance of countries affected, and takes effective political control of large portions of so-called ungoverned national territory.
- Despite some concern regarding the fact that FARC insurgent leaders are getting old and may not live to see the fruition of the organization's Leninist-Maoist revolutionary efforts, the current leaders appear to be unconcerned with speeding up or energizing their deliberate plan of action to seize the power of the state.
- In that connection, the major protagonists appear to think that time is on their side. As an example, there is evidence that FARC is moving from a theoretically quick military approach to taking control of the state to a broader and slower political-psychological-military approach.
- The Colombian and U.S. responses to the narco-insurgent-paramilitary nexus have been ad hoc, piecemeal, and without a holistic strategic civil-military campaign plan. As a consequence, Colombia and its U.S. ally have not addressed the real war that is taking place in the hemisphere. That war continues to fester and

grow toward the ultimate objective of controlling, deposing, and radically changing the political, economic, and social system of the state.

The Colombian insurgency and its associated TCO phenomenon have been ongoing from at least the mid-1940s to date. In that time, violence and destruction have varied like a sine curve from acute to tolerable. However, just because a situation improves to the point of being "tolerable" does not mean that the problem has gone away or should be ignored. Sun Tzu reminds us that "there has never been a protracted war from which a country has benefited."[69]

CHAPTER 4

HUGO CHAVEZ'S USE OF POPULAR MILITIAS AND OTHER INSTRUMENTS OF POWER

Achieving a Populist Antidemocratic and Antisystem Agenda

Since his election as president of Venezuela in 1998, Hugo Chavez has encouraged and continues to encourage his Venezuelan and other Latin American followers to pursue a confrontational "defensive," populist, and nationalistic agenda that will liberate Latin America from the economic dependency and political imperialism of the North American "Empire" (the United States).[1] Chavez argues that liberation, New Socialism, and Bolivarianismo (the dream of a Latin American liberation movement against the United States' hegemony) will be achieved only by (1) radically changing the traditional politics of the Venezuelan state to that of "direct" (totalitarian) democracy;[2] and (2) destroying North American hegemony throughout all of Latin America by building a new Bolivarian state, beginning with Venezuela and extending to the whole of Latin America; and conducting a "super insurgency," war of all the people, or fourth-generation war (4GW) to depose the illegitimate external enemy.[3] This is not the rhetoric of a "nut case." It is, significantly, the rhetoric of an individual who is performing the traditional and universal Leninist-Maoist function of providing a strategic vision and the operation plan for gaining revolutionary power. In pursuit of this Bolivarian dream, President Chavez has stirred the imaginations of many other interested observers all around the world. And he is now providing political leaders—populists and neopopulists, New

Socialists, disillusioned revolutionaries and oppositionists, and submerged *nomenklaturas* around the globe—with a relatively orthodox and sophisticated Marxist-Leninist-Maoist model for the conduct and implementation of a regional "super insurgency" (fourth-generation war):[4] the only kind of conflict the United States has ever lost.[5] An explanation of Hugo Chavez's Bolivarian dream begins with the political-historical context of the general Latin American and Venezuelan reality.

POLITICAL-HISTORICAL CONTEXT

A handful of powerful political-historical factors dominate Venezuelan and Latin American politics and inspire President Chavez's behavior. The first three factors are closely related and more or less universal within Latin American culture: *caudillismo* (political domination by a strongman), its associated populism, and the political-economic "modernization" that has been experienced since World War II are all strongly rooted in the culture and politics of the Latin American region. The fourth factor is relatively unique to Venezuela: a robust oil economy in post–World War II Venezuela produced an experiment in democracy that was diminished by a strong centralized government.

Caudillismo

Caudillos—including "The Liberator," Simon Bolivar, himself—dominated Venezuela and most of the other Hispanic American countries in a succession of civilian and military dictatorships from independence to the late 1980s. During that period of over 140 years, more than twenty constitutions were drafted, promulgated, rewritten, and ignored. More than fifty armed revolts (coups) took their toll of life and property. Popular approval of and support for government meant little. Political principles meant even less.[6] In all, Venezuela exhibited the characteristics of a traditional, centralized, and authoritarian *(caudillistic)* state.[7]

Over the past twenty to thirty years, there has been pressure from abroad for Latin American countries to move away from the caudillo tradition toward the ideals of representative democracy. In many countries of the region, however, presidential power is not institutionalized, and the president must be de facto the whole government—executive, legislature, and judiciary. Therefore, the president must maintain himself in office by his own ingenuity and political skill. If these attributes fail him, then fraud and force come into play. Generally, the people of Latin America expect the president to be all-powerful. He must be the caudillo. There is not much middle political ground.[8]

Populism

The linkage between caudillismo and populism is straightforward. One defining element of populism is the emergence of a strong leader in whose hands the fate of a nation will be carried.[9] Historically, populism arises out of political crises and the inability of the traditional system to respond to peoples' demands. Also, historically, populist leaders tend to come from outside the traditional political system and the ruling elites. They appeal to the people by presenting themselves as "uncontaminated." They appeal to the need to restore whatever is perceived to be missing—national dignity, socioeconomic justice, honesty, leadership, or anything else.

In that connection, populist leaders and demagogues tend to blame all the people's and the country's problems on the poor performance of weak elected civilian leaders.[10] Once a populist leader rises to power, he tends to bypass, dismantle, or erode institutions that restrict the concentration of power in his hands. He has been known to devise mechanisms, such as popular demonstrations, reform referenda, and unscheduled elections, that are designed to indirectly circumvent the rule of law and other elements of representative democracy.[11] If necessary, coercive means have been employed (including state-supported gangs or popular militias) to generate (or diminish) popular enthusiasm for a given "reform."[12] Thus, populist leaders tend to use totalitarian and coercive methods to achieve popular support for their purposes.[13] By doing this, they set the stage to justify closing whatever channels might remain open for real popular political participation—and dissent (and democracy).[14]

The Development of Venezuelan Democracy

Beginning with the elections of 1958 that followed the dictatorship of President Marcos Perez Jimenez and a subsequent military junta, Venezuelans began to elect their political leadership. However, their concept of democracy was not derived from the Anglo-American tradition of limited state power and strong individual human rights. Rather, the current tradition of Venezuelan democracy has its roots firmly in the outcome of the French Revolution and the perversions of Jean Jacques Rousseau's concept of "total" democracy, wherein the individual surrenders his rights and personal interests to the state in return for the strong enforcement of social harmony and the "general will."[15] Prior to the French Revolution, kings ruled by "divine right" and were sovereign. With the revolution, however, sovereignty was shifted from the king to the nation-state. Thus, the state enjoys absolute (total) power—through the enforcement of the general will—as an essential right.[16]

As a result, the political forces set in motion by a robust oil economy produced a democracy that was controlled by a strong central government. That government included a corporatist executive authority and security apparatus organized to direct the general will and control the political and economic life of the country.[17] This was a perversion of the tradition that comes out of the French Revolution and the question of who interprets and enforces the general will.[18] Thus, the Venezuelan political system was built on a pact among members of the corporate elites, preserving a democratic façade, under which the dominant political parties and their caudillo leaders have been the principal actors. As Robespierre did after the French Revolution, contemporary Venezuelan political actors determine what they believe is best for themselves, and for all citizens (the general will).[19] Accordingly, the Venezuelan state controls the wealth produced by its petroleum and other industries and is the principal distributor of the surpluses generated in a highly regulated and subsidized economy. In that connection, to one extent or another, all the people and every enterprise in Venezuela feed off what has been called the piñata (a suspended breakable pot filled with candies and other sweets for children's parties) of the state treasury.[20]

In sum, populist caudillo-type leaders such as Hugo Chavez exploit popular grievances to catapult themselves into political power, and stay there. Their success stems from solemn promises made directly to the people to solve national and individual problems without regard to slow, obstructive, and corrupted representative democratic processes. That these kinds of leaders may, from time to time, employ deceitful antidemocratic methods and Leninist-type propaganda-agitator gangs (popular militias) to "nudge" the people in the "right" directions seems not to matter. Thus, demagogic populist leaders are in a position to place themselves above constitutions, legislatures, and the rule of law—and govern and distribute the national piñata as they see fit.[21] To this date, the evolution of the Chavez government in Venezuela has consistently moved in that direction.[22]

Context for Developing a Strategic Vision

This is the contextual starting point from which to understand where Hugo Chavez intends to go and how he expects to get there. Whether he eventually achieves his aims is irrelevant: the first-, second-, and third-order 4GW effects of his efforts will shape the security environment in which Latin America and the rest of the hemisphere must struggle and survive over the next several years. This is also the starting point from which to develop the strategic vision to counter caudillismo, radical populism, and the purposeful instability and chaos they engender.

CHAVEZ'S BOLIVARIAN DREAM: FOUR ESSENTIAL ENABLERS

The creation, protection, and expansion of the Bolivarian dream depend on four enabling concepts. The first enabler is the New Socialism. With that concept in place, one can envision building a new, neopopulist, antisystem social democracy, beginning with Venezuela and extending eventually to the whole of Latin America. In turn, that concept dictates a new system of power. Hugo Chavez calls this system "direct democracy." Its main tenets dictate that the new political authority must be a leader who communicates directly with the people; elections, plebiscites, Congress, and the courts will provide formal democracy and international legitimacy but will have no real role in governance or the economy, which are the responsibility of the leader; the nation-state, through the leader, will own or control the major means of production and distribution; and the national and regional political-economic-military integration function will be performed by the leader by means of his financial, material, and political-military support of "people's movements" and popular militias.[23]

The second enabler centers on social-economic programs designed to provide tangible benefits to the mass of Venezuelans who were generally neglected by previous governments. These benefits are intended to strengthen the leader's internal power base.[24]

The third enabler focuses on communications with the intent of enabling the media (radio, television, newspapers, and magazines) to create a mass consensus. President Chavez has used the media skillfully to communicate his ideas, develop positive public opinion, and generate electoral successes. In connection with the Bolivarian dream, he has directed communications to audiences all over Latin America. And, not surprisingly, the Chavez government has shut down some elements of Venezuela's opposition media to ensure the "irreversibility of the process for establishing Socialism for the 21st Century."[25]

The fourth enabler involves the reorganization of the security institutions of the country. In addition to the traditional armed forces, the following independent forces have been created and funded by Chavez's government: a national police force (Guardia Nacional); a 1.5-million-person military reserve organization; a paramilitary (popular militia) called the Bolivarian Liberation Front (Frente Bolivariano de Liberación); and another paramilitary militia, the Army of the People in Arms (Ejercito del Pueblo en Armas). All these institutions are outside the traditional control of the regular armed forces, and each organization is responsible directly to the leader (President Chavez). This institutional separation is intended to ensure that no one military or paramilitary organization can control another, but the centralization of these institutions directly under the leader guarantees absolute control of security and social harmony in Venezuela.[26]

In sum, what President Chavez has achieved by restructuring the Venezuelan government and its democratic institutions, improving the physical well-being of many poor Venezuelans, and verbalizing these successes on television and in the press is the formation of a unity of political-psychological-military effort and the development of a large, popular, internal and external base of support. Moreover, the reorganization of the government and its security apparatus provides for presidential control of the political, economic, social, informational, and security instruments of state power that are intended to "deepen and extend" the bases of the regional liberation effort—and to enable the implementation of fourth-generation (asymmetric) warfare.[27] Once all these enablers function together, they will destroy traditional representative Venezuelan and Latin American democracy and the old Venezuelan and Latin American political-economic system.[28] The old democracy and the old system will be replaced by a new kind of democracy and a new type of political system—socialism for the twenty-first century.

THE PROGRAM FOR THE LIBERATION OF LATIN AMERICA

Hugo Chavez consistently identifies the origins of the Bolivarian revolution and defines the central strategic problem in Latin America as the lack of legitimacy of the U.S.-dominated governments of the region. He further identifies the primary objective of the revolution as power. Power is generated by an intelligent, motivated, and disciplined leader and his organization for direct democracy, with a vision of Latin American greatness. Accordingly, President Chavez is planning for a long-term, three-stage, multiphase program for gaining power (regional hegemony). Though Chavez's three stages use different terminology, they are similar to those of Lenin: (1) organization, (2) development and use of coercive political and limited military power, and (3) the capture of a targeted government.[29]

The Three Basic Stages of the Bolivarian Revolution

Stage One: Organization. This is the essential first effort. It requires taking the time necessary to lay the strongest possible organizational foundations for the subsequent political-psychological-military struggle. In this stage, the revolutionary leadership must concentrate on doctrine and leadership development; creation of the political-military architecture necessary to conduct the revolution; expansion of the organization's relationship with other political-military movements; and, generally, the creation of a receptive sociopolitical environment for the revolutionary movement. More specifically, one of Hugo Chavez's mentors, Abraham Guillen, teaches that the revolutionary leadership must propagate Latin American nationalism; educate and prepare for combat, organizational duties, and governance several hundred professionals who are prepared to lead the masses through the revolution and into the proverbial halls of power; and create a popular front of not only "a few true believers but [also] a combination of Christians, Socialists, trade unionists, intellectuals, students, peasants, and the debourgeoised middle class who will march together to defeat sepoyan (regional) militarism and U.S. imperialism."[30]

Stage Two: Development of Political and Military Power. As with the organizational stage, the second stage of the revolution is to be preparatory and long term. And the leadership must again take the time necessary to develop and nurture popular support while increasing the size of the organization and establishing and defending liberated zones. This kind of effort allows the consolidation and expansion of political logistical support bases, the extension of influence throughout the various Latin American countries, and the establishment of de facto control in areas uncontrolled or abandoned by a given state.

More specifically, the political-military effort requires the formation and nurturing of a number of ancillary multinational organizations. The most important would include a united anti-imperialist popular political party (front); a united central trade union organization; a united Latin American youth federation (league); a united labor party; and a united army of unity and liberation. The general purposes of these organizations would be to continue to raise the level of direct popular action against "indigenous feudalism, aboriginal capitalism, sepoyan militarism, and *yanqui* imperialism."[31] The organizations would also provide leadership experience and human skills that will be necessary when it is time to form a direct popular government and install a socialist mode of production and distribution.

As might be expected, Guillen and other contemporary revolutionary theorists who do not follow the teachings of Ernesto "Che" Guevara argue that the military effort is more political and psychological than military. According to Vladimir Ilyich Lenin, revolutionary war does not propose to decide anything by means of battles or by occupying somebody's national territory. Nevertheless, an army of national liberation must eventually be formed in each Latin American country, with a central Latin American strategic command. The army would be further organized into local militias that fight only in their own zones, provincial or district militias that would fight in their own zones, and an army that fights in all parts of a targeted geographical area, with the cooperation of local and provincial/district militias.[32] The objective of the military effort, however, is not to destroy the enemy but to wear down the opposition, over time, until the opponent's resolve collapses. As a result, "political and moral factors are more decisive for victory than heavy armament and ironclad units."[33]

Stage Three: Take Control of a Targeted Government or Geographical Area. Theoretically, this stage of the revolution is reached when, and only when, the enemy is completely demoralized and only a relatively small military force is required to finalize the total collapse of the targeted state. The collapse of the state will not be the result of any one spectacular action but, rather, the result of several small and successive actions. Ideally, that collapse will not take place until interior and urban support bases are consolidated; the revolutionary leadership cadre is sufficiently prepared and large enough to administer *and* govern the new state; and the revolutionary organization is prepared to both hold its ground against a concerted "imperialist" counterattack from outside the country and move against the next targeted state in a subsequent phase of the general Latin American liberation effort.[34]

The Application of the Three Stages. The theoretical intent of the first two stages of the Bolivarian revolution is to take the necessary time to let one's enemies become accustomed to a given purposeful action and slowly move toward new stages of the revolution in a phased and deliberate manner. Thus, by staying under his opponents' threshold of concern, Hugo Chavez expects to "put his enemies to sleep—to later wake up dead."[35]

Six Phases That Elaborate the Role of the Popular Militias

A minimum of six phases elaborate that paradigm and outline the role of the paramilitary popular militias. General Gustavo Reyes Rangel Briceño articulated the phases that might well have been written by Lenin or Guillen when he accepted the office of minister of defense for the national reserve and national mobilization on July 18, 2007:

1. Organize to propagate Latin American nationalism, train a cadre of professionals (propagandists and agitators/popular militias) for leadership duties and political-military combat, and create selected environments of chaos.
2. Create a popular (political) front out of the "debourgeoised" middle classes and other like-minded individuals, who will work together to disestablish opposed societies and defend the new social democracy.
3. Foment regional conflicts. This would involve covert, gradual, and preparatory political-psychological-military activities ("seeding operations") in developing and nurturing popular support. As the number of recruits grows and the number of activities increases, the fomentation of regional conflicts would also involve the establishment and defense of "liberated zones."
4. Plan overt and direct intimidation activities, including popular actions (such as demonstrations, strikes, civic violence, personal violence, maiming, and murder) against feudal, capitalistic, militaristic opponents and against yanqui imperialism. The intent is to debilitate target states and weaken enemy military command and control facilities.
5. Increase covert and overt political-psychological-economic-military actions directed at developing local popular militias to fight in their own zones, provincial or district militias to fight in

their particular areas, and a larger military organization to fight in all parts of the targeted country with the cooperation of local and district militias.

6. Directly, but gradually, confront a demoralized enemy military force and bring about its desired collapse—or invade a targeted country with the objective of imposing appropriate New Socialist governance.[36]

Until the last moment in the last and decisive phase of the Latin American liberation process—when the targeted government is about to collapse—every action is preparatory work and not expected to provoke great concern from the enemy or its bourgeois allies.[37] Only at the point of enemy collapse and the radical imposition of New Socialist governance will the people begin to enjoy the benefits of love, happiness, peace, and well-being.[38]

Clearly, the revolutionary vision outlined above will not be achieved through a conventional war. This antidemocratic challenge is rooted in the assumption that incumbent Latin American governments and the United States are not doing what is right for the people of the hemisphere, whereas the New Socialist political philosophy and leadership will do what is best for the people. Thus, regime legitimacy will be key to the general 4GW conflict. Hemispheric regimes that fail to understand this fact and respond only militarily to phantom revolutionary military forces (popular militias) are likely to fail.[39]

Chavez's Strategy

At present, however, President Chavez is only in the beginning phases of his preparatory organizational stage of the program for the liberation of Latin America; the culmination of stage one is still a long time away. Stages two and three must be several years down the revolutionary path. At the strategic level, then, Chavez appears to be trying to consolidate his base position in Venezuela, taking a relatively low revolutionary profile, and waiting for a propitious time to begin the expansion of the revolution on a supranational Latin American scale. He will likely continue to focus his primary attack on the legitimacy of the U.S. economic and political domination of the Americas and on any other possible rival. And he will likely continue to conduct various rhetorical and political-military attacks on adversaries; cultivate diverse allies in Latin America, the Middle East, and Asia; and engage his allies and his popular militias in propaganda and agitation "seeding operations." The intent of these actions is to create a receptive political climate throughout the Western Hemisphere.[40] The fact that Venezuelans have been arrested in Peru who are accused of engaging in some form or another of propaganda and agitation activities indicates that "seeding operations" are in progress.[41]

WHERE THE BOLIVARIAN DREAM LEADS

The stages and phases of President Chavez's program for the liberation of Latin America presuppose the conduct of 4GW as an integral part of the entire revolutionary process—from beginning to end. In turn, 4GW leads to the coerced imposition of the radical political-economic restructuring of targeted states and/or the process of state failure.

Fourth-Generation Warfare

Hugo Chavez understands that, in essence, 4GW is a long-standing methodology of the weak against the strong. Its primary characteristic is that of asymmetry (the use of disparity between contending opponents to gain relative advantage). He also understands that this kind of conflict (war) is no longer limited to using military violence to bring about desired political-economic-social (neopopulist, antisystem) change. Rather, all means that can be brought to bear on a given situation must be used to compel a targeted government to do one's will. Moreover, former Lieutenant Colonel Chavez understands that contemporary nontraditional/unconventional/irregular/peripheral war is not a kind of lesser or limited appendage to the more comfortable first- through third-generation attrition and maneuver warfare (1–3GW) paradigms but is instead a great deal more. The "battlefield" is everywhere and involves everyone and everything. This kind of war is in no way limited: it is unrestricted (total).[42]

In that connection, 4GW is complex, ambiguous, and hard to deal with for several interrelated and multidimensional reasons.

- A wise challenger slowly and deliberately uses a variety of internationally legal and illegal, democratic and antidemocratic, and military and nonmilitary approaches to avoid direct confrontation with a stronger enemy.
- At the same time, that challenger will slowly and deliberately develop an internal and external political-economic-psychological support base before escalating the level of indirect aggression that is ultimately intended to defeat the rival competitor, without violating the clearly defined international (Westphalian) principles under which a country is legally considered to be at war.
- 4GW applies to nation-state actors that surreptitiously challenge other state, as well as nonstate, actors.
- Those actors would first send advisors, small arms, and money to their allies in Country A, B, or C, then military trainers and "volunteers," proxy, or surrogate forces (popular militias), and finally, heavy weapons and regular forces as the fighting and the stakes of the conflict escalate.
- Man is the active element in 4GW; technology and firepower are passive. The human factor and human terrain are decisive.
- In that connection, the struggle will be predominantly political-psychological, and the outcome will likely be determined in the media rather than on any kind of conventional battlefield.
- In the final analysis, the struggle is total in that it uses all (unrestricted) means to accomplish its ends and gives the winner absolute (total) power to control or replace an existing order. That, in turn, brings about the radical restructuring of political and economic systems, which, if that does not work as scripted, exacerbates the state failure process.[43]

The End of the Dream? The Process of State Failure

Contemporary 4GW threats to national stability, sovereignty, and well-being are not necessarily direct attacks on a government. They are, however, proven means for weakening governing regimes. These new threats reflect a logical progression from the problems of institutional and state weaknesses to the partial collapse of the state and, finally, to failure of the state.[44] That progression allows us to infer that several small, weak states in the Caribbean and Latin America are at serious risk of failure to perform their sovereign governance, securing, and well-being functions. The problems of diminished governance take us to the real threat engendered by personal and collective insecurity together with diminishing national stability and sovereignty: state failure.

The state failure (destabilization) process tends to move from personal violence to increased collective violence and social disorder to kidnappings, bank robberies, violent property takeovers, murders/assassinations, personal and institutional corruption, criminal anarchy, and internal and external population displacements. In turn, the momentum of this process of violence tends to evolve into widespread social violence, serious degradation of the economy, and diminished governmental capabilities of providing personal and collective security and guaranteeing the rule of law to all citizens. Then, using complicity, intimidation, corruption, and indifference, an irregular political actor can quietly and subtly co-opt politicians, bureaucrats, and security personnel to gain political control of a given piece of the human or geographical national territory. As the destabilization process continues, the state will control less and less of its national territory and fewer and fewer of the people in it. The individual or organization (state or non-state; traditional or irregular) that takes control of a series of networked pieces of such "ungoverned territory" can then become the dominant political actor and can create (or control) a state-within-a-state or a group of states.[45]

Nevertheless, just because a state fails does not mean that it will simply go away. The diminishment of responsible governance and personal security generates greater poverty, violence, and instability—and a downward spiral in terms of development and well-being. It is a zero-sum game in which aggressive irregular actors are the winners and the people of a targeted society are the losers. Ultimately, failing or failed states become dysfunctional states dependent on other states or international organizations, or they become tribal states, rogue states, criminal states, narco-states, "new people's republics," draconian states (military dictatorships), or neopopulist states (civilian dictatorships). Moreover, failing or failed states may dissolve and become parts of other states or may be reconfigured into entirely new entities.[46]

In the end, experience demonstrates that most failing and failed states do not or cannot bring themselves back to political-economic viability without considerable outside help. Sooner or later the international community and relatively wealthy individual nation-states must pay the indirect social, economic, and political costs of state failure. Accordingly, the current threat environment in the Western Hemisphere is not a traditional security problem, but it is no less dangerous. The consistency of these kinds of experiences throughout the world, and over time, inspires confidence that these lessons are valid.[47]

Responses

One school of thought in Latin America—expressed privately if not publicly to a Norteamericano (North American)—firmly supports Chavez and his supranational Bolivarian dream. Those who oppose Chavez are against his "lack of realism," are ambivalent, or just do not want to take him seriously—and hope that he will go away. While the Chavez supporters are organizing and preparing for the future, the opposition waits, watches, and debates.[48]

The United States has tended to ignore the larger problem of responsible representative democratic governance and has instead concentrated on the war on drugs. If there is another North American concern, it would be the problem of possible nuclear proliferation and the associated Venezuelan-Iranian alliance. Countries such as Bolivia, Ecuador, and Nicaragua appear to support the Bolivarian dream. Others that might be affected by the destabilizing consequences of Chavez's neopopulist political-psychological-economic efforts throughout the Western Hemisphere have not yet adjusted to the reality that transnational aggression can be something other than the Napoleonic massing of troops and the subsequent conventional invasion of another country's national territory.[49] Apparently, very few individuals or governments will acknowledge Chavez's goal as a clearly defined, universally recognized threat until large numbers of uniformed troops of one sovereign state directly invade the sovereign territory of another.[50]

KEY POINTS AND LESSONS

- Although seemingly overambitious, Chavez's concept of a regional superinsurgency conducted primarily by popular militias appears to be in accord with Lenin's approach to the conduct of irregular asymmetrical political war. This notion is quietly opening a new era in which much of the world is ripe for those who wish to coerce political-social change and change history, avenge grievances, find security in new structures, or protect old ways.

- Asymmetric war may be accomplished by those familiar with the indirect approach to conflict, using the power of dreams and the importance of public opinion, along with a multidimensional flexibility that goes well beyond conventional forms. The consequent interactions among all these factors in asymmetric war prevent the military dimension from functioning as the traditionally dominant actor.

- The threat, thus, is not an enemy military force or the debilitating instability generated by an asymmetric aggressor. Rather, at base, the threat is the inability or unwillingness of the government in office to take responsible and legitimate measures to exercise effective sovereignty and to provide security for and ensure the well-being of all of its citizens. That governmental failure to protect the people is what gives an oppositionist aggressor the opening and justification for its existence and action.

- As a corollary, the ultimate threat is either state failure or the violent imposition of a radical socioeconomic-political restructuring of the state and its governance in accordance with the values (good, bad, or nonexistent) of the victor.

- Targeted regimes and their international allies that fail to understand Chavez and his intentions, and respond militarily to his rhetoric and the phantom people's militias and other state-associated and state–supported gang phenomena, are not likely to be successful in their attempts to counter the Bolivarian dream.

That the world's only superpower does not have a unified strategy and a multidimensional interagency organizational structure to deal with 4GW superinsurgency is surprising and dismaying. No number of ad hoc "actionable recommendations" at the tactical and operational levels of conflict will be of much help in generating a strategy and an appropriate architecture to deal with contemporary irregular asymmetric conflict. The strategic level requirement, thus, involves two different levels of analysis: the need for civilian and military strategic leaders to better understand the nature of contemporary conflict and implement an realistic and holistic ends, ways, and means program to deal with it; and the need for an organizational structure to ensure high levels of individual, national-institutional, and transnational unity of effort. Substantive changes in leadership and strategy development and in the unity of national and international effort require a carefully staffed, phased, and long-term validation, planning, and implementation program—the sooner the better.

These lessons are all too relevant to the "new" 4GW political wars of the twenty-first century. General Sir Rupert Smith warns us that "war as cognitively known to most noncombatants, war as a battle in a field between men and machinery, war as a massive deciding event in a dispute in international affairs; such war no longer exists."[51] Instead, we have irregular asymmetric conflict that will require an entirely new and flexible approach.

CHAPTER 5

DEFENSIVE JIHAD IN
WESTERN EUROPE

Al Qaeda's Elevation of Nonstate Irregular Asymmetric Warfare onto the Global Arena

International relations scholarship generally focuses on the nation-state, and conflict is defined generally in conventional military terms. The one area of divergence in this dialogue is that terrorism and revolution scholars recognize that nonstate actors can sometimes play more than bit parts in the global security arena. Nevertheless, the mainstream international relations literature articulates that nonstate actors are, at base, local law enforcement problems and do not require sustained national security policy attention.[1] Al Qaeda is somewhat of an anomaly because it does not fit completely into any one set of the international relations literature. Were Al Qaeda a rival state power, it could easily fit into the hegemonic stability/power transition theories. Were it a terrorist organization mostly confined to seeking limited goals, it could fit into the traditional terrorism literature. Were it a revolutionary organization seeking the overthrow of a nation-state through sequential warfare, with or without the use of terror tactics, it could fall within the traditional revolutionary warfare literature. But Al Qaeda's global reach, combined with its strategic ability, elevates it onto a different plane. That is, Al Qaeda is a nonstate hegemonic terrorist insurgency and a serious threat to the West that, for the most part, has not yet been perceived as such.[2]

Al Qaeda has succeeded in doing what no other terrorist organization accomplished: elevating asymmetric, insurgent warfare onto the global arena.[3] Far from being apolitical and unique, Al Qaeda acts in accordance with a political logic that is a continuation of politics by indirect and violent means. Al Qaeda and its leadership do not pretend to reform an unjust order or redress perceived grievances. The intent is to destroy perceived Western regional and global enemies and replace them as the world hegemonic power. Thus, Al Qaeda's asymmetric global challenge is not abstract; it is real.[4] The point from which to begin to understand the threat and respond effectively to it is the organizational context.

THE ORGANIZATIONAL CONTEXT

A popular term being used to describe Al Qaeda's organizational structure is "leaderless jihad."[5] That term accurately characterizes the concept of no formal chain of command and further illustrates the fact that killing or neutralizing Al Qaeda leadership only causes a basic cell to lie dormant for a season—then it renews itself automatically.[6] The term, however, is deceptive. "Leaderless jihad" implies that there is no central directing authority, no focus of purpose and effort, no coordination of movement and action, and no real threat. Al Qaeda, in fact, is anything but leaderless or benign. Osama bin Laden organized Al Qaeda very carefully to take advantage of human and physical terrain and used multiple and modifiable methods to compel enemies to serve his purposes and comply with his will.[7] In these terms, Al Qaeda can and does elevate nonstate asymmetric insurgent warfare into the global security arena and engages in hegemonic actions—just as if it were a nation-state attempting to force political change in other nation-states.[8] Yet Al Qaeda does not rely on highly structured organization, large numbers of military forces, or costly weaponry.

The leadership of Al Qaeda understands that anyone wishing to compel an adversary to accede to its will must organize and employ a relatively small body of propagandists and agitators (cells or gangs). The purpose is clear. These irregular, asymmetric instruments of statecraft are integral parts of the revolutionary process, and their purpose is "to expedite the fall of the common enemy": the globally hegemonic West.[9] This unacknowledged Leninist dictum is illustrated in the general application of Al Qaeda's strategy globally and (as more specific examples) in Western Europe and Spain.[10] The use of gangs as components of strategy and tactics, however, is not unique to Al Qaeda or confined to Europe or Spain.[11] Instead, armed nonstate groups all over the world find their perceived notions of the Al Qaeda model for asymmetric global challenge to be salient.[12] The key role of the Al Qaeda propaganda-agitator gang operating in Western Europe, however, can be understood more completely within the context of the general organizational structure.

The Leader and His Organizational Vision

Experience and an expanding understanding of Al Qaeda in Western Europe indicate that Osama bin Laden represents a militant, revolutionary, and energetic commitment to a long-term approach to returning to Islamic governance, social purpose, and tradition. He has further identified the primary objective of the movement as power.[13] Power is absolutely necessary in order to implement the political, religious, economic, and social changes that are explicit and implicit in the idea of a return to Islamic governance of Muslim peoples and the resurrection of the Islamic caliphate of the year 711 A.D.[14] Power is generated by an enlightened, well-educated, well-motivated, and disciplined organization that can plan and implement an effective program for gaining control of societies and states. Power is maintained and enhanced as the organization acts as a "virtual state" within a state (the nonterritorial Islamic state) and replaces the artificial and illegitimate (apostate) governments that impose their rule on contemporary Muslim societies.[15] Thus, Al Qaeda members—from those in the highest positions to new recruits—have had to pledge their lives for the achievement of this vision and, as in the time of the empire, pledge their allegiance to the leader.[16]

The Base Organization

Osama bin Laden's first and continuing concern must center on organization. The preparatory activities necessary to achieve his long-term vision are classical Leninist and Maoist. He created a motivated and enlightened cadre, a political party type of infrastructure, a small and loosely organized guerrilla network, and a support mechanism for the entire organization.[17] Organizational vitality, breadth, and depth provide the basis for local, regional, and global effectiveness. Thus, the base organization, *not operations*, is considered key to Al Qaeda's success. Importantly, the term "Al Qaeda" means "the base."

Generally, and at first glance, Al Qaeda appears to be structured much like a classical hierarchical movement along rigid, close-knit, secretive lines in a pyramid structure. A closer examination of that multitiered structure, however, indicates a substantial corporate enterprise, designed especially for conducting large- and small-scale business operations and terrorist activities all around the globe. As a result, this organization looks much like transnational criminal gang organizations in the Americas that can quickly and flexibly respond to any kind of changing situation. Thus, it is more helpful to look at Al Qaeda's structure as being arranged in horizontal concentric circles rather than as a traditional vertical pyramid.[18]

The First Ring. The inner circle of the horizontal Al Qaeda organization consists of a small council *(shura)* of elders and a few hundred carefully selected, talented members (coordinators) who operate the functional structures considered essential to long-term effectiveness and durability—regardless of who serves as the leader. There are at least six of these functional organizations within the base organization: military, funding, procurement, manpower and logistics, training and personnel services, and communications and propaganda.[19] This inner circle provides strategic and operational-level guidance and support to its horizontal network of compartmentalized cells and allied (franchised) associations (groups or networks). This structure also allows relatively rapid shifting of operational control horizontally rather than through a slow vertical chain of command. This organization can, then, respond to an unexpected problem or to a promising opportunity in a timely manner.[20]

The Second Ring. The next ring of the concentric organizational circle consists of an unknown number of "holy warriors" who are veterans of the campaigns against the Russians in Afghanistan and subsequent efforts in Iraq, the Middle East, and North Africa. They are proven and trustworthy (committed) and provide leadership and expertise to the worldwide, multidimensional network.

The Third Ring. Al Qaeda's third ring consists of thousands of Islamic militants (aspirants and sympathizers) from around the globe. These individuals make up a loose alliance of political parties and groups, as well as transnational criminal, insurgent, and terrorist organizations and cells that can be called on virtually any time for aid, sanctuary, and personnel. (A cautionary note should be added here: leaders of many Islamic communities have consistently condemned the terrorist activities of Al Qaeda and do not want to be associated with it or Osama bin Laden. Thus, Al Qaeda is not a universally accepted organization within the various Islamic communities around the globe and should not be perceived as representing other Islamic political points of view. The Islamic "sympathizers" in the third ring of the base organization are only a small portion of the entire Islamic community.)

The Fourth Ring. The outer ring of the Al Qaeda organizational structure consists of amorphous groups of Muslims and non-Muslims (outsiders), in ninety countries around the world. They generally support Osama bin Laden's view of the West as the primary enemy of Islam and of humanity.[21] Accordingly, active support for Al Qaeda comes from a broad range of social classes, professions, and various Muslim and non-Muslim groups. A highly respected Al Qaeda expert, Michael Scheuer, asserts that the next generation of members will be more diverse and larger, more professional, less operationally visible, and more adept at using modern communications and military tools.[22]

One example of the quality and talent of the people who are working in bin Laden's contemporary base structure is his world-class media organization. This apparatus is already very sophisticated, flexible, and omnipresent in virtually every country in the world. Al Qaeda's media people produce daily combat reports, videos of attacks on enemy targets, interviews with various Al Qaeda and other Islamic leaders, and a steady flow of news bulletins to feed 24/7 satellite television networks around the globe. Thus, the Al Qaeda media are providing Muslim and other communities around the world with Al Qaeda's version of the war in Iraq and Afghanistan—and elsewhere—professionally, reliably, and in real time.[23] If Scheuer is right, then the next generation can only be more sophisticated and formidable than the present one and can only enhance Al Qaeda's position as a global hegemonic power in an environment in which public opinion, correct and incorrect perceptions, and deep religious and political beliefs dominate the human terrain.[24] The resultant radicalization of parts of the Islamic and anti-Western world—particularly young people—has already generated general sociopolitical problems, as well as specific immigration, law enforcement, foreign policy, and national security issues in virtually all of Western Europe.[25]

AL QAEDA'S REGIONAL AND GLOBAL CHALLENGE

Al Qaeda documents and statements envisage what Osama bin Laden calls a "defensive jihad" that calls for three different general types of war—military, economic, and cultural-moral—divided into four stages and with well-defined strategic, operational, and tactical-level objectives.[26] The intent is to organize indirect and direct violence to sow panic and instability in a society; to destabilize, weaken, or depose perceived enemies; and to ultimately bring about radical political change. This kind of violence "shades on occasion into guerrilla warfare and even a substitute for war between states."[27]

This concept also allows military, political, and other facets of an Al Qaeda insurgency to be conducted in tandem. The different types of war and their associated stages are sometimes overlapping and may be altered. Additional stages may be assumed as various milestones are met or not met. Moreover, objectives and the types of military and nonmilitary ways and means chosen to achieve them may be adjusted as a given situation dictates. This kind of ambiguous war intentionally blurs the distinction between and among crime, terrorism, and conventional war—which makes it substantially more difficult to counter. Flexibility in organizational planning and implementation of the program to achieve power is thus an important consideration when analyzing the Al Qaeda model.[28]

The dominating characteristic of a given war is defined as military, economic, or cultural-moral. The difference between the dominant

sphere and the whole is an important one in the context of "combinations" or "collective activity"; that is, there is a dynamic relationship
between a dominant type of general war (such as military, economic,
or moral) and the supporting elements that make up the whole. As an
example, military war is always supported by media (information) war
and a combination of other types of war that might include—but will
not be limited to—psychological war, financial war, trade war, cyber-
network war, or diplomatic war.[29]

At base, the intent of every type of Islamic war, with its dynamic
combinations of multidimensional efforts, is to support directly one or
more of the five main political objectives in Al Qaeda's currently stated
intermediate end state: (1) eject the United States from the Middle East;
(2) open the path to destroy the apostate Arab regimes in the area, as
well as Israel; (3) preserve regional energy resources for Islamic ben-
efit; (4) enhance Muslim unity; and (5) install sharia rule throughout
the region—one geographical place or one part of the human terrain
at a time.[30] The intermediate end game, however, must always be seen
in the light of Al Qaeda's long-term political objectives: take down all
governments that are considered apostate or corrupt; recover all territories that were, at one time or another after 711 A.D., Islamic (including Spain and Portugal, the south of France and Italy, the islands of
the Mediterranean, and some Balkan states); attain regional and global
hegemony; and reestablish the caliphate.[31]

Al Qaeda's Program for Gaining Power: An Elaboration

Al Qaeda's program for gaining power is further divided into four general, multiphased, and overlapping stages.

The First Stage. Inspiring Muslims all around the globe to support the
restoration of the caliphate is the first stage of Islamic conflict against the
House of War (that is, the part of the world ruled by infidels or apostates).
This is a classic Leninist-Maoist first organizational stage, in which bin
Laden concentrates on motivation, discipline, and leadership development (enlightenment), expanding his base organization's relationships
with potential supporters—Muslim and non-Muslim, permanent and

temporary—and developing small propaganda-agitator cells (gangs) all over the globe. With this comprehensive foundational effort, Al Qaeda does not have to depend on any one or two or three sources of logistical, financial, or political support, personnel, or sanctuary. Instead, like the propaganda-agitator cells and networks, Al Qaeda's support organizations are small and diversified to the point that an enemy cannot completely shut them down.[32]

The Second Stage. The next stage of Islamic war involves the creation of loosely organized corporate-type franchise action and support organizations. This is a logical organizational step directed at generating loosely organized, "rhizomatic," hard-to-eradicate networks, relatively reliable infrastructure, and alliances out of first-stage support. Additionally, these support organizations contribute toward the unification of efforts "under the banner of monotheism."[33] When ready, these organizations can open new fronts (stages of war) virtually anywhere in the world that Al Qaeda considers useful within its grand strategy.

The Third Stage. The next stage, overtly more active and military/ terrorist-oriented, might be called "moving onto the offensive." At this point, Al Qaeda and its allied and supporting organizations can begin to attack the symbols of power in enemy states and the global community. The kinds of attacks would range broadly from hanging dogs and cats from lampposts to assassinating and kidnapping apostate functionaries and supporters of illegitimate states or multinational corporations to bombing buildings, railroad stations, groups of people, and any other symbol of perceived illegitimate or corrupt national, regional, and global power. The classic Leninist intent of this terrorist violence (armed and unarmed propaganda and agitation) is to destroy infidel opposition or apostate governmental authority, thereby creating a political vacuum that will allow Al Qaeda and its allied franchise organizations to become the de facto governing authority in areas uncontrolled or abandoned by the targeted state (the human terrain), creating "the nonterritorial Islamic state." This intent should also be applied to socially isolated Muslim societies functioning within a larger society, such as those in Britain, France, Germany, Italy, and Spain.[34]

The Fourth Stage. The final stage of Al Qaeda's Islamic war is the gradual widening of the global battlefield to the point where Al Qaeda becomes less relevant and the Islamic caliphate begins to take control of the general struggle against the House of War. This may mistakenly be considered to be one or a short series of spectacular events, but this stage of conflict is intended to be a long, slow, deliberate, and virtually unnoticed process that will allow a small—but possibly direct—military/terrorist assault to bring about the desired ultimate end state. In any event, the resultant caliphate will expand by one piece of human terrain or geographical territory or country at a time, unevenly, over a lengthy period.[35]

The Success of Al Qaeda's Strategy

At the strategic level, then, Al Qaeda might be expected to conduct combinations of various wars, using diverse battlefields and methods throughout the global community. At the same time, Al Qaeda will continue working toward broader support in the Islamic world and in any non-Islamic state that pledges not to attack Muslims or intervene in their affairs. In short, Al Qaeda will do what it can with its small propaganda-agitator cells to move closer and closer to the achievement of the five objectives (listed above) that define an intermediate political end state.[36] To be sure, there are those in the global Muslim community who do not hold these extreme views.[37] But Al Qaeda does hold these views and to date is one of the best organized and most successful revolutionary (insurgent) movements in Islam. Currently, Al Qaeda is also the only Islamic revolutionary movement that is globally oriented, that is, not limited in scope and geography.

PROPAGANDA AND AGITATION IN THE AL QAEDA PROGRAM

At first glance, Al Qaeda's asymmetric global challenge might appear to be ad hoc, piecemeal, and without reason. However, a closer look at Al Qaeda operations in Spain and Western Europe is instructive. The roles of small cells or gangs within the conceptual framework of the first, second, and third stages of Islamic war mark a slow but perceptible movement toward the organizational ability to increase, intensify, and enlarge second- and third-stage operations within Western Europe. Incidents such as the brutal terrorist bombing of the Atocha train station in Madrid in March 2004, for example, although seemingly random and senseless criminal acts, in fact have specific objectives that serve as part of the subtle implementation of Al Qaeda's intermediate and long-term political-psychological-hegemonic objectives.

Roles and Functions of Propaganda-Agitator Gangs

The term "propaganda" connotes the dissemination or promotion of ideas, doctrine, and practices to further one's cause or damage the opposition's cause. Most commonly, the term is used pejoratively to imply deception or distortion of the truth. Lenin and Al Qaeda use the term in both senses. The intent is to indirectly and directly alter the political-psychological factors that are most relevant to one's own and targeted cultures, that is, to spread "a proper understanding of the present social and economic system . . . [and] an understanding of the historical task of international Social-Democracy" (or Al Qaeda's global jihad).[38]

Inseparably connected with propaganda is agitation. Agitation means that the gangs foment and take part in the various manifestations of the revolution and "all the conflicts between workers and the capitalists" (or believers and infidels).[39] Moreover, "there is no issue in the political field that does not serve as a subject for political agitation."[40] As a consequence, small propaganda-agitator organizations must be organized, trained, and utilized to support the political-psychological struggle and to act as the "midwives" of new social orders.[41]

Together, propaganda and agitation will generate the political-psychological-economic-social-military support for the whole revolutionary organization and for its immediate, intermediate, and ultimate objectives.[42] Thus, Al Qaeda does not need a formed or formal army. There are no maneuver forces, no design for conventional battle, and no obvious connectivity with any other operation elsewhere. Each engagement is particular to itself and in its setting, though all are connected together through a system of networks and an overarching political idea (global jihad and the reestablishment of the caliphate).

Propaganda. Until March 2004, Al Qaeda doctrinal and organizational requirements limited propaganda-agitator cells to a narrow set of support roles for stage one of the global jihad. These beginning activities were propaganda related. The cells acted to expand the number and geographical distribution of sympathizers. They also recruited fighters to join Iraqi, Afghani, and other Al Qaeda–sponsored holy wars in Southeast Asia, the Middle East, and North Africa. At the same time, the cells worked to attain material and financial support for their own franchise group and for the larger global organization. They obtained and distributed videos, documents, posters, magazines, pamphlets, websites, and other propaganda materials around Madrid and other Spanish cities in which Islamic communities are located.[43]

The main intent of Al Qaeda propaganda in Spain is to shift Islamic public opinion and the Muslim religious leadership toward the radical change necessary to regenerate the glories of the eighth century, as advocated by Osama bin Laden. Generally, the main themes directed at the Muslim community in Spain center on the existence of a Western and Jewish conspiracy to enslave and exterminate Muslims and the need to join the struggle against those enemies. Accordingly, Islamic communities in Spain are encouraged to isolate themselves from the host community, immerse themselves in religion, and identify with and support Al Qaeda's global and regional jihad. In turn, this personal isolation and the abundance of Al Qaeda–oriented information enable Muslims to belong to a global community whose values are contrary to those of the host society—and to establish and maintain sharia rule (the nonterritorial Islamic state) one place at a time, over time.[44] Al Qaeda propaganda is not directed only at the Muslim community, however. At a different level, propaganda is also directed at the Spanish society and its government. The main themes in this situation are to leave the Muslim communities to themselves and to refrain from opposing Al Qaeda's objectives and actions in the Middle East and North Africa.[45]

If simple persuasion fails to achieve the objectives pertaining to either the Muslim or the Spanish communities, the next step in the propaganda-agitation process is one level or another of coercion. Insurgents all around the world tend to call that type of action "armed propaganda"; illegal drug traffickers tend to call these activities "business incentives." Lenin called those persuasive-coercive activities "repression and terror."[46] In any case, Al Qaeda is involved in insurgency and narco-trafficking and has been known to apply repression and terror methods—or whatever else they may be called—to shift popular support and political leadership (both Muslim and Spanish) in its favor.[47]

Thus, both Al Qaeda and the Spanish government have a stake in the outcome of the propaganda-agitation process. The government can lose its legitimacy and effective sovereignty (moral and de facto control of significant numbers of people within its national territory), while Al Qaeda can gain the forfeited legitimacy and sovereignty—and the human terrain—lost by the government. This is a zero-sum game in which there can only be one or, possibly, no winner.

An Example of Agitation: The Madrid Bombing, March 2004. Before and shortly after March 11, 2004, Al Qaeda's asymmetric global challenge appeared to many to be ad hoc and senseless. Nevertheless, a closer look at the ruthless terroristic violence in Spain in March 2004 reveals some interesting and important lessons.

On March 11, 2004, ten rucksacks packed with explosives were detonated in four commuter trains at Madrid's Atocha train station. That terrorist act killed 191 innocent and unsuspecting people and seriously injured over 1,800 more. That act was considered to be the most violent in Western Europe since the 1988 bombing of Pan American Flight 103 over Lockerbie, Scotland, that killed 270 people. Despite its length, the 1,470-page official summary of the investigation of the Madrid bombings provided very little information. It indicated that 29 men were involved in that attack, including 15 Moroccans, 9 Spaniards, 1 Syrian with Spanish citizenship, 1 Syrian, 1 Algerian, 1 Egyptian, and 1 Lebanese. The summary also indicated that the accused individuals were members of a radical political group active in North Africa and that Al Qaeda exercised only an inspirational influence. Moreover, the official summary indicated that these terrorists might have learned their bomb-making skills not from Al Qaeda but from the Internet.[48]

Subsequent British and other Western European investigations of terrorist attacks in Western Europe provided considerable additional information regarding the March 2004 bombings in Madrid and the twenty-nine-man organization that was responsible for that act. Those investigations indicated more than a casual relationship with Al Qaeda. Four of the bombers were Al Qaeda "veterans" from the second ring of the base organization who provided leadership and expertise for the operation. Most of the nonveterans involved in the planning and implementation of the attack were operating as part of the third ring of the base organization and were involved in criminal gang activities such as drugs-for-weapons exchanges, providing false documentation (passports, other personal identification, and credit card fraud), and jewel and precious metals theft. Additionally, the nonveteran members of the gang were involved in disseminating propaganda and recruiting Spanish Muslim fighters to join Iraqi and other Al Qaeda–sponsored insurgencies. The intent of these day-to-day activities was to help support and fund regional and global Al Qaeda jihadi operations.[49] In this instance, the normal criminal gang activities of the twenty-nine-man group were interrupted so that they could take on the mission of bombing the Madrid train station.[50] Not until the bombing of the Atocha station in Madrid, then, did this particular gang transition from an implicit political agenda (that is, recruiting personnel and criminally generating financial support for Al Qaeda's political-military operations in the Middle East, North Africa, and elsewhere) to an explicit political challenge to the Spanish state and the global community. Therefore, that was the point at which these "delinquents" became "militants." The purpose of the action was not to achieve any military objective, and it was not a random act. Instead, the bombing was deliberately intended to generate strategic-level political-psychological results. (Nevertheless, the militancy continued to be treated as social and law enforcement issues.)[51]

The Establishment of Al Qaeda Support Centers in Western Europe. The long, but almost irrelevant, official legal Spanish summary of the bloody Madrid bombing left more than a few people wondering why and how a massacre of that size could be carried out by just a few delinquents.[52]

The answers to those questions did not begin to become clear until after similar attacks in London over a year later, in July 2005. The British and, later, other similar investigations of terrorist attacks in Western Europe provided several frustrating and sobering findings.

Among those findings was the discovery that several active Al Qaeda cells were operating throughout Europe with the intent of establishing support centers from which to conduct second- and third-stage Islamic war.[53] At the same time, it is obvious—and Britain is a good example—that these support organizations are now composed of radicalized second- and third-generation ("homegrown") Islamic cadres who have been trained and given experience in Al Qaeda–associated facilities and conflicts ranging from North Africa through Iraq and south and east into Asia (Afghanistan and Pakistan). The result is a rapidly expanding "homegrown" terrorist threat.[54]

After the March 2004 bombings in Madrid, Spanish police began finding large numbers of Islamic militants in the major cities of the country. Police began to verify the latent Spanish fear that their country—called Al-Andalus by Muslims—is a priority target of Al Qaeda's: that there is an Islamic obsession to reincorporate the richest part of the old caliphate into Dar al-Islam (the land of Islam). Indeed, Al Qaeda argues that the Spanish and Portuguese reconquest (711–1492 A.D.) of Al-Andalus marked the initiation of Western European colonialism against Islam.[55] Additionally, recent statements by an Al Qaeda leader, Abdel Makik Droukedel (also known as Abu Musab Abdel Wudud), in a "[m]essage to our nation in the Islamic Maghreb" further validate that Spanish perception of an existing and genuine threat.[56]

The main activities of the Islamic militants in Spain (no longer considered merely delinquents) appear to center on recruiting fighters to join the Iraqi and other Al Qaeda insurgencies, expanding the capability to support operational missions, and influencing governance within the various Islamic communities. These militants are also found to be engaged in other supporting operations for the global jihad, in terms of money, equipment, drugs, and arms. Police also claim to have foiled numerous operational missions (attacks) that are allegedly directed at internal Spanish infrastructure. Importantly, the large majority of the Islamic militants apprehended in Spain since 2004 are North African immigrants—over 500,000 of whom are Moroccan. As a consequence, the support-cell mission of radicalizing Muslims living in Spain appears to constitute an enormous political-social challenge for now and the future.[57] Yet the Spanish government appears to concentrate its national security efforts on the Basque and Catalan separatist movements.[58] To date, the only effort aimed at legal and illegal immigrants is a government plan to provide up to two years' worth (about 18,000 euros) of up-front unemployment benefits in return for giving up Spanish work and residence papers and returning to their countries of origin.[59]

In the United Kingdom (UK)—as well as France and Italy—we see patterns similar to those in Spain. Al Qaeda's terrorist activity is not only broadening in geographical scope but also escalating. In a rare public statement, the director-general of the British security service known as MI5 has made clear that "[t]here is a steady increase in the terrorist threat to the UK"; that "Al Qaeda-related terrorism is real, here, deadly, and enduring"; that "[s]ome 200 groupings or networks, totaling more than 1,600 identified individuals, are actively engaged in plotting and facilitating terrorist acts here or overseas"; and, again, that plots in the UK "often have links back to Al Qaeda in Pakistan."[60] As a result, the United Kingdom, as of mid-2008, is the only country in Western Europe that is beginning to think and act in terms of Al Qaeda and its radicalization of British Muslim youth being a serious national security problem.[61]

In France, Al Qaeda's main efforts are thought to continue to center on the trafficking that funds and supports jihadi operations in Iraq and elsewhere in the world. That "triangular trade" consists of weapons, stolen goods, and narcotics. Also, France, because of its geographical location (along with Spain), is thought to be used as a convenient transshipment point for funneling recruits and material support to and from Al Qaeda affiliates in North Africa and the Middle East.[62]

Last, Italy is thought to be another Al Qaeda base of operations in Europe. Again, as in Britain, France, and Spain, most suspected terrorists in Italy are Muslim immigrants with significant military/terrorist training and experience. The return of jihadists to Italy and elsewhere in Europe from their sojourns in Afghanistan, Iraq, the Middle East, and North Africa is causing some concern. As a result, suspected militants are generally convicted on minor charges (such as transporting illegal explosives) or for drug-related crimes.[63] In the meantime, Italian Army troops are supplementing the police in several major cities of the country. Reportedly, the intent is to "curb illegal immigration and combat crime."[64]

Analysis of Al Qaeda's establishment of small support centers in Spain and other countries in Western Europe provides several significant lessons to observers. First, Al Qaeda's primary concern in pursuing its strategic objectives centers on small, loosely organized, hard-to-eradicate networks. Although passive and active support for Al Qaeda comes from a broad range of social classes, professions, and other Muslim groups, these groups in no way represent the entire Islamic community. Active guidance and support for the entire Al Qaeda network is provided by a few hundred individuals who manage the functional military, funding, procurement, logistical, training, and communications structures of the base organization. Second, Al Qaeda's intent is to generate reliable infrastructure and franchise organizations that can begin to attack symbols of power and open new fronts (stages of war) virtually anywhere in the world. This deliberate and slow process is intended to facilitate the creation and expansion of the desired caliphate by one piece of human or physical terrain at a time. And third, Spain is perceived by many Spaniards to be a priority target for enhanced second- and third-stage Islamic war, yet except in the United Kingdom, Al Qaeda activities in Western Europe tend to be treated as social and law enforcement problems.[65]

What the Propaganda-Agitation Effort Has Demonstrated. Since March 2004, Al Qaeda has demonstrated that it can skillfully apply irregular asymmetric war techniques to modern political war and has done so with impunity. Indeed, its terroristic actions were executed in a way that made virtually any kind of Spanish, Western, or U.S. military response impossible. After over three years of investigation and the trial, the Spanish court acquitted seven of the twenty-nine defendants and found twenty-one individuals guilty of involvement in the 2004 Madrid train bombings. (One of the accused had been previously convicted on charges of illegal transporting of explosives. Also, four of the twenty-nine accused men committed suicide three days after the bombing.) Two Moroccans and a Spaniard were sentenced to 42,924 years in prison. Nobody else in the gang was sentenced to more than 23 years in prison. Of great importance is the fact that the men accused of planning and carrying out the attack were not convicted for the train bombing: they were found guilty of belonging to a terrorist group or for illegally transporting explosives.[66]

The Madrid attack also sent several messages to the Spanish people, the rest of Europe, the United States, and Muslim communities around the globe. The various messages went something like this:

- It is going to be very costly to continue to support the United States in its global war against terrorism and in Iraq.
- Countries not cooperating fully with Al Qaeda might expect to be future targets.
- Understand what can be done with a minimum of manpower and expense.
- Al Qaeda is capable of moving into stage three (offensive) operations in Europe and elsewhere, should the organization make the political decision to do so.
- Al Qaeda demonstrated that the Madrid, London, and other subsequent bombings were deliberately executed in a way that made virtually any kind of Western or U.S. military response impossible.
- Al Qaeda stood up against the United States and its allies—and succeeded.[67]

As a result, the publicity disseminated throughout the Muslim world has been credited with generating new sources of funding, new places for training and sanctuary, new recruits to the Al Qaeda ranks, and additional legitimacy.[68]

Additional Strategic-Level Results of the Bombing. Even though the information gathered throughout Western Europe from the investigations and trials connected with the Madrid bombing was treated cautiously and without alarm, the results achieved by the twenty-nine-man cadre (gang) were dramatic and significant. The sheer magnitude and shock of the attack changed Spanish public opinion and the outcome of the parliamentary elections that were held just three days later. In those elections, the relatively conservative, pro–U.S. government of Prime Minister José Maria Aznar was decisively defeated. That defeat came at the hands of the anti–U.S./anti–Iraqi War leader of the socialists, José Luis Rodriguez Zapatero. Prior to those elections, the Spanish government had been a strong supporter of the United States, U.S. policy regarding the global war on terror, and the Iraq War. Shortly after the elections, Spain's 1,300 troops were withdrawn from Iraq, and Spain ceased to be a strong U.S. ally within the global political and security arenas.[69]

These political-psychological consequences advance the intermediate and long-term objectives of political war that bin Laden and Al Qaeda have set forth. The most relevant of those objectives, in this context, are intended to erode popular support for the war on terrorism among the populations of American allies and to gradually isolate the United States from its allies.[70] All that was accomplished by a small, twenty-nine-man agitator gang with little impunity and at a cost of only $80,000.[71]

The Larger Effects of Propaganda-Agitator Gangs

Al Qaeda propaganda, the bombing of Madrid's Atocha train station in 2004, and the establishment of support centers in Western Europe have significantly opened the path to (1) weaken the influence of the United States in the Middle East and Western Europe; (2) weaken the position of the apostate Arab regimes in the area, as well as Israel; (3) enhance radical Muslim morale and unity throughout the world; and (4) demonstrate Al Qaeda's capability to conduct second- and third-stage conflict in Western Europe.

WHERE AL QAEDA OPERATIONS LEAD: THE LONG WAR

Osama bin Laden and Al Qaeda have abruptly and violently contradicted the traditional ideas that war is the purview of the nation-state and that nonstate and irregular actors' ways and means of conducting contemporary war are simple aberrations.[72] Al Qaeda also demonstrated that limited conventional motives for conducting war can be dramatically expanded to strive to achieve the Clausewitzian admonition to "dare to win all"—the complete political overthrow of a government or another symbol of power—instead of merely "using superior strength to filch some province."[73] Thus, Al Qaeda represents a militant, revolutionary, and energetic commitment to a long-term approach to the renewal of an extremist interpretation of Islamic governance, social purpose, and tradition—that is, the renewal of the eighth-century caliphate.[74]

Those disciples of Osama bin Laden who dream of a return to the glories of the eighth through fifteenth centuries understand that such a dream cannot be fulfilled overnight. Those dreamers also know that this kind of ultimate political objective cannot be achieved by *blitzkrieg* or "shock-and-awe" tactics that can deliver a final victory in a few weeks. They realize that the objective of a new Islamic society and caliphate will be achieved as a result of a deliberate and lengthy struggle that generates the destabilization and slow destruction of targeted states. This confrontation includes no compromise or other options; this is a conflict with an absolute and unalterable objective, in which there is nothing to negotiate or compromise on. This unlimited objective, then, requires a long war.[75]

The long war, however, is more than a lengthy war. It begins with a challenge to Western political and military leaders to adapt to some new realities of contemporary conflict. It ends with another challenge to Western leaders to contemplate the notion of interim "virtual states" (nonterritorial Islamic communities) within traditional sovereign nation-states and a type of war that includes no place for compromise or other options short of the achievement of the ultimate political objective—the renewal of the caliphate. As a consequence, the long war is total war in terms of scope and geography, as well as time.[76]

New Realities: New Enemies and Centers of Gravity

The legal-traditional concept of threats to national security and sovereignty is based on the assumption that war is fought between geographically distinct nation-state adversaries, by means of well-equipped military forces. The ending of that type of war generally involves some sort of compromise (armistice or surrender terms) publicly concluded between the parties to the conflict. Thus, national security and sovereignty depend primarily on the ability of a nation-state to protect its political borders and interests at home and abroad against conventional external military aggression.[77] Traditionally, then, the enemy is a nation-state, with recognizable military formations, that violates national borders and threatens the major institutions, natural resources, and external interests of another state. In these terms, the primary centers of gravity (the hub of all power on which all depends) are recognizable enemy military forces, coupled with the nation-state's industrial-technical capability to support military operations.[78]

Experience gained from the hundreds of small, uncomfortable revolutionary wars that have taken place over the past half-century teaches us differently. At base, the enemy has now become any state or non-state political actor that plans and implements the multidimensional kinds of indirect and direct, nonmilitary and military, and nonlethal and lethal internal and external activities that threaten a given society's general well-being and exploit the root causes of internal instability.[79] The primary and specific effort, however, that ultimately breaks up and defeats an adversary's political-economic-social system and forces radical change is the multidimensional erosion of people's morale and political will.[80] The better one protagonist is at that persuasive-coercive effort, the more effective that protagonist will be relative to the opposition.[81] Accordingly, the center of gravity has now become an adversary's public opinion and political decision-making leadership.[82]

The basic reality of this new center of gravity is that information and the media (propaganda)—not military firepower or technology—is the primary currency upon which "modern war amongst the people" is run.[83] Contemporary irregular asymmetric war thus takes place in an environment shaped by words, ideas, beliefs, expectations, deceptions, and political will—and the unifying political and intelligence organizations that can effectively challenge any given enemy of "the people."[84] In the final analysis, the central idea in contemporary conflict is to influence and then control people and their values (the human terrain rather than the geographical terrain). This psychological-political effort also defines victory or defeat. Once an adversary compels radical political change, there is not much need for a formal surrender document or a public ceremony acknowledging that that fundamental change has taken place. In these terms, public opinion and political leadership provide the architecture from which to develop a viable ends, ways, and means strategy that can win a long war.

Al Qaeda's Challenge to State Sovereignty

Osama bin Laden does not appear to be particularly interested in taking de facto control of any given state. Nor is he sending conventional military forces across national borders. His focus is on influencing governments to allow his organization maximum freedom of movement and action within and between national territories and on influencing and controlling the Muslim human terrain now living within various national territories in Spain, other parts of Western Europe, and elsewhere. Rather than trying to control or depose a government in a major stroke (coup or *golpe*) or a Maoist revolutionary war, as some insurgents have done, Al Qaeda and its various networks slowly take control of specific pieces of human terrain within the geographical-political territory of targeted states. This is accomplished one individual, one street, one neighborhood, or one mosque at a time. Thus, whether Al Qaeda's pursuit of freedom of movement and action is specifically criminal, terrorist, ideological, or religious is irrelevant. The putative objective is to neutralize, influence, and control people and communities to begin the long-term process to renew the caliphate. This final objective defines insurgency, a serious political agenda, and a messianic determination to radically change entire political-economic-social systems and their values.[85] In addition, it is an indirect assault on the sovereignty of targeted states.

Al Qaeda's assault on state sovereignty in Spain and other Western European countries represents a quintuple threat to the authority and legitimacy of targeted governments. First, the ability of the state to perform its legitimizing security and public service functions is undermined by petty crime, protectionism, intimidation, impunity from serious punishment, and the illegal triangular trade in weapons, drugs, and stolen goods. Second, by isolating themselves from the rest of a host country's society, Islamic communities become alienated; remove themselves from the constraints of local, regional, and national governments' authority; and begin to replace that authority with their own sharia law. Third, by making the host government irrelevant to the Muslim community while taking control of a given piece of human terrain and performing the tasks of government, Al Qaeda enclaves can transform themselves into virtual states within a state. Fourth, this non-territorial virtual state would have no centralized bureaucracy and no official armed forces. It would have an endlessly flexible and mobile fighting force made up of small groups or gangs, supported by small support groups located in over eighty countries around the globe. Additionally, this multilevel assault on state sovereignty threatens the liberal democratic values of much of the West. Together, these threats (challenges) are capable of generating high-damage, low-cost actions calculated to maximize impact and to yield a series of carefully staged media events that may or may not reflect reality.[86] The intent of all this is to slowly and deliberately compel the radical change of targeted political-economic-social systems.

WIZARD'S CHESS AND THE LONG WAR

The seriousness of Al Qaeda's ultimate objective of renewing the caliphate, and the irregular asymmetric ways and means of achieving it, cannot be dismissed as too ambiguous, too difficult, and too far into the future to deal with. The consequences of nonaction can be derived from a game described in a Harry Potter adventure: wizard's chess. Osama bin Laden is a master of this deadly game, which serves as a metaphorical example of Al Qaeda's long war. "In that game, protago-nists move pieces silently and subtly all over the game board. Under the players' studied direction, each piece represents a different type of direct and indirect power and might simultaneously conduct its lethal and nonlethal attacks from differing directions. Each piece shows no mercy against its foe and is prepared to sacrifice itself in order to allow another piece the opportunity to destroy or control an opponent—or to checkmate the king."[87]

Irregular asymmetric war, such as that seen in wizard's chess, is the only type of conflict that the United States has ever lost.[88] A loss to Al Qaeda in this long war would have even greater consequences, for "[o]ver the long term ... this game is not a test of expertise in creating instability, conducting violence, or achieving some sort of moral satisfaction. Ultimately, it is an exercise in survival. Failure in Wizard's Chess is not an option."[89]

KEY POINTS AND LESSONS

In light of the new world security environment that has been initiated by Al Qaeda, there is ample reason for worldwide concern. The results of that effort stress the following:

- Al Qaeda has succeeded in doing what no other terrorist organization accomplished: demonstrate that a nonstate actor can effectively challenge a traditional nation-state and the symbols of power in the global system—without conventional organization, weaponry, and manpower.
- Experience with Al Qaeda's activities in Western Europe indicates that Osama bin Laden represents a militant, revolutionary, and energetic commitment to a long-term approach to return to Islamic governance, social purpose, and tradition.
- The premise is that ultimate success in renewing the eighth-century caliphate can be achieved as a result of the careful application of a complex multidimensional paradigm that begins with innovations in political-psychological war, combined with the ruthless application of terror.
- That paradigm is enhanced by the addition of informational (media), economic, cultural, and other components of power that give a relative advantage to Al Qaeda over an opponent that uses a unidimensional military-police approach to address the long-term conflict.

- These various dimensions of contemporary conflict are further combined with military and nonmilitary, lethal and nonlethal, and direct and indirect methods of attacking an enemy. Together, these combinations generate a powerful irregular asymmetric substitute for conventional war.

- Osama bin Laden's first and continuing concern centers on organization. The activities necessary to achieve his ultimate political vision include the creation of a motivated and enlightened cadre, a loosely organized propaganda-agitator (guerrilla) network, and small multiform support mechanisms for the entire organization.

- Al Qaeda's program for gaining power is divided into four general multiphased and overlapping phases: (1) establishing a basic organization; (2) creating loosely organized, corporate-type franchise action and support organizations; (3) taking control of human and geographical terrain that is uncontrolled or abandoned by a targeted state, that is, "moving onto the offensive"; and (4) gradually widening the global battlefield to the point where Al Qaeda becomes less relevant and the Islamic caliphate begins to take control of the long-term struggle (the long war).

- The long war is more than a lengthy war: it begins with a challenge to Western political and military leaders to adapt to new realities (such as a new concept of enemy and new centers of gravity) and ends with another challenge to Western leaders to contemplate the notion of interim "virtual states" (nonterritorial Islamic communities) located within traditional sovereign nation-states.

- Al Qaeda's assault on state sovereignty represents a quintuple threat: (1) to undermine the ability of a government to perform its legitimizing functions; (2) to isolate Islamic communities from the rest of a host nation's society and begin to replace traditional state authority with sharia law; (3) to transform Islamic communities into "virtual states" within the host state, without a centralized bureaucracy and no official armed forces; (4) to conduct low-cost actions calculated to maximize damage and display carefully staged media events that lead to the erosion of an enemy state's political-economic-social system; and (5) as a corollary, to not only impinge on the effective sovereignty, stability, and security of a targeted society but also challenge liberal democratic values.

The global struggle for power, influence, and resources continues into the twenty-first century with different actors, different names, and different rhetoric. Thus, Lenin's strategic vision for the achievement of political power and radical political-economic-social change is no longer the property of strict Leninists. Antidemocratic populists, antisystem populists, antiglobalists, New Socialists and the revolutionary left, and radical Islamists alike are free to study it, adapt it, and use it for their own purposes. Osama bin Laden and his organization, Al Qaeda, is a case in point. As uncomfortable as this conclusion might be, however, Lenin reminds us that there is a viable solution to the problem: all who want to retain the freedoms we enjoy "should have but one slogan—seriously learn the art of war."[90]

CHAPTER 6

THE NEIGHBORS DOWN THE ROAD AND ACROSS THE RIVER

The Mexican Zetas and Other Private Armies That Do Nasty Things and "Go Bump in the Night"

Leftist insurgent groups such as Comandante Zero's Zapatista National Liberation Army (EZLN) are not the only nonstate political actors in Mexico, the Western Hemisphere, or anywhere else in the world that exercise violence to advertise their cause, radicalize the population, and move slowly but surely toward the achievement of their ideological and self-enrichment dreams.[1] One careful observer of the Mexican scene, Lincoln Krause, has catalogued thirty-seven currently active left-oriented insurgent organizations that trace their origins back to the political activism that swept that country in the 1950s and have been inspired by the heroic images of Fidel Castro, Che Guevara, and the Cuban Revolution. They continue to persist—and flourish—in the present unstable internal security environment.[2]

At the same time, a new and dangerous dynamic has been introduced into the Mexican internal security environment along with that of the Western Hemisphere more generally. In Mexico, that new dynamic involves the migration of traditional hard-power national security and sovereignty threats from traditional state and nonstate adversaries to hard- and soft-power threats from small, nontraditional, private nonstate military organizations.[3] This "privatized violence" tends to include a complex and enigmatic mix of transnational criminal organizations, or TCOs (cartels and mafia); small private military organizations such as the Zeta enforcer gangs, including the Aztecas, Negros, and Polones; mercenary groups such as the Central American Maras, Guatemalan

121

Kaibiles, and paramilitary triggermen (*gatilleros*); and other small paramilitary or vigilante organizations. (All of these groups, in combination, are hereafter cited as the gangs-TCO phenomenon.)[4]

What makes these small private armies so effective is the absence of anyone to turn to for help. Weak and/or corrupt state security institutions, as in Mexico, are notoriously unhelpful and tend to be a part of the problem—not the solution. In such a vacuum, only a few relatively well-armed and disciplined individuals are capable of establishing their own rule of law. The dynamic of privatized violence (which has been on the global scene for centuries and is not really new) involves a powerful and ambiguous mix of terrorism, crime, and conventional war tactics and operations. This violence and its perpetrators tend to create and consolidate semiautonomous enclaves (criminal free states) that develop into quasi states—and what the Mexican government calls "zones of impunity."[5] Leaders of these quasi-state (nonstate) political entities promulgate their own rule of law, negotiate alliances with traditional state and nonstate actors, and conduct an insurgency-type war against various state and nonstate adversaries. Additionally, criminal quasi states may operate in juxtaposition with the institutions of weak de jure states and force the populations to adapt to an ambivalent and precarious existence that challenges traditional values as well as local law.[6]

The dynamics of privatized military force in Mexico signal two cogent trends. The first, addressing the threat, illustrates a "new" and unconventional battlefield that represents a nontraditional security threat to Mexico and its northern and southern neighbors. The second trend deals with response to the threat. These dynamics signal a new stability-security reality that is changing relations and roles among and between state security and service institutions. The "new" threat is not just a law enforcement problem, a national security issue, or even a social issue. It is much more, requiring a whole-of-government approach to dealing with the causes as well as the perpetrators of terrorism, criminality, and military violence. Ultimately, depending on the response to the threat, there is another signal that will define an underlying shift in state identity, either toward or away from some manifestation of state failure.

The mention of a possible shift in state identity here does not imply that Mexico is now a "failed state." That country has a vibrant middle class that supports law and order, and it has a relatively robust economy that can sustain a president willing to use the powers of the state to confront the gangs-TCO phenomenon. Under President Felipe Calderon, Mexico is responding constructively to the threat and can be seen as shifting away from the possibility of state failure.[7] Nevertheless, the threat exists; it is exacerbating the "new" privatized violence, and it cannot be wished away. As a consequence, this cautionary tale is intended to help political, military, policy, academic, and opinion leaders think strategically about explanations and responses that might apply to many of the unconventional, irregular, and ambiguous threats that Mexico and other countries face now and will face in the future. At the same time, it should help to generate a more relevant response in the United States and the rest of the hemispheric community to the strategic reality of the "guerrillas next door."[8]

Directly applicable to this effort are the macro "What," "Why," "Who," "How," and "So What?" questions concerning the resultant type of conflict that has been and is being fought in Mexico. A useful way to organize these questions is to adopt a matrix approach. The matrix may be viewed as having four sets of elements: (1) the contextual setting, that is, the "What" and the beginning "Why" questions; (2) the protagonist's background, organization, operations, motives, and linkages, which lay out the fundamental "Who," "Why," and "How" questions; (3) the strategic-level outcomes and consequences, or the basic "So What" questions; and (4) key points and lessons that summarize the "So What" issues. These various elements are mutually influencing and constitute the political- and strategic-level cause-and-effect dynamics of a given case. This approach is helpful and important in policy, practical, and theoretical terms.[9]

THE CONTEXTUAL SETTING

Two contextual themes are relevant to the analysis of Mexico's past, present, and future criminal and militarized violence. First, armed insurgent groups have arisen and prospered primarily as a response to historical sociopolitical factors. Yet the Mexican political structure has not developed programs and policies to remedy the societal ills that have generated and supported all these "revolutionary" movements.[10]

Second, the continuing existence of political insurgents and armed criminal groups in Mexico "since forever" says much for their ability to adapt to and use the political system for their own purposes. This ability says much about both the motivational dedication of the insurgent-criminal leadership and the basic corruption within the postrevolutionary political system. Such corruption is likewise a result of long-standing political-historic factors, as well as new political-economic-social-military dynamics being introduced into the Mexican internal security situation.[11]

Historical-Political Context of Mexican Politics

Many scholars agree that the key to understanding the contemporary Mexican political system lies in its origins in the social upheaval of the Revolution of 1910–20. The radical change precipitated by that event almost completely destroyed Mexico's past and forged a new and somewhat different nation. Some important old political habits did survive the revolution, however.[12]

Caudillismo (political control by "strong men") never has been very far under the surface of Mexican politics, and the constitution that emerged out of the revolution did not promulgate the kind of democracy that liberals might champion. Thus, every president of Mexico since the revolution has been a "great revolutionary leader" *(caudillo)*, and the Mexican constitution is mostly an expression of hopes and wishes for future political, economic, and social justice. Accordingly, every president of the Republic represented historical continuity with the revolution and defined the revolutionary goals that would be pursued during his six-year term of office. And in true *caudillistic* fashion, the president provided justice. All actions of government—executive, legislative, and judicial—were taken in his name and were administered by his loyal political appointees.[13]

If the president was the leader (strong man) of the revolution, the Institutional Revolutionary Party (PRI) was his functional representative. The PRI was the single, all-powerful mechanism of electoral activity, recruitment, and social control. Through the manipulation of the party mechanism and all its symbols during each six-year term of presidential office, the political elites were able to maintain and enhance their power and wealth—and to enshrine the Mexican personal freedom of political opinion, while systematically repressing political organizations that operated outside the limits allowed by the PRI.[14]

A New National Security Context

With the malaise of corrupt caudillistic self-aggrandizement rooted at all levels of the Mexican political-economic-social system, forces for new and fundamental change began to emerge in the 1980s. At that time, a set of economic measures designed to reduce inflation, control currency devaluation, and cut back on government spending led to bankruptcy in the business sector, increased unemployment, growing income inequality, and a much larger role for the private business sector in the government-controlled economy. Politically, the middle class, disaffected by public-sector inefficiencies generated by PRI corruption and resistance to serious reform—and declining living standards—began to abandon the PRI and vote for other party candidates for public office. As a consequence, Mexico began to devolve from a strong, centralized, de facto unitary state to what former ambassador David C. Jordan calls an "anocratic" democracy, a state that has the procedural features of democracy but retains the characteristics of an autocracy, in which the ruling elites face no scrutiny or accountability.[15] At the same time, Mexico has become a market state that is moving toward "criminal free state" status. That is, Mexico is a state in which political power is migrating from the state to small, nonstate actors who organize into sprawling networks that maintain private armies, treasury and revenue sources, welfare services, and the ability both to make alliances with state and nonstate actors and to conduct war (the gang-TCO phenomenon).[16] This correlation of political, economic, and military forces, in turn, has generated an extremely volatile and dangerous internal security situation in Mexico that has been all but ignored in the United States.

The Anocratic Democracy. The policy-oriented definition of democracy that has been generally accepted and used in U.S. foreign policy over the past several years is best described as "procedural democracy." This definition tends to focus on the election of civilian political leadership and, perhaps, on a relatively high level of participation on the part of the electorate. Thus, as long as a country is able to hold elections, it is considered a democracy—regardless of the level of accountability, transparency, resistance to corruption, and ability to extract and distribute resources for national development and the protection of human rights, liberties, and security.[17]

In contemporary Mexico, we observe important paradoxes in this concept of democracy. Elections are held on a regular basis, but leaders, candidates, and elected politicians are regularly assassinated; hundreds of government officials considered unacceptable to the armed nonstate actors have been assassinated following their elections. Additionally, intimidation, direct threats, kidnapping, and the use of relatively minor violence on a person or his or her family play an important role prior to elections. As a corollary, although the media institutions are free from state censorship, journalists, academicians, and folk musicians who make their antinarco-gang opinion known too publicly are systematically assassinated.[18]

Consequently, it is hard to credit most Mexican elections as genuinely "democratic" or "free." Neither political party competition nor public participation in elections can be complete in an environment where violent and unscrupulous nonstate actors compete with legitimate political entities to control the government both before and after elections. Moreover, crediting Mexico as a democratic state is difficult as long as elected leaders are subject to corrupting control and intimidation or to informal vetoes imposed by criminal nonstate actors. Regardless of definitions, however, the persuasive and intimidating actions of the gang-TCO phenomenon in the Mexican electoral processes have pernicious effects on democracy and tend to erode the will and ability of the state to carry out its legitimizing functions.[19]

The Market State and the Gang-TCO Phenomenon. John Sullivan has identified an important shift in state form: from nation-state to market state and thereupon from market state to criminal free state status. As the ability to wage war (conflict) devolves from traditional hierarchical state organizations to Internet-worked transnational nonstate actors, we can see the evolution of new war-making entities (small private armies) capable of challenging the stability, security, and sovereignty of traditional nation-states. These private entities (terrorists, warlords, drug cartels, enforcer gangs, criminal gangs, and ethno-nationalistic extremists) respond to illicit market forces (such as illegal drugs, arms, and human trafficking) rather than the rule of law and are much more than "stateless" or nonstate groups. They are powerful organizations that not only can challenge the rule of law and the sovereignty of the nation-state but also are known to promulgate their own policy and laws—and impose their criminal values on societies or parts of societies (creating criminal free zones and "badlands and bad neighborhoods" all around the world).[20]

In Mexico, as an unintended consequence of devolving political power from the state to private nonstate entities, we see not only the erosion of democracy but also the erosion of the state. Jordan argues that corruption at all levels is key to this problem and is a prime mover toward "narco-socialism."[21] Narco-politics has penetrated not only the executive, legislative, and judicial branches of the Mexican federal government but also the state governments and municipalities.[22] The reality of corruption at any level of government favoring the gang-TCO phenomenon discourages responsible governance and the public well-being. In these terms, the state's presence and authority is at best questionable in over more than 233 "zones of impunity" that exist throughout large geographical portions of Mexico. At the same time, the corruption reality brings into question the issue of effective state sovereignty. This is a feudal environment defined by extreme violence, patronage, bribes, kickbacks, cronyism, ethnic exclusion, and personal whim.[23]

Given the rise of the market state and violent privatized market-state actors, long-standing assumptions about national security and law enforcement are being challenged. Most notably, the ability (and power) to conduct conflict is moving from the traditional hierarchical nation-state to the privatized, horizontally networked market state. Again, as noted above, that transition of power blurs the distinctions between and among crime, terrorism, and warfare.[24] At the same time, privatized violence is becoming (in many regions has become) a feature of the transition to the market state and beyond. In this milieu, terrorists and organized crime come into conflict with warlords, insurgents, governments, private corporations, and nongovernmental organizations (NGOs). Any and all of these types of state and nonstate entities can hire and operate a small private army. In addition, all these entities can interact and blend or share attributes at given points in time. This is particularly relevant in the case of Al Qaeda *jihadi* terrorists operating in Spain, state-supported popular militias operating out of Venezuela, and nonstate criminal-political gangs operating in Colombia that seek to foment global, regional, national, or subnational instability, conflict, and political change. The linkage between war, terrorism, and crime is especially relevant in cases in which we see these types of actors making alliances with or declaring war against other similar privatized organizations, transnational criminal organizations, NGOs, and governments.

Typically, private armies and warlordism are the providence of failed or failing states. The common wisdom predicts that failed or failing states will sooner or later dissolve into nothing and provide no problems. Yet the experience of reality warns us that failed states do not simply go away. They normally devolve into international dependencies, people's democracies, narco-socialist states, criminal states, military dictatorships, or worse.[25]

The Resultant Internal Security Situation in Mexico. In the mid-1980s and later, a new political-economic force inserted itself into the changing internal security milieu. At a time when the political system was weakening and the economy privatizing, illicit drug trafficking started to become very big business. This is not to say that the illegal drug trafficking industry had theretofore not been operating in Mexico. It was. But in the 1990s, air and sea routes to the U.S. market from South America's "White Triangle" (the main cocaine-producing regions in Colombia, Bolivia, and Peru) were being shut down. The narcotics-producing cartels, along with their TCO allies, began to use land routes through Central America and Mexico to transport their products to the U.S. market. As a consequence, between 60 and 90 percent of the illegal cocaine entering the United States is estimated to transit Central

America and Mexico. Estimates of the money involved—in the billions of dollars—are mind-boggling.[26]

In this context, gangs and their TCO allies in Mexico, as in other countries, share many of the characteristics of a multinational Fortune 500 company. Thus, the phenomenon is reified in the form of an organization striving to make money, expand its markets, and move and act as freely as possible in the political jurisdictions within and between which it works. By performing its business tasks with superefficiency and for maximum profit, the general organization employs chief executive officers and boards of directors, councils, system of internal justice, lawyers, accountants, public affairs officers, negotiators, and franchised project managers. And, of course, this company has a security division, though somewhat more ruthless than one of a bona fide Fortune 500 corporation.[27]

Authorities have no consistent or reliable data on the gang-TCO phenomenon in Mexico. Nevertheless, the gang phenomenon in that country is acknowledged to be large and complex. In addition, the gang situation is known to be different in the north (along the U.S. border) than it is in the south (along the Guatemala-Belize borders). Second, the phenomenon is different in the areas between the northern and southern borders of Mexico. Third, a formidable gang presence is known to exist throughout the entire country (regardless of the accuracy of the data estimating the size and extent of this gang presence), and—given the weakness of national political-economic institutions—there is considerable opportunity for criminality to prosper.[28] As a result, the rate of homicides along the northern and southern borders is considered epidemic, and Mexico has the highest incidence of kidnapping in the world. Finally, violent gang and TCO activity in Mexico clearly threaten the socioeconomic and political development of the country.[29]

More specifically, the Central American Mara Salvatrucha 13 and Mara Salvatrucha 18 gangs (referred to collectively as the "Maras") have made significant inroads into Mexican territory and appear to be competing effectively with Mexican gangs. In the south—along the Belize-Guatemalan borders—the Maras have gained control of trafficking in illegal immigrants and drugs moving north through Mexico to the United States. The Central American Maras are also used as mercenaries by the northern drug cartels. Between the northern and southern borders, an ad hoc mix of up to fifteen thousand members of the Mexican gangs and Central American Maras are reported to be operating in more than twenty of Mexico's thirty states. Additionally, members and former members of the elite Guatemalan special forces (Kaibiles) are being recruited by the Gulf Cartel and the Zetas as mercenaries.[30]

The gangs operating on the northern border of Mexico are long-time, well-established, "generational" (that is, consisting of Mexican grandfathers, sons, and grandsons) organizations with forty- to fifty-year histories. There are, reportedly, at least 24 different gangs operating in the city of Nuevo Laredo and 320 active gangs operating in the city of Juarez—with an estimated seventeen thousand members. The best-known gangs in the north are the Azteca, Mexicles, and Zeta organizations, whose members generally work as hired guns and drug runners for the major cartels operating in the area. The major cartels include "the big four"—Juarez, Gulf, Sinaloa, and Tijuana cartels, which operate generally in the north. Despite the fact that most of the reported violence is concentrated in three northern states—Chihuahua, Sinaloa, and Baja California—the Juarez Cartel maintains a presence in twenty-one of the Mexican states; the Gulf Cartel is found in thirteen states; the Sinaloa Cartel (see the later discussion of El Chapo) has located itself in seventeen states; and remnants of the reportedly disintegrating Tijuana Cartel (led by Areliano Felix) are present in fifteen states. There are also the Colima, Oaxaca, and Valencia cartels, which generally operate in the southern parts of Mexico. To further complicate the Mexican gang-TCO picture, there is the Mexican Mafia (EME). At one time, all gangs operating south of Bakersfield, California, and into northern Mexico had to pay homage to and take orders from EME. That is no longer a rigid requirement, however; the Central American Maras are known to have broken that agreement as early as 2005.[31]

This convoluted array of gangs and TCOs—Central American Maras, Mexican Zetas, Guatemalan Kaibiles, Mexican drug cartels, and the Mexican Mafia—leaves an almost anarchical situation throughout Mexico. As each gang and TCO violently competes with others and within itself and works against the Mexican government to maximize market share and freedom of movement and action, we see a strategic internal security environment characterized by ambiguity, complexity, and unconventional (irregular) war. In addition, we see the slow erosion of the Mexican state and the establishment of small and large criminal free enclaves in some of the cities and states of Mexico. Moreover, the spillover transcends the supposedly sovereign borders of Mexico and its neighbors (both south and north). This situation reminds one of the feudal medieval era. Violence and the fruits of violence—arbitrary and unprincipled political control—seem to be devolving to small, private, criminal nonstate actors. This is a serious challenge to democracy, stability, security, and sovereignty in Mexico and its neighbors.[32]

Unconventional Nonstate and Intrastate War

The internal security environment that we see in Mexico today is dangerous and volatile, and it goes well beyond a simple law enforcement problem. Thus, the internal security situation is characterized by an unconventional battlefield that no one from the traditional-legal Westphalian school of conflict would recognize or be comfortable in dealing with. Instead of conventional, direct interstate war conducted by uniformed military forces of another country, we see something considerably more complex and ambiguous.

First, thanks to Steven Metz and Raymond Millen and their theory-building efforts, we see unconventional *non*state war, which tends to involve gangs, insurgents, drug traffickers, other transnational criminal organizations, terrorists, and warlords who thrive in "ungoverned or weakly governed space" between and within various host countries. At the same time, we also see unconventional *intra*state war, which tends to involve direct and indirect conflict between state and nonstate actors.[33] Regardless of any given politically correct term for unconventional intrastate war, all state and nonstate actors involved in unconventional intrastate conflict are engaged in one common political act—war. That is, the goal is to control or radically change a government and to institutionalize the acceptance of the victor's will.[34] Additional strategic-level analytical commonalties in the contemporary battle space include the following: no formal declarations or terminations of war; no easily identified human foe to attack and defeat; no specific geographical territory to attack and hold; no single credible government or political actor with which to deal; and no guarantee that any agreement between or among contending actors will be honored.[35]

Experience in unconventional nonstate and intrastate war further demonstrates that there are no national or international laws, conventions, or treaties that cannot be ignored or utilized; there is no territory that cannot be bypassed or utilized; there are no national boundaries (frontiers) that cannot be bypassed or utilized; and there are no instruments of power (military, diplomatic, economic, political, informational, or psychological) that can be ignored or left unused. In these strategic-level terms, contemporary war (conflict) involves everyone, and the battlefield is everywhere. There are no front lines, no visible distinctions between civilian and irregular forces personnel, and no sanctuaries.[36]

In this fragmented, complex, and ambiguous environment dominated by political and psychological violence, conflict must be considered and implemented as a whole. The power to deal with these kinds of situations is no longer hard combat firepower or even the more benign police power. Rather, power consists of multilevel combined political, psychological, moral, informational, economic, social, police, and military activity that can be brought to bear holistically on the causes and consequences—as well as the perpetrators—of violence.[37]

ZETAS: THE "WHO," "WHAT," AND "WHY" ARCHITECTURE

The "Who," "What," and "Why" case study methodological architecture focuses on protagonist leadership and organization, operations, motives, and linkages. Long-standing common wisdom has it that virtually any nonstate political actor with any kind of resolve can take advantage of the instability inherent in anything like the current Mexican internal security situation. The tendency is that the best-motivated and best-armed organization on the scene, or an alliance of these entities, will eventually control that instability for its own purposes. Carlos

Marighella, in his well-known *Manual of the Urban Guerrilla*, elaborates on that wisdom: "A terrorist act is no different than any other urban guerrilla tactic, apart from the apparent facility with which it can be carried out. That will depend on planning and organization [and its resultant shock value]."[38] Thus, even though other privatized military organizations (including enforcer gangs) are operating in Mexico today, the Zetas appear to be the group most likely to be able to achieve its objectives. Zeta organization and planning has been outstanding, and the shock value of Zeta operations has been unequaled. Thus, as Marighella teaches, terrorism is a major force multiplier—"a weapon the revolution cannot do without."[39]

Background

During the eighty years, from 1920 through 2000, when Mexico was effectively a one-party unitary state controlled by the PRI, the drug cartels and the party made an accommodation. The question was, "Silver or lead?" Silver was a bribe; lead was a bullet to the head. The understanding that existed between the cartels and the party was that the political functionary would be better off to choose silver—simple as that! This does not mean that everyone was compromised, but many party officials who were not compromised directly nevertheless chose not to see much that was going on. Vicente Fox's election to the Mexican presidency in 2000 broke the PRI's grip on Mexico and changed the status that allowed the cartels to quietly go about their business and share some of the wealth with their "friends." President Fox and, later, President Calderon became progressively more aggressive in confronting both the cartels and the police and politicians whom the cartels had corrupted and co-opted. At about the same time, the flow of illegal narcotics through Mexico increased to the point such that drugs in Mexico are now estimated to produce $25 billion (in U.S. dollars) per year.[40]

Everything changed. The party and government were no longer as cooperative with the cartels as they had once been. The government, trying to exercise its traditional sovereignty over the Mexican national territory and finding that to be more difficult than expected, recognized the possibility that the country might be moving toward "failed state status."[41] The various cartels were competing more violently than ever before, fighting with each other—and the government—for position in the new milieu. The profits to be had for the cartels, and the stakes for Mexico, were enormous. So, what is a businessman to do? Somehow, he must protect and enhance his resources, including trafficking routes and political and physical space from which to operate more freely, and he must simultaneously protect and expand his share of the market.

As a result of carefully watching the indicators noted above, the Gulf Cartel started to recruit members of the Mexican Army's elite Airborne Special Forces Group (GAFES) in the late 1990s. The GAFES members who defected to the Gulf Cartel called themselves Los Zetas. The intent of the cartel's recruitment effort was to provide protection from government forces and other cartels, and the Gulf Cartel paid the Zetas salaries well beyond those paid by the army to make the effort worth their while. The idea proved to be a great success. Once the former soldiers were in place and functioning, their superior training, organization, equipment, experience, and discipline led them from simple protection missions to operations that were more challenging. The Zetas began to collect Gulf Cartel debts, secure new drug trafficking routes at the expense of other cartels, discourage defections from other parts of the cartel organization, and track down and execute particularly worrisome rival cartel and other gang leaders all over Mexico and Central America.[42] Subsequently, the Zetas expanded their activities to kidnapping, arms trafficking, money laundering, and creating routes to and from the United States, as well as developing access to cocaine sources in South America.[43] All this has been accomplished using the means delineated by Carlos Marighella, "often with grotesque savagery."[44]

The Zetas is the first private military organization in the Western Hemisphere to be made up of former military personnel from a regular army. Because of its considerable military expertise, previous experience in counterinsurgency combat, and guerrilla and urban warfare against leftist Mexican insurgent groups, the Zetas has made itself into a major private military-criminal organization in its own right. As a result, it has been labeled by Mexican scholar and TCO authority Raul Benetez as "the biggest, most serious threat to the nation's security."[45]

Organization and Operations

Despite the lack of precise figures and specific and authoritative organizational charts, the Zetas appears to be much more than an ordinary enforcer gang organization working within a larger business model of a contemporary Mexican drug cartel. At first glance, there appears to be a hierarchical pyramid structure that is common among military organizations and some TCOs around the world.[46] A closer examination of the multilayered and networked structure, however, indicates a substantial corporate enterprise designed to conduct small and larger-scale business operations, along with terrorist, criminal, and military-type activities over large pieces of geographical territory and over time. As a result, the Zeta private military organization looks very much like any global Fortune 500 business organization that can quickly, flexibly, and effectively respond to virtually any opportunity, challenge, or changing situation. As a consequence, there is probably more analytical utility in placing the traditional pyramid on its side and conceptualizing the Zeta organization as constituted by horizontal concentric circles.[47]

Organizational Structure. At the top, or at the center of the organizational structure, depending on whether one is looking at a pyramid or at concentric circles, is a small command structure. This group of senior individuals provides strategic- and operational-level guidance and support to its network of compartmentalized cells and to allied groups or associations. This structure allows relatively rapid shifting of operational control horizontally rather than through a relatively slow vertical military chain of command. Then, a second layer (circle) of leadership exists. These individuals oversee or manage guidance received from above, particularly in the areas of intelligence, operational planning, financial support, and recruitment and training. Additionally, this leadership group may manage special geographically and functionally distributed "project teams."[48]

At a third level, cell members may be involved in lower-level national and subnational, as well as international, activities of all kinds. The fourth, and last, level (circle) of the generalized and horizontalized organizational pyramid comprises a series of groups *(clickas)*. These groups may be constituted by aspirants (that is, new recruits trying to prove themselves), by specialists, or by some combination of the two. The specific subgroups include the following: (1) Los Halcones (The Hawks), who keep watch over distribution zones; (2) Las Ventanas (The Windows), who whistle or signal to warn of unexpected dangers in an operational area; 3) Los Manosos (The Cunning Ones), who acquire arms, ammunition, communications, and other military equipment; (4) Las Lepardas (The Leopards), who are, as prostitutes, attached to the intelligence section of the functional organization and are trained to extract information from their clients; and (5) Direccion (communications experts), who intercept phone calls, follow and identify suspicious automobiles and persons, and have been known to engage in kidnapping and executions.[49]

The Zeta organizational structure strongly indicates that it is much more than an ordinary enforcer gang subordinate to a cartel's general structure. The Zeta organization has its own agenda and timetable and appears to be quite successful in achieving its short- and longer-term objectives. Militarily, and in the short term, the organizational structure and mystique have allowed a relatively small force to accomplish the following objectives: convince the people of a given area that the Zeta organization—not local politicians or local police, not federal authorities, and not other cartels—is the real power in that specific geographical terrain; exert authority within its known area of operations, even if not physically present at a given moment; and fight both a larger force (such as police or the military or a rival gang) and another political actor at the same time.

Examples of terrorist means of convincing populations regarding prowess would include but not be limited to the following:

- November 2008–March 2009—several very senior police officials, including the commander of the federal police, were murdered in Mexico City.
- December 2008—the severed heads of eight Mexican soldiers were found dumped in plastic bags near a shopping center in Chilpancingo, capital of the southern state of Guerrero.
- February 2009—another three severed heads were found in an icebox near Ciudad Juarez in the northern state of Chihuahua.

- February 20, 2009—The chief of police for Ciudad Juarez, Roberto Orduña, resigned under pressure—after his deputy was murdered and it was revealed that another police officer would be killed every forty-eight hours until the chief (a former army major) resigned. As the body count grew, Chief Orduña resigned and left the city.[50]

Over the longer term, the Zetas' first priority is to operate a successful business enterprise, with more than adequate self-protection and self-promotion. This private military organization encourages diversification of activities, diffusion of risk, and the flexibility to make quick adjustments, correct mistakes, and exploit developing opportunities. The organization can deliberately expand or contract to adjust to specific requirements, and to new allies or enemies, while increasing profits. And, of course, this organization maintains a coherent mechanism for safeguarding operations at all levels and enforcing discipline throughout the structure. Consequently, over the past ten or more years, the Zeta organization has slowly but surely moved from protecting the Gulf Cartel to developing drug trafficking routes of its own, expanding from drug trafficking to arms and human trafficking and money laundering, and conducting an ambitious expansion policy into new territories and markets. In short, the Zeta organization appears to have taken over the main structure of the Gulf Cartel and launched an aggressive expansion strategy.[51]

Motives and Program of Action. The Mexican Zeta organization is credited with being self-reliant and self-contained. In addition to its own personnel, it has its own arms, communications, vehicles, and aircraft. The general reputation is one of high efficiency and absolute ruthlessness in pursuit of its territorial and commercial (self-enrichment) interests. As such, the Zeta organization is credited with the capability to sooner or later take over the Gulf Cartel and expand operations into the territories and markets of the other cartels. And as it progresses toward the control or incapacitation of rival organizations, it dominates territory, community life, and local and regional politics. Thus, the explicit commercial motive is also implicitly and explicitly a political motive. Yet unlike some other enforcer gangs, TCOs, other private military organizations, insurgent groups, and neopopulists, the Zeta organization does not appear to be intent on completely destroying the traditional Mexican state political-economic-social system and replacing that system with its own. Rather, the organization demonstrates a less radical option; it apparently seeks to incrementally "capture" the state.[52]

To accomplish this aim, the leaders of the Zetas have determined that—at a minimum—they need to be able to freely travel, communicate, and transfer funds all around the globe. For this, they need to be within easy reach of functioning population centers. Thus, the Zeta organization does not find the completely failed state particularly useful; it would prefer to have Mexico as a weak but moderately functional international entity. The shell of traditional state sovereignty protects the Zetas from outside (U.S.) intervention, but Mexican state weakness provides freedom to operate with impunity. And, importantly, although continued pressure from the United States will prevent Mexican authorities from abandoning the fight against illegal drug trafficking, there are many ways a functional state could exhibit a kind of cosmetic conformity while doing little in practice to undermine the power of the drug trafficking organizations.[53]

John Sullivan and Robert Bunker tell us exactly how the incremental capture of a state might conceivably take place. This pragmatic model of military and nonmilitary methods demonstrates the ways and means by which a transnational nonstate actor, such as the Zetas, can challenge and capture the de jure sovereignty of a given nation-state. This model has already proved to be the case in parts of Mexico, Central America, South America, and elsewhere in the world. This is how it works:

> If an irregular attacker—criminal gangs, terrorists, insurgents, drug cartels, private military organizations, militant environmentalists, or a combination of the above—blends crime, terrorism, and war, he can extend his already significant influence. After embracing advanced technology, weaponry, including weapons of mass destruction (including chemical and biological agents), radio frequency weapons, and advanced intelligence gathering technology, along with more common weapons systems, the attacker can transcend drug running, robbery, kidnapping, and murder and pose a significant challenge to the nation-state and its institutions.

Then, using complicity, intimidation, corruption, and indifference, the irregular attacker can quietly and subtly co-opt individual politicians and bureaucrats and gain political control of a given geographical or political enclave. Such corruption and distortion can potentially lead to the emergence of a network of government protection of illicit activities, and the emergence of a virtual criminal state or political entity. A series of networked enclaves could, then, become a dominant political actor within a state or group of states. Thus, rather than violently competing directly with a nation-state, an irregular attacker can criminally co-opt and begin to seize control of the state indirectly.[54]

This model represents a triple threat to the authority and sovereignty of a government and those of its neighbors. First, murder, kidnapping, intimidation, corruption, and impunity from punishment undermine the ability and the will of the state to perform its legitimizing security and public service functions. Second, by violently imposing their power over bureaucrats and elected officials of the state, the TCOs and elements of the gang phenomenon compromise the exercise of state authority and replace it with their own. Third, by neutralizing (making irrelevant) government and taking control of portions of the national territory and performing some of the tasks of government, the gang phenomenon can de facto transform itself into quasi states within a state. And the criminal leaders govern these areas as they wish.[55]

Objectives

As one watches television and reads newspapers, the asymmetric Zeta challenge might appear to be ad hoc, without reason, and inordinately violent (terroristic). Nevertheless, a closer examination of organization and activities illustrates a slow but perceptible movement toward the capability to increase the Zetas' freedom of movement and actions in Mexico, Central America, and elsewhere in the Western Hemisphere. After reviewing the basic facts of the brutal methods the Zetas use to insinuate their power over people, one can see that these seemingly random and senseless criminal acts have specific political-psychological objectives. After getting even closer to the situation, one can see that these objectives are not being lost on the intended audience.

Commercial enrichment seems to be the primary objective of gang-TCO phenomenon protagonists playing in the Mexican internal security arena. This is a serious challenge to existing law and order in Mexico and to the effective sovereignty of Mexico and the other nation-states within and between which the Zetas and other TCOs move. It is that, but it is also more. Sullivan warns us that resultant "para-states or criminal-free states fuel a bazaar of violence where [warlords, drug lords,] and martial entrepreneurs fuel the convergence of crime and war."[56] At the same time, because political, military, and opinion leaders do not appear to understand how to deal with this ambiguous mix of intra-state violence, Peter Lupsha, a wise and long-time observer, argues that those leaders "are doing little more than watching, debating, and wrangling about how to deal with these seemingly unknown phenomena. As a consequence, territory, infrastructure, and stability are slowly destroyed, and thousands of innocents continue to die."[57]

OUTCOMES AND CONSEQUENCES: SOME CONTEMPORARY REALITY IN ONE DAY IN THE LIFE OF AN AMERICAN REPORTER SEEKING TO INTERVIEW A DRUG KINGPIN IN SINALOA

This vignette, based on a very interesting and instructive article written by Guy Lawson,[58] is an attempt to capture the essence of the article. The intent here, however, is to briefly examine contemporary sociopolitical life in Sinaloa with a critical eye on the reality of effective state sovereignty.

The Individual Being Interviewed: Joaquin Guzman Loera, Better Known as "El Chapo" (Shorty)

El Chapo controls the Sinaloa Cartel, which operates in the Arizona border towns of Nogales and Mexicali. He has opposition, however. First, there are erstwhile friends who have developed a personal feud with El Chapo that seems to go on and on and become more and more violent. These antagonists are two brothers, Mochomo (Red Ant) and

Barbas (The Beard), who are leaders of the Beltran-Leyva cartel. Then there are the seemingly ever-present Zeta agents trying to expand their own and the Gulf Cartel's illegal drug routes into the United States. The Gulf Cartel and the Zetas appear to have teamed together with Mochomo and Barbas in an attempt to eliminate El Chapo from the market.

In the capital of the Mexican state of Sinaloa, Culiacan, El Chapo is known as "a kind of folk hero—part Robin Hood, part Billy the Kid."[59] He has more money, more women, and more weapons than any other TCO in the area—except the Zetas. Because El Chapo is relatively generous with some (actually, very little) of his money, people "respect him." He grew up poor, planting corn and marijuana. Over time, he built massive underground tunnels to smuggle cocaine into Arizona, and he subsequently assembled a fleet of boats, trucks, and aircraft that made him one of the most wanted drug dealers in the world. He now— among other things—finances new entrepreneurs as they grow both marijuana and poppies for heroine. El Chapo, however, is most famous for his "miraculous escape" from a federal prison in 2001, just before he was to be extradited to the United States for trial on U.S. drug charges. He reportedly had a plush suite in prison, complete with a personal chef, plenty of whisky, an endless supply of Viagra, and a girlfriend called Zulema.[60] The common wisdom is that El Chapo gave all that up to go back to Sinaloa and help out his friends and neighbors.

Moreover, the people of Sinaloa are convinced that the federal government in Mexico City let El Chapo escape because he is the only drug lord who has the resources and intelligence to face up to the other cartels and to the Zetas.[61] The argument, simply put, is that the federal government cannot do much. The police are incompetent and corrupt; laws constrain government, while a TCO can do whatever it wants; and regular army troops are a poor match for the much better armed, equipped, and trained Zetas. In short, it is better to let the TCOs destroy themselves rather than fight them directly.

Principal Locations Where the Search for "Shorty" Took Place, and Some of the Topics of Conversation That Helped Pass the Time

The State of Sinaloa, Mexico. Sinaloa is a small state on the Mexican Pacific coast across the Gulf of California from the Baja California peninsula.

It is situated between the sea and the almost impassable Sierra Madre Occidental on the east. There are probably not many more than a million inhabitants of the entire state, but an average of three drug-related murders are estimated to take place every day of the year in Sinaloa. That statistic explains the front-page headline of the local newspaper on the day that our American reporter arrived in Culiacan: "Worse Than Iraq."

The Capital City of Culiacan, Sinaloa. That first day in Culiacan, everyone in the city was wondering what El Chapo might do to take revenge for the death of his twenty-year-old son a few weeks earlier. The young man was shot and killed in broad daylight during a drive-by attack by fifteen gunmen, one of whom fired a bazooka. The murder was attributed to the Beltran-Leyva cartel. Weeks later, four more decapitated bodies were dumped in the center of Culiacan with a note addressed to El Chapo, saying, "You're next." Three days later, three more bodies—this time with legs as well as heads severed—were found. Among them was a former police *comandante*. Within hours, another police officer was shot and killed, along with a companion and a bystander. Within another few days, two more grotesquely decapitated bodies were dumped outside a farm owned by a *capo* (criminal chieftain) allied with El Chapo.

That was just one series of events discussed on that first day in Culiacan. Something less important than the murder of El Chapo's son was also a topic of conversation. Only a few days before the arrival of our reporter, a gang of gunmen pulled up in front of an auto shop in the center of the city. They opened fire with AK-47s and AR-15s. Within minutes, nine people were dead. Then, as the assailants fled along Zapata Boulevard, they gunned down two police officers. On Insurgentes Avenue, the killers opened fire on federal troops stationed outside a judicial building. There was no pursuit and no arrests. All that anyone seemed to know was that the gunmen were after a small time *narcotraficante* known as "Alligator." A local official succinctly explained, "No one will talk."[62]

As one might have guessed, "Culiacan is a drug-industry town the way Los Angeles is an entertainment town. Every business is connected, directly or indirectly, with illegal drugs. There are narco discos and narco restaurants. In the upscale malls scattered around town, high-end jewelers sell gaudy and expensive necklaces favored by narco wives, and girlfriends, and hookers. Narco chic is Valentino and Moschino pants, ostrich-skin boots, a black belt with a narco nickname (such as 'Alligator') engraved on it, and a Versace hand bag big enough to hold a stash of drugs and cash needed to pay off the police."[63] Thus, every day, Culiacan stages a sort of ongoing soap opera. But Culiacan is much smaller than Los Angeles. In Culiacan, one can see everyone and everything in one or two episodes.

On the Road and into Tamazula de Victoria. The American reporter was hoping to meet El Chapo and interview him. Through professional connections, he was introduced to "Julio," an opium (poppy) farmer, who considers himself a good and great friend of El Chapo. He has partied many times with El Chapo and his friends, and El Chapo supplies him with the seeds for the poppies he grows. Julio told the reporter that he could take him to a town called Tamazula, where El Chapo lives—"if he isn't in Guatemala or El Salvador."[64]

The highway inland and toward the mountains from Culiacan is dotted by large haciendas (ranches), sheltered behind thirty-foot-high walls. Tamazula boasts a new school and condo developments—signs of the prosperity bought with narco dollars. In the middle of the village, on a hill overlooking the valley, a mansion stands behind large black steel gates. "At the bottom of the hill, just under the gaze of the narco mansion, there is a kind of contradiction common in the Sierra Madres. It is an army outpost ironically illustrating that the fortunes of the law and outlaws are inextricably entwined."[65] Julio explained that the house belongs to one of El Chapo's allies. But El Chapo is not there, "he is up there, at a ranch of a *capo* named Nachito."[66] Julio pointed to a rough dirt track that could be seen leading up into the mountains from Tamazula.

On the way out of town and toward the mountains, Julio stopped and ducked into a tiny office to collect the monthly subsidy he receives from the Mexican government for not growing illegal drugs—despite the fact that he does grow opium and marijuana. This is another closely related contradiction and irony in Sinaloa, illustrating the "you leave me alone and I'll leave you alone" armistice that exists between the narcos and the government. A few minutes later, in the distance they spotted what appeared to be a platoon of soldiers. Julio suddenly decided that they should turn around and go back. He insisted that it would be unsafe to go any farther. He argued that the armed men could be federal troops, El Chapo's men, *gatilleros* (triggermen) for the Beltran-Leyva cartel, or Zetas. In any case, they would recognize a *gringo* (American) in the car and assume that he was DEA (U.S. Drug Enforcement Agency) or CIA (U.S. Central Intelligence Agency). Julio was prickly and insistent: "If you want to find El Chapo, you should look near the village of La Tuna. I know people who can take you there."[67]

On the way back to Culiacan, the conversation stayed centered on the inordinately high level of violence and impunity to prosecution for it in Sinaloa. In the capital city, the front page of the newspaper now featured a street-by-street diagram of the most recent beheadings and assassinations: "El Mapa De La Muerte" (the death map).

Our reporter never did find out how the vendetta between El Chapo and Mochomo and Barbas came out. It really did not matter. The violence, back and forth, continues apace and seems to blur into a deep gray fog. In that fog, the violence between and within the rival cartels, the enforcer gangs, and government forces does not appear likely to end anytime soon. There is too much money to be made. In a lull in the almost ever-present self-enrichment process, a bunch of headless bodies—or just the heads—will be dropped somewhere conspicuous. And there may or may not be another note. Messages in Sinaloa no longer have to be written or explicit.

ADAPTING TO CRIMINAL ANARCHY

The TCOs, their enforcer gangs, and the Zetas operating in Sinaloa have marginalized Mexican state authority and replaced it with a criminal anarchy. That anarchy is defined by bribes, patronage, cronyism, violence, and personal whim. The present vision of the human capacity to treat automatic weapons fire and the terrified screams of victims from "down the street" as mere background noise to the Sinaloa soap opera should create, at the least, a vague unease. A future vision of larger and larger parts of Mexico and the global community adapting to criminal values and forms of behavior should be, at a minimum, unsettling.

This cautionary tale of a significant criminal challenge to effective state sovereignty and traditional Western values takes us to the problem of response. Even though commercial enrichment remains the primary motive for TCO and Zeta challenges to state security and sovereignty in Mexico, the strategic architecture of the Zetas (organization, motive, practices, and policies) resembles that of a political or ideological insurgency. The primary objective of the political insurgents, drug cartels, and private armies such as the Zetas is to attain the level of freedom of movement and action that allows the achievement of the desired enrichment. This defines insurgency: coercing radical change of a given political, economic, and social system to neutralize it, control it, or depose it. Rephrased slightly, this also defines war: compelling an adversary to accede to an aggressor's policy objectives.[68]

By responding to this kind of challenge to security, stability, and sovereignty with a piecemeal and incoherent law enforcement approach or with an ad hoc and violent military approach, political leaders are playing into the hands of the cartels and TCO-gang phenomenon. Even worse, by condoning corrupt practices and hoping that the problem will go away, legitimate leaders are letting their adversaries play all the proverbial cards. Contemporary political, military, and opinion leaders must change their fundamental thought patterns (mindsets) and strengthen national and multilateral organizational structures in order to deal more effectively with this overwhelming reality.

KEY POINTS AND LESSONS

A new and dangerous dynamic has been introduced into the Mexican internal security environment. That new dynamic involves the migration of power from traditional state and nonstate adversaries to small private military organizations such as the Zetas; enforcer gangs such as the Aztecas, Negros, and Polones; and paramilitary triggermen.

- These quasi-state (nonstate) actors promulgate their own rule of law, negotiate alliances with traditional nation-state and nonstate actors, and conduct war against various state and nonstate adversaries.

- The gang-TCO phenomenon in Mexico is a response to historical-sociopolitical factors, as well as new political-military dynamics being introduced into the internal security arena. In the 1980s, Mexico began to devolve from a unitary caudillistic state with ruling elites to a market state, and private, nonstate war-making entities (the gang-TCO phenomenon) used their profits (legal and illegal) to position themselves to challenge the traditional nation-state. The resultant erosion of democracy and the erosion of the state take the internal security situation in Mexico well beyond a simple law enforcement problem: it is also a sociopolitical problem and a national security issue with implications beyond Mexico's borders.

- The component parts of the gang-TCO phenomenon are at war with each other and with the Mexican government.

- Among the various privatized military organizations operating in Mexico today, the Zeta organization is the most likely to be able to achieve its aims. Because of members' considerable military expertise and previous experience in counterinsurgency combat and guerrilla and urban warfare, the Zeta organization has made itself into a major private military-criminal organization in its own right.

- As a result, the Zetas organization is credited with the capability to sooner or later take control of the Gulf Cartel and expand operations into the territories and markets of the other cartels— and further challenge the sovereignty of the Mexican state.

- The power to deal effectively with these kinds of criminal-military threats to traditional Western values does not lie in hard military firepower or even in police power but instead requires a whole-of-government approach that can apply the full human and physical resources of a nation-state and its international partners to achieve the individual and collective security and well-being that leads to societal peace and justice.

War has changed. Adversaries have changed. Motives have changed. Ways and means of conducting operations at all levels have changed. And centers of gravity have changed. In these terms, contemporary war (conflict) reflects some hard facts:

- Combatants are not necessarily armies; they tend to be small groups of armed soldiers who are not necessarily uniformed, not necessarily all male but also female, and not necessarily all adults but also children.
- The small groups of combatants tend to be interspersed among ordinary people and have no permanent locations and no identity to differentiate them clearly from the rest of a given civil population.
- There is no secluded battlefield far away from population centers upon which armies can engage; armed engagements may take place anywhere.
- Combat or confrontation uses not only coercive military force but also co-optive and coercive political and psychological persuasion.
- All of that is intended to capture the imaginations of the people and harness the will of their leaders. Thus, the struggle is total in that it gives the winner absolute power to control or replace an entire existing government or other symbol of power.

Contemporary political, military, and opinion leaders must change their fundamental thought patterns (mindsets), as well as national and international organizational structures, to deal effectively with this overwhelming reality. It is time to take the wisdom of Sun Tzu seriously. He left for posterity his exhortation from the opening of his famous *Art of War*: "War is a matter of vital importance to the State. The province of life or death; the road to survival or ruin. It is mandatory that it be thoroughly studied."[69]

CHAPTER 7

SOME FINAL THOUGHTS

*Toward a New Paradigm for Irregular Wars
among the People*

We find ourselves in a time of revolutionary activity all around the globe. The certainties of the past are devolving more and more into uncertainties and irrelevancies every day. As an example, the long-accepted conventional military-economic-political fundamentals of power are changing. And even though the primary purpose of war—to compel an adversary to acquiesce to one's will and bring about radical political change—remains as it has been for millennia, secondary motives and ways and means of conducting war have changed and continue to change slowly but dramatically.[1]

The reasons for these changes are evident. The lessons of the Persian Gulf War, the Iraq War, the Afghanistan War, and the many other conflicts that have been taking place around the world over the past several years are not being lost on the new state and nonstate powers emerging into the contemporary multipolar global security arena. Ironically, strategies being developed to protect or further the interests of many traditional and nontraditional political actors are inspired by the idea of evading and frustrating superior conventional military or police power. The better a government or a nonstate actor has become at the operational level of conventional war or law enforcement, the more that external and internal state or nonstate adversaries have turned to the more political-psychological types of asymmetric conflict that are being called "knowledge-based" war and "wars amongst the people."[2]

The concepts of conventional attrition and maneuver war are being superseded by those of Sun Tzu's "indirect war," B. H. Liddell-Hart's "camouflaged war," Qiao Liang and Wang Xiangsui's "unrestricted war," John Holloway's "radical change without taking power," Jorge Verstrynge's "peripheral war," or the more generic asymmetric war and irregular war.[3] Regardless of what any contemporary irregular indirect war may be called, each one is closely related to knowledge-based (brain-force) war.

Normally, the primary aim of a war is to politically and psychologically gain control of a population or government, not simply to gain some sort of limited territorial, political, or military concession. Consequently, the stakes in contemporary conflict are total from the standpoint of both the eventual winner and the loser. Contemporary conflict is total on at least two additional levels. First, this kind of war is not just a singular military effort; it is a multidimensional civil-military effort that employs all (a totality or a combination) of the instruments of state and international power, that is, military and nonmilitary, lethal and nonlethal, and direct and indirect. Second, contemporary asymmetric indirect war must involve everyone and everything—there are no front lines, no noncombatants, and no restrictions. Again, war is total.[4]

This reality translates itself into constant and subtle, and not-so-subtle, multidimensional struggles that dominate life throughout much of the world today. The results of these dynamics can been seen in an explosion of weak, incompetent, misguided, insensitive, and corrupt governments, as well as the creation of new social orders. Weak governments and their resultant successors tend to require the shadowy support of illicit mercenary organizations. Traditionally, this has meant that governments are waging war on their citizens, are fighting to survive assaults from their citizens, or have become mere factions among other competing political factions claiming the right to govern all or part of a destabilized national territory. This leads to the slow but sure destruction of a targeted state, government, society, and hundreds of thousands of innocents—and, finally, the creation of some kind of new social order.[5]

Although perhaps less violent than the attrition and military maneuvers of conventional war, the conduct of asymmetric indirect war does not change the essence of war. War is compulsion and control, and indirect war does not alter that cruel outcome. Thus, the methodology of war, not its ultimate purpose, is what has changed. The new multidimensional methodology of contemporary conflict requires the astute use of "brain power" rather than the traditional application of technology and "brute force." That dictates nothing less than a paradigm change.[6]

The primary challenge of such a change is to come to terms with the fact that contemporary security, at whatever level, is a holistic, long-term, strategic political and civil-military effort to address the legitimate and meaningful preservation (security) of a state and its society.[7] The main task in that regard is to construct policy and strategy on the same strategic foundations that have supported success and effectiveness in the past. There are no secrets to preserving the legitimate integrity of a targeted state against asymmetric indirect threats propagated by old and new adversaries. Despite ambiguity, complexity, and uniqueness in the various forms of asymmetric indirect war, there are analytical commonalities—strategic-level principles ("rules")—that remain relevant in time and experience.[8]

THREE GOVERNING RULES THAT MAKE WAR POLITICALLY EFFECTIVE

The strategic-level analytical commonalities derived from our purposive sample of state-supported gangs, state-associated gangs, and non-state-actor-associated gangs transcend different parts of the world, as well as different types and stages of the state or nonstate-actor gang phenomena. They apply to virtually any situation in which the gang phenomenon is generating the instability and violence that is intended to bring about radical political change. And they focus on the long-forgotten populace-oriented political-psychological-social aspects of conflict (war) that constitute the hub of all power and movement on which success or failure in the contemporary security arena depends.[9] Additionally, these commonalities stress that objectives, organization, and the appropriate instruments of power are the primary resources that, when developed and integrated into a legitimizing and holistic strategic vision and strategy, make the difference between winning and losing the illicit internal and external indirect challenges inherent in twenty-first-century conflict (war).[10]

The resultant governing rules (whether called commonalities, generalizations, or lessons learned) inferred from our sample of cases would not have been news to Sun Tzu, Machiavelli, Lenin, or to a contemporary populist, neopopulist, New Socialist, or criminal nonstate actor (such as Argentine Piqueteros, Venezuelan popular militias, and Colombian narco-criminal gangs) or to a hegemonic state (such as Iran and Syria) or nonstate actor (such as Al Qaeda and Hezbollah) that uses agitator gangs, criminal gangs, "super gangs," and popular militias for national, regional, or global hegemonic purposes.[11] The consistency of the lessons learned inspires confidence that these lessons represent the essential ingredients that make war politically effective and that they are more than adequate to initiate the process of rethinking the state-supported gang phenomenon and reshaping a strategic response.[12] In these terms, the case study methodology that serves as the foundation for this volume indicates that there are at least three long-standing political-strategic rules that determine success or failure (the different sides of the same proverbial coin) of the kind of asymmetric and indirect war generated by the state-supported gang phenomenon: perceived legitimacy, multidimensional combinations of hard and soft power, and unity of effort.[13]

What the Gangs Teach Us: It Is All about Perceived Legitimate Governance

When we speak of legitimacy, we speak of legitimate governance. The distinguished contemporary French philosopher Jacques Maritain, like many of his classical predecessors, argues that the state is an instrument in the service of man. "The highest functions of the State [are to] ensure the law and facilitate the free development of the body politic. . . . Then only will the State achieve its true dignity, which comes not from power and prestige, but from the exercise of justice."[14] Thus, legitimate governance is more than de facto or de jure legitimacy: legitimate governance concerns the manner of governing rather than the fact of international recognition that a given legal entity represents a nation-state or the fact that a given regime claims to represent a nation-state. Legitimacy, in this context, is defined as governance that derives its just powers from the governed and generates a viable political competence that can and will effectively manage, coordinate, and sustain collective and personal security, as well as political, economic, and social development and societal peace and prosperity. This is also a current definition of security.[15] Legitimate governance is inherently stable because it has the political competence and societal support to adequately manage internal problems, change, and conflict that affect individual and collective security and well-being. Conversely, governance that is not legitimate is inherently unstable because the hard evidence over time and throughout the world shows that human destabilizers and physical instabilities are the general consequences of misguided, corrupt, insensitive, and incompetent governance. As a consequence, illegitimate governance is the root cause and the central strategic problem of the contemporary unstable global security environment.[16]

Data show that five salient empirical indicators of legitimacy must be implemented by virtually any political actor facing nontraditional and traditional instability threats, and the resultant violence, that are inherent in the current global chaos: (1) free, fair, frequent, and culturally acceptable selection of leaders; (2) a high level of popular participation in or support for the political process; (3) a low level of corruption; (4) a culturally acceptable level or rate of political, economic, and social development; and (5) a high level of regime acceptance by major social institutions.[17] These variables are not new in discussions dealing with the concept of legitimacy. They reflect traditional theoretical-philosophical concepts that are closely associated with the classical notion of legitimacy. In general terms, they are consent of the governed and moral rectitude on the part of the governors.[18] The degree to which a political actor effectively manages a balanced mix of these five variables enables the strengthening, stabilizing, and legitimizing of a governing regime.[19] This is the prime lesson for vulnerable states, and their more powerful allies, in the coming decades.

In sum, all five indicators of legitimacy focus on the moral right of a regime to govern. That moral right can be perceived as having been originally derived from the governed in the form of a "social contract." The social contract as described in classical political philosophy is maintained through the continuing consent of the governed and through the continuing acceptance and support provided by a country's social institutions. That consent and support are dependent on the government providing or creating propitious conditions for security and the general well-being in a culturally acceptable manner. If a regime—for any reason—is perceived as breaking that contract, then internal and external instability, violence, and possible radical political change are the likely result. Legitimacy is the basis of stability or instability, as well as the positive or negative consequences of stability or instability. It cannot be passed off as too difficult to deal with. The essence of any given contemporary threat situation relies heavily on grievances such as political, economic, and social discrimination as the means through which a vulnerable or failing political actor or regime is attacked. This is the fundamental nature of the threat from virtually any illicit challenger, and any response must begin there. The logic is compelling. The only realistic durable counter to those who would coerce radical political change to create a new social order is legitimate democratic governance.[20] That counter, however, must begin to deal with a state as it exists. Change to legitimate governance takes time, political will, and resources. Above all, the effort must be implemented from within the context of the existing culture.

All the diverse cases examined in this study provide strong support for this strategic-level analytical commonality (rule or lesson). However, as noted earlier, nothing of the centrality of the concept of legitimate governance to the success or failure of war (conflict) is new. Twenty-five-hundred years ago, Sun Tzu wrote, "Those who excel in war first cultivate their own humanity and justice and maintain their laws and institutions. By these means they make their governments invincible."[21]

What Gang Operations Teach Us: This Kind of Conflict Is a Multidimensional Combination of Soft and Hard Elements of State and International Power

At the beginning of this century, much of the world is ripe for those who wish to change history, find security in a new structure, protect old ways, or avenge old or new grievances. Those who are apt to destabilize global order to change history and society are not easily deterred, because they do not seek tangibles: they seek the realization of dreams. This implies that they will reify their dreams through new and different wars, through conflict (war) that is a matter of perception and takes place in an environment shaped by words, ideas, beliefs, expectations, convictions, and the political will to challenge an opponent. This type of war is won by altering, over time, indirectly and directly, the political-psychological-cultural factors that are most relevant in a targeted culture.[22]

Political and military leaders and opinion makers all over the world have been struggling with these political-psychological aspects of war since the end of World War II, especially since the ending of the cold war and the beginning of the postmodern era. Yet the nature of the war phenomenon is still not well understood.[23] Western leaders tend to think of the legalistic and military dictums generated from the Treaty of Westphalia (in 1648) and their particular experiences as the only guidelines or examples concerning war that are worth considering. As result, there has been too much military operational-tactical crisis response to very discrete situations, while strategic theory and action have played little part in the debate and actions involving contemporary irregular war as a whole.[24]

Strategic theory and action must center on Sun Tzu's indirect approach to war, with soft power in general and the power of dreams in particular—and a mental flexibility that goes well beyond conventional forms. The principal tools (instruments of power) in this situation include public diplomacy at home and abroad; intelligence, information and propaganda operations; cultural manipulation measures to influence or control public opinion and political-military decision making; and foreign alliances and partnerships. All of this requires actions that are indirect and direct, state and nonstate, military and nonmilitary, lethal and nonlethal, and a combination of some or all of the above. In turn, this requires rethinking and redefining concepts of centers of gravity versus nodes of vulnerability, political-psychological objectives versus military operational objectives (human versus physical terrain), in addition to enemy power, deterrence, and victory. A major consideration is that the anarchic environment of global politics allows each political actor to be the only and the final judge of his interests and actions. Thus, we must go back to the basics: concepts of what victory, enemy power, and deterrence might mean in a given situation must be centered on public opinion and political decision making at home and abroad.[25]

As an example, deterrence is not necessarily military—although that is important. Nor is it necessarily negative or directly coercive— although that, too, is important. Deterrence is much broader than that. Deterrence can be direct or indirect applications of political-diplomatic, social-economic, psychological-moral, and nonmilitary-military dimensions and can be persuasive as well as coercive. In its various forms and combinations of forms, it is an attempt to influence how and what an enemy or potential enemy thinks and does. Deterrence, in other words, is the creation of a state of mind that either discourages one thing or encourages something else. Motives and culture, therefore, become crucial. In this context, political-military communication and preventive diplomacy become vital parts of the deterrence equation at home and abroad.[26]

Conflict is no longer a simple military-to-military confrontation. Conflict now purposely blurs the distinction between and among crime, terrorism, and warfare. Conflict now involves entire populations, as well as a large number of indigenous national civilian agencies, other national civilian organizations, international organizations, nongovernmental organizations, private voluntary organizations, and subnational indigenous actors involved in dealing politically, economically, socially, morally, criminally, and/or militarily with ambiguous and complex threats to national and global security and well-being.[27] Thus, nonprofessional warriors who can understand and cope with the ambiguous chaos of conflict among the people—imposed by diverse state, nonstate, and transnational political-criminal actors—must now be included in an organizational architecture for conducting asymmetric irregular indirect war. Qiao and Wang remind us, "Warfare is no longer an exclusive Imperial garden where professional soldiers alone can mingle."[28] At the same time, an almost unheard-of unity of effort is required to coordinate the multilateral, multidimensional, and multiorganizational paradigm necessary for success on either or all sides of a contemporary conflict. And General Anthony Zinni warns us, "If we can't learn [the need for a complete unity of effort] from our experience, we are doomed to the status quo—and ad-hoc-ing it every time."[29]

What Success and Failure Teach Us: It Is Primarily a Political-Psychological-Military Combination of Unified Effort

Regardless of whether a war took place twenty-five-hundred years ago or last year, our data indicate that all victories or failures display one common denominator—the winner is the national power, international power bloc, or nonstate political actor that best organized and implemented a combination of multidimensional efforts. The loser, thus, is the political actor that "ad-hoc-ed" a generally singular military effort. As a consequence, the global community must come to grips with the fundamentally transformed nature of defense and security challenges in the twenty-first century. To do so requires a significant change in how actors are organized to plan and implement contemporary war (conflict). Above all, effective combinations of multidimensional efforts require a unity of effort.

Combinations. All the political actors who support or are associated with the political-psychological agitator/criminal gang phenomena—whether they dream of "A New Argentina" (that is, a new political-economic system that can replace North American hegemony in Latin America), or a new political-economic (socialist, populist, or criminal) system, or a return to the glories of the eighth century—understand that a new political-economic system cannot be achieved by military "shock-and-awe" tactics. They realize that a new social order will be achieved only as a result of a slow, deliberate, and lengthy struggle (a long war) that exacerbates the destabilization and incapacitation of a targeted actor.

Moreover, all ways and means that can be brought to bear on a given target must be used to apply persuasion and coercion to slowly but surely create a new social order. This type of political-ideological/commercial-criminal/global-hegemonic confrontation accepts no compromise or other options. There is nothing to negotiate or compromise on, short of the achievement of the ultimate political objective—whether it is radical political change or absolute control. Conversely, if a targeted government wants to create the security necessary to preserve and enhance a traditional political-economic-social system, it must understand what is happening and counter the persuasion and coercion with a decisive and appropriate organization and strategy of its own. The ultimate threat, in these terms, is not instability, violence, or chaos, for these are but symptoms. The ultimate threat is that unless and until leaders at the highest levels recognize the symptoms for what they are, and reorient thinking and actions appropriately, it is only a matter of time before the debilitating problems brought on by those who would destroy a state will create a failing or failed state—and then establish a "new" political-economic-social system. That is why Lenin consistently referred to propaganda-agitator gangs as "midwives" of new social orders.[30]

The dominating characteristic of a war of this kind is defined as political-military, economic-commercial, or cultural-moral. Within the context of combinations (collective activity or multidimensional conflict), there is a difference between the dominant sphere and the whole, although a dynamic relationship exists between a dominant type of general war (political, economic, or cultural) and the supporting elements that make up the whole. As an example, military war must be strongly supported by media (information/moral) war and a combination of other types of war that might include but are not limited to psychological war, information war, financial war, trade war, cyber-network war, diplomatic war, or narco-criminal war.[31] The combination of all available ways and means of conducting conflict includes military and nonmilitary, lethal and nonlethal, and direct and indirect methods. As only a few examples, combinations of military, transmilitary, and nonmilitary warfare would include but are not limited to the following:

- Conventional war/network war/persuasion-coercion-propaganda war;
- Surrogate or proxy war/intelligence war/media war;
- Biochemical war/insurgency war/resources war;
- Narco-criminal war/financial war/trade war; and
- Atomic war/diplomatic war/ideological war.

Any one of the above types of or combinations of war can be combined with others to form completely new methods and combinations of conflict. There are no means that cannot be combined with others. The only limitation would be one's imagination.[32] As a consequence, politically effective contemporary warfare requires the services of nonprofessional warriors who can conduct persuasion-coercion-propaganda war, media war, financial war, trade war, psychological war, network (virus) war, insurgency war, chemical-biological-radiological war, and so forth—as well as professional soldiers and policemen.[33]

The interaction among the many possible dimensions of conflict prevents the military, technological, or any other dimension from serving as the automatic dominant factor in any given war situation. That interaction also forces an adversary to fight on multiple fronts that are determined by his opponent's strengths. The intent would be to organize a system of offensive and defensive power that is a great force multiplier and facilitator within the global security arena—and that would deprive the enemy of the same advantages. This gives new and greater meaning to the idea of a nation-state or other political actor using *all available* instruments of national and international power to protect, maintain, or achieve its perceived vital interests.

The primary and specific effort, however, that exacerbates the process of state failure and forces the desired radical political change is the multidimensional erosion of people's morale and will to resist. The better an actor is at the persuasive-coercive political-psychological-military/police effort, the more effective he will be relative to his adversary. Accordingly, this effort defines victory or defeat. One of Carl von Clausewitz's translators, Michael Howard, makes the point that the "forgotten" nonmilitary social-psychological dimensions of power play key roles in determining success or failure in contemporary conflict.[34] Again, this requires the understanding of warfare as a whole, coupled with the need to develop the necessary organization and doctrine to enable a comprehensive unity of effort.[35]

Unity of Effort. In the past, small- and large-scale peace and stability efforts tended to be viewed as providing military solutions to military problems. Presently, the complex realities of contemporary asymmetric indirect conflict within entire societies must be understood as a holistic process that relies on various national and international civilian and military agencies and organizations working together in an integrated manner to achieve a common political objective. In such situations, responses must be well organized, highly cooperative, carefully coordinated, and conducted with considerable political skill. Otherwise, "strategic ambiguity" is introduced; belligerents are given the opportunity to "play in the seams" of the operation and frustrate objectives; allies are allowed to pursue their own agendas; political, personnel, and monetary costs rise; and the probability of mission failure increases. As an example, the ongoing tragedy in Afghanistan is a reminder that "trying to do good is not as much futile as exceptionally complicated. Succeeding is a product of shrewd planning, not wishful thinking."[36]

Thus, the creation of unity of effort must be addressed at several different levels. First, at the highest level, the primary parties to a given conflict must be in general agreement with regard to the objectives of a political vision and the associated set of operations that will contribute to the achievement of the political objective. Although such an agreement regarding a strategic or operational end state is a necessary condition for unity of effort, however, it is not sufficient. Sufficiency and strategic clarity are achieved by adding appropriate policy implementation and civil-military structure—and "mind-set adjustments"—at the following three levels.

The second level of effort requires an executive-level management structure that can and will ensure continuous cooperative planning and execution of policy among and between relevant civilian and military agencies (vertical coordination). That structure must also ensure that all political-military actions at the operational and tactical levels directly contribute to the accomplishment of the mutually agreed-on strategic political end state. This requirement reflects a need to improve coordination within the operational theater and between the theater and its political masters.

Third, steps must be taken to ensure clarity, unity, and effectiveness by integrating coalition (partner or proxy) civil-military, international organization, and nongovernmental organization processes with one's own political-military planning and implementing processes (horizontal coordination). It has become quite clear that the political end state is elusive and operations suffer when no strategic planning structure is empowered to integrate key multinational and multiorganizational civil-military elements of a given conflict situation. Duplication of effort—or no effort at all—is clearly the immediate consequence of the absence of such a strategic planning and implementing body. The result is costly in personnel, financial, and political-psychological terms. And, again, the achievement of the agreed-on objective is—at best—elusive.

At a base level, however, unity of effort requires education (mind-set adjustments) as well as organizational solutions. Even with an adequate planning and organizational structure, ambiguity, confusion, and tensions are likely to emerge. Only when and if the various civilian and military leaders involved in an operation can develop the judgment and empathy necessary to work cooperatively and collegially will they be able to plan and conduct operations that meet the mandates of the guiding strategic vision. Thus, unity of effort ultimately entails the type of professional civil-military education and leader development that leads to effective diplomacy and the achievement of a twenty-first-century end state (game plan or campaign plan). Lenin's admonition to his followers in 1918 remains all too relevant to anyone who wants to succeed in the twenty-first-century security arena: "The chief task of our day is to learn from [history] and pursue the principle of discipline, organization, and harmonious cooperation."[37]

In sum, without an organization at the highest levels to establish, enforce, and continually refine a coherent soft and hard power ends, ways, and means strategy, authority is fragmented and ineffective in resolving the myriad problems endemic to contemporary irregular conflict. It is time to extend the spirit and intent of "military jointness" to the entire interagency process, to international and interalliance venues, to coordination with nongovernmental organizations, and to any other civil-military partnership that is involved in the conduct of a holistic effort against those who would violently, criminally, or indirectly threaten the existence of any given political-economic-social system.

Implementing a Paradigm Shift

Implementing the conceptual and organizational change, as well as the regeneration implied in this call for a paradigm shift, will not be easy. Nevertheless, it will be far less demanding and costly in political, military, monetary, and ethical terms than to continue a traditional, generally military, tactical-operational-level crisis management approach to contemporary global security. Importantly, the alternative cannot be acceptable. This is not simple idealism. It is a marriage of North American pragmatism, or *realpolitik*, and our empirical data that provides a viable foundation for national, regional, and global stability and well-being. But, again, the elements of this paradigm are not new. Machiavelli reminds us that the use of political-psychological instruments of power *en unison* (in unity) with military power allowed Republican Rome to conquer and rule the (then) known world.[38]

PILLARS OF SUCCESS

In the past, the United States worked hard to develop coherent theories of engagement. A great deal of intellectual energy, including national debate and writing, to say nothing of war gaming, went into the question of how and under what circumstances the United States could contain the Soviet Union. Now the United States must seek to understand a new central strategic problem and be able to deal with more than television images and the symptoms of global instability. The days of delineating a successful strategic end state as simple short-term self-protection or short-term compassion for a human problem are over. The American public expects U.S. efforts, especially if they involve the expenditure of large amounts of tax revenue or the expenditure of even a few American lives, to make the world a better place.[39]

Thus, U.S. decision makers and policy makers have an obligation to go beyond simple self-protection, cosmetics, and compassion and to advocate and defend the principles for which America stands. To do this, we must combine realism, pragmatism, and idealism to secure "an organized and effectively enforced system of general international peace."[40] Accordingly, contemporary conflict—at whatever level—must be understood as essentially a sociopolitical matter. We must also rethink the political-economic ways, means, and measures of effectiveness to counter international instability caused by the lack of legitimate governance.

This discussion brings us back to where we began—to the core strategic problem of legitimate governance in the postmodern world that foreign policy and conflict management must address. To be sure, nuclear prolif-eration, weapons of mass destruction (WMD), the security issues posed by Russia, China, India and Pakistan, Iraq and Afghanistan, and ethnic and irredentist conflicts, human starvation, refugee flows, and trade wars all over the world are all serious problems and potential threats. Underlying all these issues, however, is a core security problem of state gangs, state-associated gangs, and nonstate-actor-associated gangs exacerbating the processes of state failure and generating "wars of national debilitation, a steady run of uncivil wars sundering fragile but functioning nation-states and gnawing at the well-being of stable nations."[41]

The main task in the search for security now and for the future is to construct stability and well-being on the same strategic pillars that supported success and effectiveness in the past. The first pillar of suc-cess is a conceptual requirement: the development of a realistic "game plan," strategic vision, philosophy, or theory of engagement to deal legitimately with gang phenomena and the human and physical disas-ters they create. The second pillar is an organizational requirement: the creation of planning and management structures to establish a viable unity of effort to plan and implement a legitimacy theory of engage-ment. The third is an organizational and operational requirement. Orga-nizationally, it involves developing and implementing the appropriate combination of political, economic, informational, moral, and coercive instruments of national and international power to pursue the multi-dimensional requirements of the contemporary irregular asymmetric security environment. Operationally, it involves learning to understand friends as well as adversaries (and potential adversaries) culturally, so as to better influence their thought and behavior. Most important is that it involves educating leaders at all levels to carry out a twenty-first-century game plan among the people.[42]

KEY POINTS AND LESSONS

In this era of geopolitical change, the United States has the opportu-nity and responsibility to redirect policy from one that is essentially ad hoc, negative, and reactive crisis management to one that is coherent, positive, and proactive—and to which the American people can relate. Additionally, competing pressures can be sorted out and decisions rationally made if we can stay with the basics. The recommended basic direction for such an effort would include principled actions to

- Develop a coherent legitimacy theory of engagement;
- Develop clear supporting political-economic-informational-military/police objectives;
- Develop an executive branch organizational and leadership structure to effectively merge the diverse soft and hard assets required to prevail in the contemporary global security environment;
- Develop the ability to synchronize the appropriate national and international civil-military tools of power for attacking opposition and defending friendly centers of gravity;
- Develop civil-military leadership that better understands other cultures and mores;
- Develop civil-military leadership that can understand and deal with the challenges and opportunities of "ambiguity";
- Develop civil-military leadership that understands the ways in which coercive force and indirect coercive and noncoercive force can be employed to achieve political ends, as well as ways in which political considerations affect the use of coercive and noncoercive force;
- Develop civil-military leadership that can interact collegially and successfully with representatives of U.S. civilian and military agencies, non-U.S. civilian and military agencies, international organizations, nongovernmental organization, civilian populations, and local and global media;
- Develop a "self-help" doctrine to support politically, economically, informationally, and militarily free peoples and legitimate partners who are willing to fight criminal anarchy, attempted subjugation by armed minorities, organized criminals, narco-terrorists, ethnic cleansers, and outside aggressors; and
- Develop, at home and abroad, an understanding of the critical nature of winning—that is, accomplishing the ultimate strategic

political objective. Without that understanding and commitment, there is no reason to even begin a civil-military effort to help or to counter any given political actor.

Nothing in the notion of a legitimacy theory of engagement is new or radical; it is simple common sense, basic foreign policy, and rational national and international civil-military asset management. What is new is that the implementation of the proposed paradigm would be a kind of "revolution" in itself. It is a revolution that the author of *The Rebel*, Albert Camus, would support unequivocally: "He who dedicates himself to [revolution for revolution's sake] dedicates himself to nothing and, in turn, is nothing. But, he who dedicates himself to the . . . dignity of mankind, dedicates himself to the earth and reaps from it the harvest that sows its seed and sustains the world again and again."[43]

WHAT IS TO BE DONE?

Doing good is not the result of wishful thinking. Doing good, and working to help achieve the dignity of mankind, requires appropriate action. In this context, there are two basic tasks. Sun Tzu articulated the first task when he succinctly answered the "Why?" and "So What?" questions regarding involvement in conflict (war or revolution): "War is a matter of vital importance to the State; the province of life or death; the road to survival or ruin."[44]

Qaio and Wang guide us toward the answer to the "How?" question, and the second set of tasks. They remind us that the hard-won lessons learned from past experience—to include those inferred from the case study data presented in this volume—are relevant to the indirect wars of the twenty-first century and that incidents building up a body of evidence demonstrating "the same phenomenon" are not accidents but rules.[45]

As a consequence, we must remember that the study of the fundamental nature of conflict has always been the philosophical cornerstone for understanding conventional war. It is no less relevant to nontraditional irregular asymmetric war that involves nonstate actors and entire societies. Lenin caught the essence and the principle of the "How?" part of the conflict problem when he advised, "We should have but one slogan—seriously learn the art of war."[46]

By accepting these challenges and tasks, one can help destroy the romantic dream of ultimate freedom being achieved by destroying an old political-economic system in order to create something "new." At the same time, one can help replace conflict with cooperation and can harvest the hope and fulfill the promise that a new legitimacy-based paradigm offers. The sooner, the better.

Afterword

JOHN T. FISHEL

In this new book, Max Manwaring has taken the next logical step in the development of his theory of conflict, known variously as the SWORD Model, the Manwaring Paradigm, or the "Max Factors."[1] In focusing on gangs, militias, and other nonstate- and state-supported actors, Manwaring has rediscovered an ancient phenomenon of conflict that recently has reappeared in a new guise. Just how ancient it is—and how it has evolved—is the subject of this afterword.

Although the statement is often made that there is nothing new under the sun, that notion is less than totally accurate. Of course, there are new technologies, new ways of organizing, new structures, and even new functions. Most of the time, however, the new is simply an innovative way of combining the old with the new. Thus, Afghan warlords, such as Abdul Rashid Dostum, hark back to the warlords of Homer's *Iliad* (Achilles, Odysseus, and Ajax), among others. The men they lead are not much different from the men who followed those ancient warlords.

ANCIENT IRREGULARS AND PIRATES

Most of the city-states of Greece had nothing resembling a standing armed force—Sparta being a notable exception. As a result, they relied on local militia forces in which every able-bodied male citizen was expected to provide his own armor and weapons and fall in on his fellows in time of need. This was as true at sea as it was on land. Nevertheless, the men that we know from popular history as great Greek patriots—especially during the wars with the Persians—were less than 99.7 percent pure. As historian Victor Davis Hanson puts it, "[A]n entire series of gifted politicians and renegade intriguers such as Demaratus, Themistocles, and Alcibiades would aid the Persians against their own Greek kin" for gold and other personal gain.[2] Thus, we can see these famous militia leaders and heroes of Western civilization as gang leaders, pirate chieftains, and warlords, not so very different from the Afghan general Dostum. To illustrate the point, let us consider the following vignette, which could easily have been torn from today's headlines: "After a short stay there [in Bithynia] with Nicomedes, the king, in his passage back he [Julius Caesar] was taken near the island of Pharmacusa by some of the pirates, who, at that time, with large fleets of ships and innumerable smaller vessels, infested the seas everywhere."[3] This is hardly different from today's Gulf of Aden or Straits of Malacca; nor is Caesar's solution to his problem unlike that chosen by shippers worldwide or by the United States and Indian navies.

> When these men at first demanded of him twenty talents for his ransom, he laughed at them for not understanding the value of their prisoner, and voluntarily engaged to give them fifty. He presently despatched those about him to several places to raise the money, till at last he was left among a set of the most bloodthirsty people in the world, the Cilicians, only with one friend and two attendants. Yet he made so little of them, that when he had a mind to sleep, he would send to them, and order them to make no noise. For thirty-eight days, with all the freedom in the world, he amused himself with joining in their exercises and games, as if they had not been his keepers, but his guards. He wrote verses and speeches, and made them his auditors, and those who did not admire them, he called to their faces illiterate and barbarous, and would often, in raillery, threaten to hang them. They were greatly taken with this, and attributed his free talking to a kind of simplicity and boyish playfulness. As soon as his ransom was come from Miletus, he paid it, and was discharged, and proceeded at once to man some ships at the port

of Miletus, and went in pursuit of the pirates, whom he surprised with their ships still stationed at the island, and took most of them. Their money he made his prize, and the men he secured in prison at Pergamus, and he made application to Junius, who was then governor of Asia, to whose office it belonged, as praetor, to determine their punishment. Junius, having his eye upon the money, for the sum was considerable, said he would think at his leisure what to do with the prisoners, upon which Caesar took his leave of him, and went off to Pergamus, where he ordered the pirates to be brought forth and crucified; the punishment he had often threatened them with whilst he was in their hands, and they little dreamt he was in earnest.[4]

As did Caesar, many shippers today pay ransoms. As did Caesar, the U.S. Navy killed the pirates holding an American captain. As did Caesar, the Indian Navy destroyed the pirates in their base (mother ship). Lest we think that nothing has changed in two thousand years, we would be wise to note that recently (in late August 2009), pirates fired a heavy-caliber machine gun at a U.S. Navy surveillance helicopter; also, back in the 1990s, pirates in the Straits of Malacca fired AK-47s at a U.S. Navy nuclear attack submarine transiting the strait at night, running deck awash, without lights. The sub simply buttoned up and ignored the pirates while reporting the attack to its base at Pearl Harbor. The only result of the incident was the restoration of M-60 machine guns to U.S. submarine standard equipment (after a brief interval when the navy had decided they were not needed).[5]

In ancient times and in the seventeenth and eighteenth centuries, as today, piracy—criminal gangs at sea—constituted a security threat as well as a criminal one. But Caesar's pirates could not have functioned without the support and connivance of states such as Rome any more than the pirates of the Caribbean could without the support of England (which they had as long as their prey was the Spanish gold fleet). Similarly, the Barbary pirates were hardly distinguishable from the states of the coast of North Africa. In much the same way today, pirates operate in areas where the state is weak, practically nonexistent, or actively colluding with them.

TRIBAL WARRIOR FOES

Another aspect of warfare against irregulars also comes from Caesar's time (as do several more that I touch on later): war against tribal cultures on the periphery of the Roman state, in what was then known as Gaul and is now most of modern France. Caesar describes his campaign in Gaul in *The Gallic War*, where he discusses, among many other things, the beginning of his campaign against the Belgae: "To the Senones and the other Gauls who were neighbours of the Belgae, he gave the task of finding out what the Belgae were doing and of keeping him informed of developments. They all loyally reported that gangs were mustering, and an army was assembling in one place. Then he knew it was important that he set out for the territory of the Belgae."[6] Clearly, tribes such as the Belgae were organized to fight as gangs or militia; they were not regular forces even in Roman times. Gauls, Germans, Britons, Huns, Scythians, and other barbarian tribes fought as gangs for loot, booty, and honor. As for the Indians of the American plains, counting coup— or its functional equivalent—was as important as territorial conquest. Yet a prime purpose of war was the defense of turf against the outsider, who could as easily be from another tribe, a Roman legionary, or an American cavalryman. In no way does such war differ from what the British found in India's Northwest Frontier province during the nineteenth century, as told by Rudyard Kipling:

> Kamal is out with twenty men to raise the Borderside,
> And he has lifted the Colonel's mare that is the
>   Colonel's pride.
> He has lifted her out of the stable-door between the dawn and
>   the day,
> And turned the calkins upon her feet, and ridden her far away.
> Then up spoke the Colonel's son that led a troop of the Guides:
> "Is there never a man of all my men can say where Kamal
>   hides?"[7]

In the very same areas of the world outside Europe, David Kilcullen (an Australian anthropologist, soldier, and U.S. State Department advisor) has observed,

It struck me that while neo-Salafi "jihadists"—a small elusive minority in any society—are often implacable fanatics, the local guerrillas they exploit frequently fight because they perceive Western presence and the globalized culture Westerners carry with us, as a deadly corrosive to local identity. More often, they fight Westerners because we are intruding into their space. Ironically, it is partly our pursuit of terrorists that has brought us into sustained contact with traditional nonstate societal hierarchies [tribes and clans]—Wazirs, Mahsuds, Kuchi, Albu Mahal, Tuareg—whose geographical and demographic terrain interests Western governments mainly because terrorists hide (or are believed to hide) in it.[8]

POLITICAL GANGS: ANCIENT AND NOT SO ANCIENT

In Rome, shortly after Caesar's assassination (44 BCE), an incident that demonstrates the violent nature of Roman politics took place. Marc Antony had called a meeting of the Senate to propose new honors to Caesar's memory. Cicero, leading the moderates, found it wise to take no stand on the issue and so absented himself, pleading illness. "Antony was furious. During the debate he launched an outspoken attack on Cicero, threatening to send housebreakers to demolish his house on the *Palatine.*"[9] Although the gang never showed up, the incident illustrates the violent nature of Roman politics and the ease with which the legitimacy of the republic could be challenged. Soon, indeed, political violence would win out and the republic would be replaced by the empire—and Cicero would be dead (on the order of Antony with the acquiescence of Octavian, who soon would be Rome's first emperor), the victim of some of Antony's soldiers operating as no more than a political gang.[10]

During the next hundred years, as the empire expanded and Octavian (Augustus) was succeeded by lesser heirs—ending with Nero—the newly conquered province of Judea, incorporated as a subdivision of the larger province of Syria, grew restive and revolted. The rebels enjoyed some success until Vespasian moved into the Galilee to quell the revolt. Among the few prisoners taken was the former rebel commander, known to history as Josephus, who chronicled the war through the fall of Jerusalem.[11] In his telling of the siege of Jerusalem, Josephus discusses the rebel gangs, which he lumps together as "Zealots," with commentary on their various leaders, tactics, and methods.[12] E. Mary Smallwood, in her appendix entitled "Bandits, Terrorists, Sicarii, and Zealots," clearly differentiates among these groups:

> The word . . . "bandit" or "brigand" denotes . . . a terrorist, a guerrilla . . . a man working towards a political goal. Brigandage of this kind was a frequent, if not endemic, problem in Palestine. Herod's first post was a military commission to put down bandits in the Galilee in 46 BC. . . .
>
> The Sicarii were a splinter group of terrorists formed in the 50s [CE], distinct from other groups not in their aims but in their methods. Their name "daggermen" (from the Latin, *sica*, a dagger) . . . described their insidious *modus operandi*. . . .
>
> The Zealots appear in 66 [CE] as the main war party under Eleazar son of Simon. . . . But their methods were no less brutal than those of other nationalist factions.[13]

Thus, we see political gangs active both in Rome and throughout the empire. As Josephus describes the war, it is hard to determine the degree to which the various political gangs were seeking political, economic, religious, or personal power ends. This blending of ends may be one hallmark of political gangs throughout history.

Political gangs were not simply a phenomenon of ancient times; they flourished in the medieval period and are recounted in the legends surrounding Robin Hood in the England of the late 1100s and early 1200s. The Robin Hood legend, as I learned it as a schoolboy, was that Robert of Lockesley, a Saxon of noble birth and unquestioned loyalty to King Richard the Lionheart, was framed by the corrupt sheriff of Nottingham and Prince John (the regent and the king's brother) for a crime he did not commit. As a result, he took flight and organized his gang—the band of Merry Men—who robbed from the rich and gave to the poor and agitated for the return of King Richard. Separating truth from falsehood in this story is both difficult and not very important. The importance of the legend is that it has created as a culture hero a gang leader, and his gang has become the role model for many persons who have lived at, or near, the margins of the law. This is true not only in English culture and its derivatives but also in places such as Colombia where Pablo Escobar, the drug lord, had a "legitimate" political career and endowed parks and other public goods for the poor with his ill-gotten gains (from cocaine smuggling).

Political gangs have existed in America as well, not always as evil as that of Pablo Escobar, but often enough worse. Consider the situation that developed in the American South during and after Reconstruction following the Civil War.

> In the summer of 1865, President [Andrew] Johnson sent Carl Schurz, an ambitious German-American politician, to examine conditions in the South. Schurz's report was chilling:
>
> "I saw in various hospitals negroes, women as well as men, whose ears had been cut off or whose bodies were slashed with knives or bruised with whips, or bludgeons, or punctured with shot wounds. Dead negroes were found in considerable number in the country roads or on the fields, shot to death, or strung on the limbs of trees. In many districts the colored people were in a panic of fright, and the whites in an almost insane state of irritation against them."
>
> . . . . By 1866, the violence would become organized. Southern whites formed terrorist groups with chivalric names—the Knights of the Golden Circle, the Knights of the White Camellia, the Teutonic Knights, the Sons of Washington, the Knights of the Rising Sun, and the Ku Klux Klan. As many as a hundred masked and hooded riders could descend on a homestead or town, killing and maiming at will.[14]

Quite obviously, the purpose of these gangs was to, at minimum, mitigate the effects of the loss of the Civil War by the South and of emancipation of the slaves. The larger goal was to restore the antebellum power structure, In this, they had the assistance—both witting and unwitting—of the president of the United States and many of his supporters. In the end, the political gangs achieved their minimal goals and a bit more, especially as Reconstruction ended with the political compromise that made Rutherford B. Hayes president and included the passage of the Posse Comitatus Act in 1878, which removed U.S.

Army troops from the South and prohibited them from enforcing the law. Perhaps a better name would have been the American Terrorist Gang Enabling Act!

In the modern United States of America, a use of official forces as political gangs similar to that done by Antony and Octavian was the series of race riots and violent demonstrations against the Vietnam War in 1968. This all culminated in what the official federal investigation dubbed the police riot at the Democratic National Convention in Chicago. Contributing to that outcome were the events that preceded the convention and the riot recounted here, in the contemporaneous words of the official report:

> The police were generally credited with restraint in handling the first [race] riots—but Mayor Daley rebuked the Superintendent of Police. While it was later modified, his widely disseminated "shoot to kill arsonists and shoot to maim looters" order undoubtedly had an effect.
>
> The effect on police became apparent several weeks later, when they attacked demonstrators, bystanders, and media representatives at a Civic Center march. There were published criticisms—but the city's response was to ignore the police violence.[15]

What followed was a major breakdown of "normal" police behavior during the convention, with the Chicago police being used as a partially out-of-control political gang by Mayor Richard J. Daley to demonstrate his domination of his city in the face of "outside" challengers.

WHAT MAX HATH WROUGHT

The purpose of this afterword has so far been to demonstrate that Max Manwaring's analysis of gangs, militias, and other irregular adversaries—sometimes including the forces of order being used to promote an illegitimate order—is nothing new. Rather, it is a phenomenon more than two thousand years old in the West and certainly even older when other ancient civilizations are considered. But it is also designed to show that the phenomenon persists both across time and over geography, to all corners of the world and in all kinds of political systems. Legitimate government is always, at all times, and in all places challenged by irregular forces seeking both power and lucre in one combination or another. In case further evidence is warranted, the following excerpt from a letter to Horace Walpole from Voltaire, dated July 15, 1768, is offered: "Truly the history of the Yorkists and Lancastrians, and many others, is much like reading the history of highway robbers."[16] Manwaring's achievement is to have addressed this phenomenon in its many present-day manifestations. Not only has he addressed it, but he has also placed it in the broad category of threats to national security. Although the political gang is a criminal enterprise, it is not simply a law enforcement problem.

Drawing from his earlier work, Manwaring shows that political gangs attack the legitimacy of a government. This is true even when the government is the sponsor of the gang. Typical examples of such government-sponsored gangs having a negative impact on regime legitimacy include the *turbas divinas* of the 1980s Sandinista Nicaragua and the use by the current Iranian regime of its *basij* militias against political opposition that includes major regime figures such as the former president, Hashimi Rafsanjani. These actors, past and present, undermine the regime, destroying its legitimacy with its own people as well as with the international community of which it is part. The Roman republic fell to Julius Caesar, who used both Gallic militias to assist in putting down other tribes of Gaul rebelling against Roman rule (in the process making Caesar relatively more independent of the Senate) and quasi-criminal agents such as Antony and his thugs to intimidate opponents. Later, the western empire fell to barbarians who had defended the frontiers in the pay of the Romans, while the eastern empire watched and took advantage of the plight of the West to expand its power and lay claim to all of Rome's legitimacy.

Not only does Manwaring place the political gangs at the appropriate point on the threat spectrum, but he also addresses the implications for action to control them and the threat they pose. Although political gangs generally do not pose existential threats to states, there are historical examples such as the fall of the western Roman empire where, coupled with evidence of internal decay, the political gangs have pushed a state over the edge.

ON DEALING WITH THE (POLITICAL) GANG THREAT

More than two decades ago, Max and his associates began research on the factors that made for success in counterinsurgency. Over the years, this research expanded to include counterdrug operations, peace operations, and now political gangs.[17] Although this expansion happened over time, it was implicit from the beginning. In their initial analysis of the possible cases, Manwaring and his colleagues identified sixty-nine candidates. Of these, only forty-three met the criteria of insurgencies. The other twenty-six cases were different sorts of "small wars." They were, then, cases that fell into the categories of operations against drug cartels such as Operation Blast Furnace in Bolivia in 1986, peace operations such as those in Haiti and the Balkans in the 1990s, operations against terrorists from the 1970s onward, and finally interdiction of cross-border smuggling of people and drugs. What all of these studies had in common was that the factors/dimensions identified as being critical for success against insurgents were equally important for success in these other cases.

The seven dimensions of the SWORD Model are (1) military actions of the intervening power, (2) support actions of the intervening power, (3) host government legitimacy, (4) external support to insurgents (for our purposes, political gangs), (5) actions versus subversion (that is, crime),[18] (6) host government military (and police) actions, and (7) unity of effort. Each of these dimensions individually, the variables that constitute them, and all the factors collectively contribute to success or failure in small wars. The implication of the research in this book, along with previous research, is that these dimensions lead toward the appropriate policies and strategies to deal with the several threats posed by political gangs. Perhaps a few examples from the past—interspersed with observations from the present—will serve to illustrate the continued utility of the SWORD Model in these somewhat different circumstances.

The research clearly indicates that military actions taken by the intervening power are most effective when there is a small footprint that mainly addresses training and support for host government forces. However, if a major intervention was necessary, it was most effective if undertaken with what Colin Powell called "overwhelming force."

Julius Caesar's actions against the Gallic militias illustrate both points. Generally, he sought to train and use Gallic tribes to control the country, but when the Belgae revolted he brought in his legions—hard and fast. At sea, Caesar's destruction of the pirates who seized him is a second example of his effective use of overwhelming force. Similarly, for centuries, the Romans trained and equipped German auxiliaries and even brought them into the legions. The result was a long peace on the Rhine frontier until decay from within opened the frontier to the renegade legions and auxiliaries—themselves political gangs. The British in their empire building used many of the same methods, especially in areas where they chose to use methods of indirect rule. The Kipling poem cited above goes on to tell how the colonel's son gains the admiration of the tribal chief, Kamal, so much that Kamal directs his own son to join the Guides and admonishes him to protect the young British officer. Through this kind of indirect and supporting approach, the British kept a tenuous peace in the Northwest Frontier and, after failed attempts at more direct rule, in Afghanistan.[19]

One lesson that can be learned about political gangs is that if the threat they pose to the host government and intervening power is not existential, then a good strategy for the political gang is simply to wait out the intervening power. Eventually, the intervening power may tire of the conflict and decide it can live with it. The case of outlasting the intervening power is well made during the Reconstruction of the American South. The U.S. government as the intervening power was supporting the Reconstructed governments of the states formerly in rebellion. Unfortunately, support was inconsistent because of the ongoing battle between President Andrew Johnson and the Radical Republicans in Congress. Although the election of Ulysses S. Grant to the presidency put a more sympathetic Republican in charge of Reconstruction, the forces of order were being worn down by the constant low-grade guerrilla warfare of the political gangs such as the Ku Klux Klan. Moreover, the army, charged with enforcing Reconstruction, was being reduced to peacetime size, which meant that it no longer was capable of an effective occupation of the South. The end came with the disputed election of 1876. The Republican Rutherford B. Hayes became president, and in exchange Reconstruction was ended and the Posse Comitatus Act was passed. And Jim Crow governments ruled the South, aided and abetted by the political gangs. It was the price of support actions of the intervening power being neither consistent nor sustained. The patience of the national government lasted a mere ten years and was disputed all the way.

Britain's willingness to support its hosts in the Indian subcontinent varied greatly. As noted above, the British became tired of trying to dominate Afghanistan and finally settled on supporting an ally they could not control but who met their minimal requirements. In British India, by contrast, they were willing to commit to staying for as long as it took—until colonialism began to die in the wake of the Second World War. British rule in India lasted in the neighborhood of 150 years, a pretty good track record for an intervening power.

The wars with political gangs, like all small wars, are wars of legitimacy. No matter where we find them, political gangs seek recognition as legitimate players in the political, economic, and social life of the state. Gallic and German militias sought Roman recognition of their legitimate role in the security of Gaul and the Rhine frontier. The Jewish brigands sought to expel Romans as well as the Jewish kingdom and control the state for their own version of their religion. Caesar's pirates sought to control the commerce of the Mediterranean and were encouraged in their quest for legitimacy by the Roman governors. The Barbary pirates were the economic and military muscle of the rulers of the smaller states on the North African coast under the nominal rule of the Ottoman Empire. Julius Caesar and the later Caesars co-opted the militias, making them legitimate instruments of the Roman state and guaranteeing the legitimacy of Rome and Rome's frontiers. Vespasian and his son Titus successfully delegitimized the brigands known to them as the Zealots and Sicarii by defeating and destroying them. While British support for the legitimate ruler of Afghanistan was important in reinforcing his legitimacy, direct British rule of India was an important legitimating factor in the wake of the failure of the East India Company, as demonstrated by the great mutiny of 1857.

These examples from ancient times to the nineteenth century are echoed by modern clashes over legitimacy with political gangs. Colombia's Medellin Cartel under Pablo Escobar was notorious as Escobar attempted, with some success, to establish a legitimate political role for himself while the cartel provided both his wealth and his muscle. If Pablo Escobar was the first to operate this way in the post–cold war era, he was certainly not the last, as Manwaring cogently points out.

That political gangs were enhanced by outside supporters in bygone eras is attested to by Rome's support of its Gaulish and German tribal clients as well as the pirates who infested the Mediterranean and made life miserable on the *mare nostrum* for the enemies and rivals of Rome. Likewise, British sea dogs stole the wealth of Spain, France, and other rivals, often carrying letters of marque from the crown. This was no different from the Bey of Tunis or the British East India Company renting the loyalty of certain tribal leaders in the subcontinent or the French government supplying and paying Algonquian tribes to raid English settlements in America in the seventeenth and eighteenth centuries. Needless to say, the British did the same during the American Revolution and War of 1812, as shown by the actions of the British colonel known to the Americans as "Hair Buyer Hamilton." When outside support ended, either by force majeure or by choice, gang activity diminished. Would the FARC in Colombia be as great a problem as it still is without the support of Hugo Chavez's oil-money-purchased arms and equipment? Would the Afghan Taliban be as great a threat as they are without the continued support of elements of Pakistan's Inter-Services Intelligence (ISI) and the transnational drug trafficking organizations that purchase the raw opium that the Taliban receives in taxes from local cultivators?

The actions that the government and its allies take to deal directly with the threat posed by political gangs have varied over the centuries. Those actions that have proven successful have relied on effective intelligence, strategic communication (psychological operations), and population and resource control measures.[20] Caesar's successful capture of the pirates depended on the knowledge he had gained during his captivity of their behavior and security measures (or their lack). By the time his ransom arrived, Caesar knew exactly what his captors did twenty-four hours each day, seven days a week. As a result, he attacked the pirates when they least expected it and captured them all.

Similarly, good intelligence has resulted in the successful killing of the leader of Al Qaeda in Iraq, Abu Musab al-Zarqawi, and the targeted killings of Al Qaeda and Taliban gang leaders in both Afghanistan and Pakistan. Intelligence focused on the Indian Ocean shipping lanes and pirate bases in Somalia has reduced, but not eliminated, successful pirate attacks in recent weeks (as of fall 2009).

Other specific actions targeted on political gangs that have had some success have included Caesar's rallying of some of the tribes of Gaul to his side through effective "strategic communication"; Vespasian's effective psychological operation that brought the Jewish general Josephus over to his side; the marriage of Henry VII, which effectively united the warring "highway robbers," Yorkists and Lancastrians; and the British operations to woo the Pathan tribes of the Northwest Frontier of India. A modern example in the same area is the activities of the Jawbreaker teams from the U.S. Central Intelligence Agency and the military special forces in gaining the support of Taliban elements through money and other "psychological" inducements.[21]

One of the things that made the Romans, British, American cavalry, and others successful against the political gangs they faced was the discipline and training of regular forces, both military and police. Clearly, the professionalism of the legions was what struck terror into the hearts of Gaulish, German, and other tribes. When that discipline decayed and the training was passed on to the tribes, the effectiveness of the legions deteriorated dramatically. British discipline won many a fight against political gangs in every corner of the far-flung British empire. And even the greatest disasters of the American cavalry in their nineteenth-century wars with American Indians—such as the destruction of Brevet Major General George Armstrong Custer's detachment of the Seventh Cavalry at the Little Bighorn—was reversed within days with the arrival of General George Crook's forces and the return of the tribes to the reservations. In Malaya in the 1950s, much of the British success against the Chinese communist political gangs was because of the discipline and training of the British and Malayan police—perhaps more even than the military. Likewise, in the Philippines, Secretary of Defense Ramon Magsaysay replaced the corrupt police (constabulary) with professional and well-disciplined soldiers, effectively turning around the fight against the gang known as the Huks. Today, some degree of success has been shown by the actions of the U.S. Federal

Bureau of Investigation, the New York Police Department, the U.S. Central Intelligence Agency, and Scotland Yard, among other police and intelligence forces, in disrupting and thwarting attacks by terrorist gangs before they occur.

In nearly all cases of success against political gangs, there has been real unity of effort on the part of the forces of order. Failure has come when unity of effort was lacking. In his operation against the pirates who had taken him, Caesar was clearly in sole command. Yet when he attempted to follow the Roman chain of command, Junius followed his own agenda and would have derailed Caesar had the latter allowed him. Instead, Caesar simply ignored Junius and took care of matters on his own. By contrast, when the Senate was seeking to resist Antony and Octavian and the gangs they employed, the senators failed to achieve any kind of unity, and the republic fell to the newly created empire. American operations against Indian tribes tended to be most successful when command was vested in a single commander such as George Crook or Nelson Miles. When command was divided between the officer on the scene and his superior at Fort Laramie—as it was during Red Cloud's War in 1866—then the gangs tended to be more successful. The same result was seen in the Philippines from 1899 through 1902 when General Arthur MacArthur was given full authority to prosecute the war and in General John J. Pershing's 1916 Punitive Expedition to Mexico against Pancho Villa's political gang when Pershing was not given that authority.

Among the more recent examples of successful and unsuccessful unity of effort are the British in Malaya and the Americans (and United Nations) in Somalia. In the former, the British incrementally came to vesting both political and military command in a single individual, Sir Gerald Templar. When they did, they achieved the success famously predicted by the chief of the imperial general staff, Field Marshall Bernard Montgomery: "First, we need a plan. Then we need a man. When we have a plan and a man, we shall succeed. Not otherwise."[22] By contrast, in Somalia, the United Nations and American command structure—both designed by the United States—failed to even follow American doctrine for command and control. The result was a system so cumbersome and dysfunctional that it is a wonder it worked at all.[23]

IF THIS STUFF ISN'T NEW,
WHY DON'T WE ALWAYS WIN?

The subhead suggests the dilemma that faces all policy makers and scholars of small wars. How to defeat political gangs (as well as insurgents and terrorists by whatever name) has been known and practiced successfully since ancient times. Nevertheless, political and military leaders throughout the ages have failed in their efforts to subdue political gangs or reached accommodations with them that were often not advantageous to the government. Such false accords always bore the seeds of future conflict, which was usually more violent than it would have been if the problem posed by the political gangs had been addressed with greater intelligence, based on the lessons learned in many previous conflicts.

What was often forgotten was the great maxim of Carl von Clausewitz that war is an extension of politics by other means.[24] War, then, is policy made by political leaders. It is a set of goals and objectives, driven by some perceived threat, that can be achieved only through the use of force. How that force is applied along with other actions and with what resources is what is called strategy. This is true even when we do not recognize a conflict as war. But as long as force is a key method, then Clausewitz's definition of war applies. This, then, is where Manwaring has made his innovative contribution with this book. He has identified through rediscovery a whole set of nontraditional threats that must be addressed in part, at least, through the use of force. Nevertheless, he would be the first to remind us that politics is both more than and less than force. His SWORD Model integrates a set of dimensions that include both military and civil resources. That model forms the basis of the current U.S. military doctrine for counterinsurgency and stability operations, as well as other forms of small wars. As usual, Max Manwaring is leading the way in identifying new/old threats to which it applies and demonstrating the consequences of successful and failed applications.

NOTES

FOREWORD

1. John T. Fishel and Max G. Manwaring, *Uncomfortable Wars Revisited* (Norman: University of Oklahoma Press, 2006); and Max G. Manwaring, *Insurgency, Terrorism and Crime: Shadows from the Past and Portents for the Future* (Norman: University of Oklahoma Press, 2008).

2. Fishel and Manwaring, *Uncomfortable Wars Revisited*, vii.

3. Linda Robinson, *Tell Me How All This Ends: General David Petraeus and the Search for a Way Out of Iraq* (New York: Public Affairs, 2008), 86, 276–79; and Linda Robinson, "Our Man in Baghdad," *Washington Post National Weekly Edition*, September 22–28, 2008, p. 27.

4. *The U.S. Army–Marine Corps Counterinsurgency Field Manual* (Chicago: University of Chicago Press, 2007), xiii, xlv.

5. From John T. Fishel comments of July 2008, "Revising FM 3-24: What Needs to Change?" in "Small Wars Council," part of the *Small Wars Journal*, available at http://council.smallwarsjournal.com.

6. For a list of books, book chapters, and articles that have made use of the Manwaring Paradigm or SWORD Model, see the selected bibliography (which I compiled) that is included in Fishel and Manwaring, *Uncomfortable Wars Revisited*, 315–24.

7. Eliot Cohen, Lt. Col. Conrad Crane (U.S. Army, ret.), Lt. Col. Jan Horvath (U.S. Army), and Lt. Col. John Nagl (U.S. Army), "Principles, Imperatives, and Paradoxes of Counterinsurgency," *Military Review* (March–April 2006): 49–53.

8. Todd Greenlee, *Crossroads of Intervention: Insurgency and Counterinsurgency Lessons from Central America* (Westport, Conn.: Praeger Security International, 2008).

9. See Salvador Sanchez Ceren, *Con suenos se escribe la vida: Autobiografía de un revolucionario salvadoreño* (Mexico City: Ocean Press and Ocean Sur, 2008).

INTRODUCTION

1. Rupert Smith, *The Utility of Force: The Art of War in the Modern World* (New York: Alfred A. Knopf, 2007); Kimbra L. Fishel, "Challenging the Hegemon: Al Qaeda's Elevation of Asymmetric Insurgent Warfare onto the Global Arena," in *Networks, Terrorism and Global Insurgency,* ed. Robert J. Bunker (London: Routledge, 2005), 115–28.

2. Niccolò Machiavelli, *The Art of War* (New York: Da Capo Press, 1965), 196.

3. See, as examples, essays by V. I. Lenin in *The Lenin Anthology,* ed. Robert C. Tucker (New York: W. W. Norton, 1975): "What Is to Be Done?" 12–19 and 112–14; "Two Tactics of Social-Democracy in the Democratic Revolution," 134–41; and "Socialism and War," 194–95.

4. Thomas A. Marks, *Maoist Insurgency since Vietnam* (London: Frank Cass, 1996). Also see General Vo Nguyen Giap, *People's War, Peoples' Army: The Viet Cong Insurrection Manual for Underdeveloped Countries* (New York: Frederick A. Praeger, 1962), 34–37; Abraham Guillen, *Philosophy of the Urban Guerrilla: The Revolutionary Writings of Abraham Guillen,* ed. and trans. Donald C. Hodges (New York: William Morrow and Company, 1973); Qiao Liang and Wang Xiangsui, *Unrestricted Warfare* (Beijing: PLA Literature and Arts Publishing House, 1999); and Jorge Verstrynge Rojas, *La guerra periferica y el Islam revolucionario: Origines, reglas, y etica de la guerra asimetrica,* Special Edition for the Army of the Bolivarian Republic of Venezuela, IDRFAN, Enlace Circular Militar (Madrid: El Viejo Topo, 2005).

5. V. I. Lenin, "Tasks of Russian Social-Democrats," in *The Lenin Anthology,* 5. Also see pp. 3–11; and Lenin, "What Is to Be Done?" 12–19 and 112–14; "Socialism and War," 194–95; and "The State and Revolution"; all in *The Lenin Anthology,* 324.

6. Smith, *Utility of Force.* Also see Robert A. Dahl, *Modern Political Analysis* (Englewood Cliffs, N.J.: Prentice-Hall, 1976); and Dahl, *On Democracy* (New Haven, Conn.: Yale University Press, 1998).

7. See previous note. For an early discussion of these phenomena, see Samuel Huntington, *The Clash of Civilizations and the Remaking of World Order* (New York: Simon and Schuster, 1966); and Robert D. Kaplan, *The Coming Anarchy* (New York: Random House, 2000). Also see David Easton, *A Framework for Political Analysis* (Englewood Cliffs, N.J.: Prentice-Hall, 1965). David Easton formulated and elaborated the concept of "authoritative allocation of values" as the accepted definition of politics.

8. See essays by V. I. Lenin in *The Lenin Anthology:* "The Tasks of Russian Social-Democrats," 3–11; "What Is to Be Done?" 34–38, 40, 83–87; "Socialism and War," 194–95; "The Proletarian Revolution and the Renegade Kautsky," 467; "A Great Beginning," 478; and "The Dictatorship of the Proletariat," 486–89.

9. Vladimir Torres, *The Impact of "Populism" on Social, Political, and Economic Development in the Hemisphere,* FOCAL Policy Paper (Ottawa: FOCAL [Canadian Foundation for the Americas], 2006), 1–18.

10. V. I. Lenin, "The Tasks of the Youth Leagues," in *The Lenin Anthology,* 671.

11. Ibid.

12. See essays by V. I. Lenin in *The Lenin Anthology:* "The Tasks of Russian Social-Democrats," 3–12; "What Is to Be Done?" 13–14; "Socialism and War," 183–95; "April Thesis," 295–300; "The State and Revolution," 311–98; "On Revolutionary Violence and Terror," 423–32; and "The Tasks of the Youth Leagues," 661–74.

13. Carl von Clausewitz, *On War,* ed. and trans. Michael Howard and Peter Paret (Princeton, N.J.: Princeton University Press, 1976), 88.

14. Robert K. Yin, *Case Study Research: Design and Methods,* 2nd ed. (Thousand Oaks, Calif.: SAGE Publications, 1994), 31, 46.

15. Ibid., 1–15, 31–32, 46, 51, 147.

16. Ibid., 138–39.

17. Clausewitz, *On War,* 88–89.

18. See essays by V. I. Lenin in *The Lenin Anthology:* "The Tasks of Russian Social-Democrats," 3–11; "What Is to Be Done?" 84–87; "How to Organize Competition," 427; and "Capitalist Discords and the Concessions Policy," 628.

19. See essays by V. I. Lenin in *The Lenin Anthology:* "What Is to Be Done?" 12–19 and 112–14; "Two Tactics of Social-Democracy," 134–41; and "Socialism and War," 194–95.

CHAPTER 1. WHERE LENIN LEADS

1. Ian Beckett, "The Future of Insurgency," *Small Wars and Insurgencies* (March 2005): 22–36. Also see William J. Olson, "International Organized Crime: The Silent Threat to Sovereignty," *Fletcher Forum* (Summer–Fall 1997): 75–78.

2. As one important example, see Qiao Liang and Wang Xiangsui, *Unrestricted Warfare* (Beijing: PLA Literature and Arts Publishing House, 1999). Also see Thomas X. Hammes, *The Sling and the Stone: On War in the 21st Century* (St. Paul, Minn.: Zenith Press, 2006).

3. Steven Metz and Douglas V. Johnson II, *Asymmetry and U.S. Military Strategy: Definition, Background, and Strategic Concepts* (Carlisle Barracks, Penn.: Strategic Studies Institute, 2001).

4. Ralph Peters, "Constant Conflict," *Parameters* (Summer 1997): 10. Also see Peters, "The Culture of Future Conflict," *Parameters* (Winter 1995–96): 18–27.

5. Hammes, *Sling and the Stone*, 2006. Also see Col. Thomas X. Hammes (USMC, ret.), "Fourth Generation Warfare," *Armed Forces Journal* (November 2004): 40–44.

6. See essays by V. I. Lenin in *The Lenin Anthology*, ed. Robert C. Tucker (New York: W. W. Norton, 1975): "The Tasks of Russian Social-Democrats," 3–11; "Socialism and War," 183–95; "The Symptoms of a Revolutionary Situation," 275–76; "April Thesis," 295–300; "The State and Revolution," 311–98; "On Revolutionary Violence and Terror," 423–32; "Report on War and Peace," 545; and "The Tasks of the Youth Leagues," 662–64.

7. Lenin, "Tasks of Russian Social-Democrats," 3–11.

8. See note 6, this chapter.

9. Lenin, "Report on War and Peace," 545.

10. Interestingly, Lenin argued that this is what Clausewitz had in mind when he wrote, "It is possible to increase the likelihood of success without defeating the enemy's forces" (V. I. Lenin, "Capitalist Discords and Concessions Policy," in *The Lenin Anthology*, 628). See Carl von Clausewitz, *On War*, ed. and trans. Michael Howard and Peter Paret (Princeton, N.J.: Princeton University Press, 1976), 92–93.

11. See essays by V. I. Lenin in *The Lenin Anthology*: "The Tasks of Russian Social-Democrats," 3–11; "What Is to Be Done?" 38, 84–87; "The Proletarian Revolution and the Renegade Kautsky," 467; "The Dictatorship of the Proletariat," 489–96; and "Socialism and War," 194–95.

12. Lenin, "Tasks of the Youth Leagues," 671.

13. Ibid.

14. Steven J. Blank, "Class War on a Global Scale: The Leninist Culture of Political Conflict," in Blank et al., *Conflict, Culture, and History: Regional Dimensions* (Maxwell Air Force Base, Ala.: Air University Press, 1993), 26; and Robert A. Jones, *The Soviet Concept of Limited Sovereignty from Lenin to Gorbachev* (New York: St. Martin's Press, 1990), 88–91.

15. Kimbra L. Fishel, "Challenging the Hegemon: Al Qaeda's Elevation of Asymmetric Insurgent Warfare onto the Global Arena," in *Networks, Terrorism and Global Insurgency*, ed. Robert J. Bunker (London: Routledge, 2005), 115–28.

16. See essays by V. I. Lenin in *The Lenin Anthology*: "The Tasks of Russian Social-Democrats," 3–11; "Two Tactics of Social-Democracy," 134–41; "Socialism and War," 194–95; "The Proletarian Revolution and the Renegade Kautsky," 467; and "The Dictatorship of the Proletariat," 489–91. Also see Lenin, "Conducting War for Social-Democracy," 333–38; "The State and Revolution," 348–50, 371–78; and "Left-Wing Communism: An Infantile Disorder," 560–618.

17. Rupert Smith, *The Utility of Force: The Art of War in the Modern World* (New York: Alfred A. Knopf, 2007).

18. See note 16, this chapter.

19. Lenin, "Socialism and War," 188. This definition of center of gravity is very close to that expressed by Clausewitz. See Clausewitz, *On War*, 596.

20. Smith, *Utility of Force*, 375–77.

21. See notes 6, 11, and 16, this chapter.

22. Lenin, "Capitalist Discords and Concessions Policy," 628.

23. Lenin, "On Revolutionary Violence and Terror," 425.

24. See note 16, this chapter. Also see Adda B. Bozeman, "War and the Clash of Ideas," *Orbis* (Spring 1976): 73.

25. Lenin, "Symptoms of a Revolutionary Situation," 275–76.

26. Ibid. Also see Lenin, "Report on War and Peace," 545; and "Revolutionary Taking of Power," 395–414.

27. Lenin, "Tasks of Russian Social-Democrats," 4–8.

28. Ibid. Also see Lenin, "What Is to Be Done?" 34–38, 40, 83–87; "The State and Revolution," 324; "Report on War and Peace," 549; and "Left-Wing Communism: An Infantile Disorder," 559.

29. See previous note.

30. See note 28, this chapter.

31. See note 28, this chapter. Also see Lenin, "Tasks of the Youth Leagues," 661–74.

32. J. Bowyer Bell, *Dragonwars* (New Brunswick, N.J.: Transaction Publishers, 1999), 417–18.

33. Beckett, "Future of Insurgency," 34–35.

34. Lenin, "Symptoms of a Revolutionary Situation," 275–76; and "Report on War and Peace," 545.

35. Lenin, "Tasks of Russian Social-Democrats," 3–11; "Socialism and War," 183–95; "April Thesis," 295–300; "The State and Revolution," 311–98; "On Revolutionary Violence and Terror," 423–32; and "Tasks of the Youth Leagues," 661–74.

36. Lenin, "Report on War and Peace," 545. Also see Lenin, "Symptoms of a Revolutionary Situation," 275–76; "Great Beginning," 478; and "Tasks of the Youth Leagues," 671.

37. Tony Judt, *Postwar: A History of Europe since 1945* (New York: Penguin Press, 2005), 131–39; and "The Secret Policeman's Election," *Economist*, December 8, 2007, pp. 59–60.

38. Judt, *Postwar*, 139.

39. Ibid., 132.

40. Ibid., 135.

41. Ibid., 137.

42. Stephen J. Blank, "Web War I: Is Europe's First Information War a New Kind of War," *Comparative Strategy* 27, no. 3 (2008): 227–47. Also see "Tallinn Tense after Deadly Riots," April 28, 2007, BBC News, news.bbc.co.uk/2/hi/

europe/6602171.stm; "The Cyber Raiders Hitting Estonia," May 17, 2007, BBC News, news.bbc.co.uk/2/hi/Europe/6665195.stm; and "Estonian Trial of Russian Activists," January 14, 2008, BBC News, news.bbc.co.uk/2/hi/Europe/7187437.stm.

43. Lenin, "Tasks of the Youth Leagues," 669.

44. Ibid., 440–45.

45. Ibid.

46. Ibid.

47. Ibid.

48. Judt, *Postwar,* 443–44.

49. Ibid.

50. Lenin; see note 9, this chapter.

51. See note 8, this chapter.

52. Ivelaw L. Griffith, *Drugs and Security in the Caribbean: Sovereignty under Siege* (University Park: Pennsylvania State University Press, 1997); "Bubba, Bobo, Zambo and Zeeks—Domestic and International Issues Fuel Gang Violence in the Caribbean," *Economist,* November 4, 2004; and John Rapley, "The New Middle Ages," *Foreign Affairs* (May/June 2006): 93–103.

53. Richard Augustus Norton, *Hezbollah: A Short History* (Princeton, N.J.: Princeton University Press, 2007); Abas William Samii, "A Stable Structure on Shifting Sands: Assessing the Hezbollah-Iran-Syria Relationship," *Middle East Journal* 62, no. 1 (Winter 2008): 32–53; and Audry Kurth Cronin, "Foreign Terrorist Organizations," CRS Report for Congress, February 6, 2004.

54. "Out of the Underworld," *Economist,* January 27, 2006.

55. "Gang Violence in the Caribbean," *Economist,* November 4, 2004; Griffith, *Drugs and Security;* and Rapley, "New Middle Ages."

56. Rapley, "New Middle Ages," 93. Also see previous note; see Alexus G. Grynkewich, "Welfare as Warfare: How Violent Non-state Groups Use Social Services to Attack the State," *Studies in Conflict and Terrorism* 31 (2008): 350–70.

57. See previous note.

58. David C. Jordan, *Drug Politics: Dirty Money and Democracies* (Norman: University of Oklahoma Press, 1999).

59. "Out of the Underworld," *Economist,* January 27, 2006.

60. "Anti-crime Community Initiative to Be Launched," *Jamaica Gleaner,* February 6, 2006.

61. Rapley, "New Middle Ages."

62. Ibid.

63. See notes 52 and 54, this chapter.

64. Rapley, "New Middle Ages"; and "Beyond a Boundary," *Economist,* February 24, 2007.

65. "Winograd Committee Final Report," Israel Ministry of Foreign Affairs, January 30, 2008; Jeremy M. Sharp, coordinator, "Lebanon: The

Israel-Hamas-Hezbollah Conflict," CRS Report for Congress, September 15, 2006; and Stephen Biddle and Jeffrey A. Friedman, *The 2006 Lebanon Campaign* (Carlisle Barracks, Penn.: Strategic Studies Institute, 2008).

66. See previous note. Also see Alastair Crooke and Mark Perry, "How Hezbollah Defeated Israel, Part One: Winning the Intelligence War," *Asia Times,* October 12, 2006; Crooke and Perry, "How Hezbollah Defeated Israel, Part Two: Winning the Ground War," *Asia Times,* October 13, 2006; Crooke and Perry, "How Hezbollah Defeated Israel, Part Three: The Political War," *Asia Times,* October 14, 2006; Chris Zambelis, "Hezbollah Reacts to Israel's Winograd Report," *Terrorism Focus* 4, no. 13 (May 8, 2007); and Matt M. Matthews, *We Were Caught Unprepared: The 2006 Hezbollah-Israeli War,* Occasional Paper 26 (Ft. Leavenworth, Kans.: U.S. Army Combined Arms Center Combat Studies Institute Press, 2008).

67. See previous note.

68. The best analysis, in the author's opinion, of combinations in multidimensional conflict may be found in Qiao and Wang, *Unrestricted Warfare.*

69. Ibid.

70. Frank Kitson, *Warfare as a Whole* (London: Faber and Faber, 1987).

71. Ari Shavit, "A Spirit of Absolute Folly," *Haaretz,* August 15, 2006.

72. See, as one example, Robert F. Worth and Nada Bakri, "Deal for Lebanese Factions Leaves Hezbollah Stronger," *New York Times,* May 22, 2008.

73. Max G. Manwaring and John T. Fishel, "Insurgency and Counter-Insurgency: Toward a New Analytical Approach," *Small Wars and Insurgencies* 3, no. 3 (Winter 1992): 272–310.

74. This concept is really not new. Clausewitz articulated the idea in *On War,* 596, quite a few years ago.

75. Qiao and Wang, *Unrestricted Warfare,* 35.

76. Clausewitz, *On War.*

77. Qiao and Wang, *Unrestricted Warfare,* 41.

78. Sun Tzu, *The Art of War,* trans. Samuel B. Griffith (London: Oxford University Press, 1971), 38–41.

CHAPTER 2. THE ARGENTINE PIQUETEROS

1. Hubert Herring, "Argentina," in *A History of Latin America,* 3rd ed. (New York: Alfred A. Knopf, 1972), 689–785.

2. Ibid. Additionally, from 1955 through 1958, the author was in a position from which to observe personally the political-military situation in Argentina. Over the period 1955–2009, the author traveled often to the southern cone countries and interviewed more than five hundred senior U.S. and Latin American civilian and military officials. This and subsequent assertions made throughout

this book are consensus statements based on observation and interviews. The intent is to allow anonymity for those who object to their names being made public. The interviews were conducted from October 1989 through July 1994; September 1996; December 1998; November 2000; February 2001; and March 2003, 2004, 2005, and 2006; April through July 2007; and July, August, and September 2009. In subsequent notes, these statements are cited as Author Interviews.

3. See note 1, this chapter. Also see Richard Gillespie, "Political Violence in Argentina: Guerrillas, Terrorists, and *Carapintadas*," in *Terrorism in Context*, ed. Martha Crenshaw (University Park: Pennsylvania State University Press, 1995), 215; Maria Jose Moyano, *Argentina's Lost Patrol: Armed Struggle, 1969–1979* (New Haven, Conn.: Yale University Press, 1995); and (for a detailed compilation of terroristic events in Argentina from 1970 through 1979) HACER, *Evolucion de la delincuencia terorista en la Argentina* (Madrid: HACER, n.d.).

4. Isabella Alcañiz and Mellissa Scheier, "New Social Movements with Old Party Politics: The MTL Piqueteros and the Communist Party in Argentina," *Latin American Perspectives* 34, no. 2 (2007): 159. Also see Guillermo E. Gini, "Piqueteros: De la protesta social a la accion politica," *Estrategia*, CIFE (September 2004): 60–66; and Steven Levitsky, "From Labor Politics to Machine Politics: The Transformation of Party-Union Linkages in Argentine Peronism," *Latin American Research Review* 38, no. 3 (2003): 3–36.

5. Author Interviews. Also see Gillespie, *Political Violence in Argentina;* and Moyano, *Argentina's Lost Patrol.*

6. Ramiro Salvachea, "Clientelism in Argentina: Piqueteros and Relief Payment Plans for the Unemployed—Misunderstanding the Role of Civil Society," *Texas International Law Journal* 43 (Spring 2008): 295.

7. "Latin America's Ten Year Rut" (the Latinobarametro Poll), *Economist*, October 31, 2005. Also see Francisco Rojas Aravena, "Nuevo contexto de seguridad internacional: Nuevos desafios, nuevas oportunidades?" in Aravena, *La seguridad en American Latina pos 11 Septiembre* (FLAXO-Chile, 2003), 23–43.

8. See previous note. In the simplest terms, neopopulism advocates radical political-economic-social change. Also see "Cristina in the Land of Make-Believe," *Economist*, May 3, 2008; "Argentina: Party Time," *Economist*, February 16, 2008; "Crimes Past, Crimes Present," *Economist*, June 5, 2004; Nicolas Marquez, "Por qué siguen habiendo tantos izquierdistas en el 2007?" at www.hacer .org/current/ARG273.php; Moisés Naím, "From Normalcy to Lunacy," *Foreign Policy*, no. 141 (March/April 2004): 104–103; Álvaro Vargas Llosa, "The Return of the Idiot," *Foreign Policy*, no. 160 (May/June 2007): 54–61; and Jonas Wolff, "(De-)Mobilising the Marginalised: A Comparison of the Argentine *Piqueteros* and Ecuador's Indigenous Movement," *Journal of Latin American Studies* 39, no. 1 (2007): 1–29.

9. See notes 2, 3, and 4, this chapter.

10. Doug McAdams, Sidney Tarrow, and Charles Tilly, *The Dynamics of Contention* (Cambridge: Cambridge University Press, 2001). Also see Alcañiz and Scheier, "New Social Movements," 157–71.

11. Gini, "Piqueteros," 59–86.

12. Author Interviews. Also see Levitsky, "From Labor Politics," 3–36; Alcañiz and Scheier, "New Social Movements," 157–71; and Wolff, "(De-)Mobilising the Marginalised."

13. Author Interviews. Also see Gillespie, *Political Violence in Argentina*, 215–23; and Moyano, *Argentina's Lost Patrol*.

14. See previous note.

15. See note 13, this chapter.

16. See note 13, this chapter.

17. See note 13, this chapter.

18. Dinerstein argues that the roadblocks were the scene of the emergence of the Piquetero identity and the organization of the unemployed into a serious movement. See Ana C. Dinerstein, "Roadblocks in Argentina: Against the Violence of Stability," *Capital and Class* no. 74 (Summer 2001): 1–7; and Dinerstein, "Power or Counter-power? The Dilemma of the Piquetero Movement in Argentina Post-crisis," *Capital and Class* no. 81 (Autumn 2003): 1–8.

19. Wolff, "(De-)Mobilising the Marginalised." Also see "Cristina in the Land of Make-Believe," *Economist*, May 3, 2008; "Party Time," *Economist*, February 16, 2008; "Hard Times, Same Old Politics," *Economist*, March 22, 2003; "In Buenos Aires, a Friend in Need," *Washington Post*, April 11, 2005; "A Do-It-Yourself Plan for Argentina's Poor," *Washington Post*, March 14, 2004; "Argentina—Crumbling Away behind a Façade of Optimism," *Banker*, January 1, 2004; Tom Hennigan, "Argentine Leader's Fiercest Opposition," *Christian Science Monitor*, January 29, 2004; and Mary Anastasia O'Grady, "Americas: Peronist Argentina's Other Hallmark," *Wall Street Journal*, June 18, 2004.

20. "Kirchner Sets New Record for Bypassing Argentina's Congress," *Latin American Weekly Report*, June 29, 2004; and "Argentina: Political Representation Explodes into Small Fragments," *Latin American Weekly Report*, September 28, 2004.

21. See previous note. Also see Salvachea, "Clientelism in Argentina," 287–323; Javier Auyero, "When Everyday Life, Routine Politics, and Protest Meet," *Theory and Society*, special issue (June–August 2004): 417–41; and Guillermo A. O'Donnell, *Modernization and Bureaucratic Authoritarianism* (Berkeley: University of California Press, 1979).

22. Author Interviews. Also see Levitsky, "From Labor Politics," 15.

23. Levitsky, "From Labor Politics," 17–30.

24. Alcañiz and Scheier, "New Social Movements," 163. Also see Javier Auyero, *Poor People's Politics: Peronist Survival Networks and the Legacy of Evita* (Durham, N.C.: Duke University Press, 2001); German Lodola, "Popular

Mobilization and Geographic Distributive Paths: The Case of Argentine Plan Trabajar," paper delivered at the Latin American and Caribbean Economic Association Political Economy Group, Cartagena, Colombia, 2003; Gabriela Delamata, *Reporte sobre Plan Jefe y Jefas* (Buenos Aires: Centro de Estudies Legals y Sociales [CELS], 2003); and Ernest F. Calvo and Maria Victoria Murillo, "Who Delivers? Partisan Clientelism in the Argentine Electoral Market," *American Journal of Political Science* 48, no. 4 (October 2004): 742–57.

25. Salvachea, "Clientelism in Argentina," 298–317.

26. Author Interviews. Also see Alcañiz and Scheier, "New Social Movements," 160; and Gini, "Piqueteros," 68.

27. Salvachea, "Clientelism in Argentina," 304.

28. Gabriela Delamata, *Los barrios desbordades, las organicaciones de desocopados del Gran Buenos Aires* (Buenos Aires: Eudeba Libros del Rojas, 2004), 17; Salvachea, "Clientelism in Argentina," 78; and Wolff, "(De-)Mobilising the Marginalised," 15–17.

29. "Las discussiones son bravas pero con el tiempo la gente se va acomodando y el que no se acomoda se le da de baja y pierde el plan" (Author Interviews). Also see Raúl Zibechi, *Genealogia de la revuelta, Argentina: La sociedad en movimento* (Buenos Aires: Letra Libre and Nordan Comunidad, 2003), 146–47; and Gini, "Piqueteros," 75.

30. Alcañiz and Sheier, "New Social Movements," 164; Salvachea, "Clientelism in Argentina," 304–305; Gini, "Piqueteros," 68–69; and Dinerstein, "Power or Counter-power?" 3–5. Also see "Kirchner ya tiene Piqueteros proprios," INFOBAE, June 9, 2004, www.infobae.com/contenidos/118595-0-0-Kirchner-ya-tiene-piqueteros-propios.

31. See previous note.

32. See note 30, this chapter.

33. See note 30, this chapter; and Author Interviews. Also see Alcañiz and Scheier, "New Social Movements," 160; and Salvachea, "Clientelism in Argentina," 298–317.

34. See previous note.

35. Levitsky, "From Labor Politics," 28; and Salvachea, "Clientelism in Argentina," 297, 305, 310–11.

36. Dinerstein, "Power or Counter-power?" 1–7; and Wolff, "(De-)Mobilising the Marginalised," 12–13.

37. The author is grateful to Dr. Phil Williams for these and the following assertions. See Gregory Laurent and Baudin O'Hayon, *Big Men, Godfathers, and Zealots: Challenges to the State in the New Middle Ages* (Pittsburgh: University of Pittsburgh Dissertations and Theses, 2003); Hedley Bull, *The Anarchical Society* (New York: Columbia University Press, 1977); Jorge Friedrichs, "The Meaning of the New Medievalism," *European Journal of International Relations* 7, no. 4 (2001): 475–502; and Philip Cerny, "Neomedievalism, Civil War, and

the New Security Dilemma: Globalization as Durable Disorder," *Civil Wars* 1, no. 1 (Spring 1998): 36–64. Also see Steven R. David, "Saving America from the Coming Civil Wars," *Foreign Affairs* (January/February 1999): 103–16; Steven D. Krasner, "Abiding Sovereignty," *International Political Science Review* 22, no. 3 (2001): 229–52; Chester A. Crocker, "Engaging Failed States," *Foreign Affairs* (September/October 2003): 32–44; Steven D. Krasner and Carlos Pascual, "Addressing State Failure," *Foreign Affairs* (July/August 2005): 153–63; John Rapley, "The New Middle Ages," *Foreign Affairs* (May/June 2006): 93–103; and Phil Williams, *From the New Middle Ages to a New Dark Age: The Decline of the State and U.S. Strategy* (Carlisle Barracks, Penn.: Strategic Studies Institute, 2008).

38. Robert D. Kaplan, *The Coming Anarchy* (New York: Random House, 2000), 49.

39. Ibid. Also see Daniel C. Esty, Jack Goldstone, Ted Robert Gurr, Barbara Harff, and Pamela T. Surko, "The State Failure Project: Early Warning Research for U.S. Foreign Policy Planning," in *Preventive Measures: Building Risk Assessment and Crisis Early Warning Systems*, ed. John L. Davies and Ted Robert Gurr (New York: Rowman and Littlefield, 1998), 27–38.

40. Steve C. Ropp, *The Strategic Implications of the Rise of Populism in Europe and South America* (Carlisle Barracks, Penn.: Strategic Studies Institute, 2005), 2–3, 17.

41. Ibid., 23. Also see Joel Horowitz, "Populism and Its Legacies in Argentina," in *Populism in Latin America*, ed. Michael L. Conniff, 22–42 (Tuscaloosa: University of Alabama Press, 1999).

42. Vladimir Torres, *The Impact of "Populism" on Social, Political, and Economic Development in the Hemisphere*, FOCAL Policy Paper (Ottawa: FOCAL, 2006), 1–5.

43. Ibid., 1.

44. Ibid.

45. One of the main reasons for populist nationalism's reason for being is the existence of an enemy abroad. That directs popular attention away from local failures. Imperialism, the United States, the international financial institutions, and the multinational corporations of the global economy are Latin American and Argentine populism's preferred scapegoats. Thus, neopopulism is also antiglobal.

46. Torres, *Impact of "Populism,"* 4–5.

47. Thomas Legler, "Bridging Divides, Breaking Impasses: Civil Society in the Promotion and Protection of Democracy in the Americas," FOCAL Policy Paper (Ottawa: FOCAL, 2006).

48. "Quiconque refusera d'obeir a la volonte generale y sera constraint par tout le corps: ce qui ne signifie autre chose sinon qu'on le forcera de'etre libre." For another translation in English, see Jean Jacques Rousseau, *The Social*

Contract, book 1, chapter 7, translated by Charles Frankel (New York: Hafner, 1947), 18. Also see J. L. Talmon, *The Origins of Totalitarian Democracy* (New York: Praeger, 1968).

49. Legler, "Bridging Divides"; and Torres, *Impact of "Populism."*

50. That is, the impeachment of political leaders and the nullification of unpopular laws, decrees, policies, and programs.

51. See note 49.

52. See note 49. Also see Dinerstein, "Power or Counter-power"; and the following essays by V. I. Lenin in *The Lenin Anthology,* ed. Robert C. Tucker (New York: W. W. Norton, 1975): "The Tasks of Russian Social Democrats," 3–11; "What Is to Be Done?" 84–87; "Socialism and War," 183–95; "The Symptoms of a Revolutionary Situation," 275–76; "The State and Revolution," 311–98; "On Revolutionary Violence and Terror," 423–32; and "The Tasks of the Youth Leagues," 662–64. One Peronist Piquetero stated their philosophy simply: "*Peronismo* is about helping poor people. So we give them food, medicine, and maybe even a job. That's what Peronism is all about."

53. Dinerstein, "Power or Counter-power?" 3–4; and Claudio Lozano, "Acerca del programa nacional para jefes y jefas de hogar sin empleo," Central de los Trabajadores Argentina, Instituto de Estudios y Formación, www.cta.org.ar/instituto/planjefes.html.

54. This metaphor stems from Mao Zedong's literal long march during the Chinese Revolution.

55. John Holloway, *Cambiar el mundo sin tomar al poder: El significado de la revolucion hoy* (Buenos Aires: Universidad Autonoma del Pueblo, 2002), 27–98. Also see Lenin, "Tasks of Russian Social-Democrats," 3–11; and "What Is to Be Done?" 12–114.

56. See previous note; also see note 52, this chapter.

57. Holloway, *Cambiar el mundo,* 65.

58. See note 51, this chapter.

59. Holloway, *Cambiar el mundo;* and Dinerstein, "Power or Counter-power?"

60. See notes 4, 24, and 28, this chapter.

61. Holloway, *Cambiar el mundo;* also see note 52, this chapter.

62. Author Interviews.

63. Jose Maria Aznar, *Latin America: An Agenda for Freedom,* ed. Miguel Angel Cortes (Madrid: FAES, 2007), 28.

64. John Le Carré, *The Constant Gardener* (New York: Scribner, 2001), 137.

65. Esty et al., "State Failure Project"; and Crocker, "Engaging Failed States." Also see David C. Jordan, *Drug Politics: Dirty Money and Democracies* (Norman: University of Oklahoma Press, 1999).

66. See notes 37 and 38, this chapter.

67. Niccolò Machiavelli, "The Different Kinds of Militia and Mercenary Soldiers," chapter 12 of *The Prince and the Discourses* (New York: Random House, Modern Library, 1950), 44–45.

CHAPTER 3. FROM THE BARREL OF A GUN AND DEEP POCKETS

1. Author Interviews. See note 2, chapter 2.

2. Douglas Porch and Maria Jose Rasmussen, "Demobilization of Paramilitaries in Colombia: Transformation or Transition?" *Studies in Conflict and Terrorism* 31, no. 6 (2008): 520–40.

3. International Crisis Group, *Colombia's New Armed Groups*, Latin America Report no. 20 (Bogota/Brussels: International Crisis Group, May 10, 2007). Also see Diana Cariboni, "New Breed of Paramilitaries Infiltrate Urban 'Refuges,'" Inter-Press Service, June 26, 2006, http://ipsnews.net/news.asp?idnews=33769; Mayer Nudell, "Ex-paramilitaries Form Crime Gangs in Colombia," *Washington Post*, July 31, 2006; Caleb Harris, "Paramilitaries Reemerge in Pockets of Colombia," *Christian Science Monitor*, March 12, 2007; Joshua Goodman, "Report: New Criminal Gangs in Colombia," AP News, August 16, 2007; and Sibylla Brodzinsky, "Is Colombia's FARC on the Ropes?" *Christian Science Monitor*, May 21, 2008.

4. See previous note; also see Author Interviews.

5. Vladimir Torres, *The Impact of "Populism" on Social, Political, and Economic Development in the Hemisphere*, FOCAL Policy Paper (Ottawa: FOCAL [Canadian Foundation for the Americas], 2006), 1–18.

6. Over the period from 1948 to 1956, as only one example, la violencia claimed the lives of more than 250,000 Colombians. See Vernon Lee Fluherty, *Dance of the Millions: Military Rule and the Social Revolution in Colombia, 1930–1956* (Pittsburgh, Penn.: University of Pittsburgh Press, 1957). Also see Luis Alberto Restrepo, "The Crisis of the Current Political Regime and Its Possible Outcomes," in *Violence in Colombia: The Contemporary Crisis in Historical Perspective*, ed. Charles Bergquist, Ricardo Penaranda, and Gonzalo Sanchez (Wilmington, Del.: SR Books, 1992), 273–92.

7. Author Interviews.

8. Ibid.

9. Ibid.

10. Ibid. Also see Thomas A. Marks, *Colombian Army Adaptation to FARC Insurgency* (Carlisle Barracks, Penn.: Strategic Studies Institute, 2002); Marks, *Sustainability of Colombian Military/Strategic Support for "Democratic Security"* (Carlisle Barracks, Penn.: Strategic Studies Institute, 2005); and Marks, *Maoist Insurgency since Vietnam* (London: Frank Cass Publishers, 1996).

11. Angel Rabassa and Peter Chalk, *Colombian Labyrinth* (Santa Monica, Calif.: RAND, 2001), 39–60. Also see Larry Rohter, "A Colombian Guerrilla's 50-Year Fight," *New York Times*, July 19, 1999; Larry Rohter, "Colombia Rebels Reign in Ceded Area," *New York Times*, May 16, 1999; Howard LaFranchi, "Guerrilla Commander Says, 'This Is a Means,'" *Christian Science Monitor*, July 19, 1999; Garry M. Leech, "An Interview with FARC Commander Simon Trinidad," *NACLA Report on the Americas* 34, no. 2 (September/October 2000); Clifford Krauss, "Colombia's Rebels Keep the Marxist Faith," *Christian Science Monitor*, July 19, 1999; Serge F. Kovaleski, "Rebel Movement on the Rise: Colombian Guerrillas Use Military Force, Not Ideology, to Hold Power," *Washington Post*, February 5, 1999; Alfred Molano, "The Evolution of the FARC: A Guerrilla Group's Long History," *NACLA Report on the Americas* 34, no. 2 (September/October 2000); and Jane's Information Group, "FARC: Finance Comes Full Circle for Bartering Revolutionaries," January 19, 2001. The most recent public data are published at "FARC Inc.," *Semana*, February 2, 2005.

12. See previous note; also see "Survey of Colombia," *Economist*, April 21, 2001.

13. Douglas Porch, "Uribe's Second Mandate, the War, and the Implications for Civil-Military Relations in Colombia," *Strategic Insights* 5, no. 2 (February 2006): 5; Chris Kraul, "Alarming Surge of Displaced People in Colombia," *San Francisco Chronicle*, December 4, 2008, A-12; and Author Interviews.

14. See previous note. Also see Douglas Farah, "The FARC's International Relations: A Network of Deception," *NEFA Foundation Report*, September 22, 2008.

15. Author Interviews; and PC-3 Secretariat, "Rebirth of the Revolutionary Masses," *Semana*, August 16, 2008.

16. Thomas A. Marks, "Urban Insurgency," *Small Wars and Insurgencies* (Autumn 2003): 141.

17. FARC's objective remains the "taking of power for the people" (ibid.); see Author Interviews. Also see Christopher Toothacher, "Chavez Urges FARC to End Armed Struggle," Associated Press, June 8, 2008.

18. Author Interviews. Also see Brodzinsky, "Is Colombia's FARC on the Ropes?" *Christian Science Monitor*, May 21, 2008; and Kraul, "Alarming Surge of Displaced People," *San Francisco Chronicle*, December 4, 2008, A-12.

19. See previous note. Also see David Spencer, *Colombia's Paramilitaries: Criminals or Political Force?* (Carlisle Barracks, Penn.: Strategic Studies Institute, 2001); Juan Forero, "Colombian Paramilitaries Adjust Attack Strategies," *New York Times*, January 22, 2001; Juan Forero, "Rightist Chief in Colombia Shifts Focus to Politics," *New York Times*, June 7, 2001; and Tod Robberson, "Militia Leader's Revelations Igniting Fear in Colombia," *Dallas Morning News*, December 17, 2001.

20. Leon Valencia Agudelo, director, *Paramilitares y Politicos,* an investigation conducted by the Nuevo Arco Iris Corporation with the support of the Swedish Agency for International Development (ASDAI), Bogota, March 2007, 19.

21. See notes 2 and 10, this chapter.

22. Porch, "Uribe's Second Mandate," 3.

23. Ibid.; and "Survey of Colombia," *Economist,* April 21, 2001.

24. Porch, "Uribe's Second Mandate," 7.

25. Author Interviews.

26. Porch, "Uribe's Second Mandate."

27. David Bushnell, "Politics and Violence in Nineteenth-Century Colombia," in *Violence in Colombia: The Contemporary Crisis in Historical Perspective,* ed. Charles Bergquist, Ricardo Penaranda, and Gonzalo Sanchez (Wilmington, Del.: SR Books, 1992), 17–19.

28. James Rosenau, *Turbulence in World Politics* (Princeton University Press, 1990), 253.

29. David Easton formulated and elaborated the concept of "authoritative allocation of values" as the accepted definition of politics. See David Easton, *A Framework for Political Analysis* (Englewood Cliffs, N.J.: Prentice-Hall, 1965). Also see David Easton, *The Political System: An Inquiry into the State of Political Science,* 3rd ed. (Chicago: University of Chicago Press, 1981).

30. See previous note. Also see Peter A. Lupsha, "The Role of Drugs and Drug Trafficking in the Invisible Wars," in *International Terrorism: Operational Issues,* ed. Richard H. Ward and Harold E. Smith (Chicago: Office of International Criminal Justice, University of Illinois at Chicago, 1988), 181; and Peter A. Lupsha, "Towards an Etiology of Drug Trafficking and Insurgent Relations: The Phenomenon of Narcoterrorism," *International Journal of Comparative and Applied Criminal Justice* 13, no. 2 (Fall 1989): 63. Also see William J. Olson, "International Organized Crime: The Silent Threat to Sovereignty," *Fletcher Forum* (Summer/Fall 1997): 75–78.

31. See previous note. Also see "Central America and Mexico Gang Assessment" (Washington, D.C.: U.S. Agency for International Development, Bureau for Latin America and Caribbean Affairs, April 2006), hereafter cited as AID Paper.

32. See notes 30 and 31.

33. Author Interviews.

34. Ibid. Also see "The Statutes of the FARC-EP," chapter 1, article 1 in *El pais que proponemos construer* (Bogota: Editorial La Oveja Negra, 2001).

35. Rabassa and Chalk, *Colombian Labyrinth;* Spencer, *Colombia's Paramilitaries.*

36. See previous note.

37. Author Interviews.

38. Ibid. Also see Simon Romero, "Crisis at Colombia Border Spills into Diplomatic Realm," *New York Times,* March 4, 2008; and Simon Romero and James

C. McKinley, Jr., "Crisis over Colombian Raid Ends in Handshakes," *New York Times,* March 8, 2008.

39. See previous note. Also see David C. Jordan, *Drug Politics: Dirty Money and Democracies* (Norman: University of Oklahoma Press, 1999), 165–67.

40. See previous note. Also see Author Interviews; and Martha Crenshaw, ed., *Terrorism in Context* (University Park: Pennsylvania State University Press, 1995).

41. Robert D. Kaplan, "The Coming Anarchy," *Atlantic Monthly,* February 1994.

42. An early assertion of this argument was made by Rensselaer W. Lee III in *The White Labyrinth* (New Brunswick, N.J.: Transaction, 1990), 139. Another, by an eminent Peruvian jurist, is Luis Bustamente Belaunde, "Corrupción y discomposición del estado," in *Pasta básica de cocaina, abuso de drogas,* ed. Federico R. León and Ramiro Castro de la Mata (Lima, Peru: Centro de Información y Educación para la Prevención de Abuso de Drogas, 1990), 301–21. For a more recent and thorough discussion of this issue, see Jordan, *Drug Politics.*

43. V. I. Lenin, "Tasks of the Russian Social-Democrats," in *The Lenin Anthology,* ed. Robert C. Tucker (New York: W. W. Norton, 1975), 3–7. Also see the introduction to the present volume.

44. Author Interviews. Also see the discussion of the rhizomatic command system in Rupert Smith, *The Utility of Force: The Art of War in the Modern World* (New York: Alfred A. Knopf, 2007), 332–34.

45. Author Interviews. A good example of this kind of thinking and action is found in Anthony Vinci, "The Strategic Use of Fear by the Lord's Resistance Army," *Small Wars and Insurgencies* 16 (December 2005): 360–81.

46. Porch, "Uribe's Second Mandate"; and International Crisis Group, *Colombia's New Armed Groups,* 5.

47. See previous note. Many additional citations can be used here, including Spencer, *Colombia's Paramilitaries;* Mayer Nudell, "Ex-paramilitaries Form Crime Gangs in Colombia," *Washington Post,* July 31, 2006; Diana Cariboni, "New Breed of Paramilitaries Infiltrate Urban 'Refuges,'" Inter-Press Service, June 26, 2006; Caleb Harris, "Paramilitaries Reemerge in Pockets of Colombia," *Christian Science Monitor,* March 12, 2007; "Colombia: NDI Analysis Finds Parties Lack Credibility, Stability," November 22, 2005, available at http://FBIS_LAP_2005//2004003; "Pacto con el diablo," *Semana,* February 18, 2008; "The Truth about Triple-A," National Security Archive, February 18, 2008; "Paramilitaries as Proxies," National Security Archive, February 18, 2008; and "Unraveling the Paramilitary Web," National Security Archive, February 18, 2008 (the last three are available at www.gwu.edu/nsarchiv/NSAEBB/NSAEBB223/index.htm).

48. This pattern is well known in northern Mexico, where the drug cartels and hired gangs are collaborating to control specified routes for drugs and other

illegal commerce moving into the United States. Also see Max G. Manwaring, *A Contemporary Challenge to State Sovereignty: Gangs and Other Illicit Transnational Criminal Organizations in Central America, El Salvador, Mexico, Jamaica, and Brazil* (Carlisle Barracks, Penn.: Strategic Studies Institute, 2007).

49. Diana Cariboni, "New Breed of Paramilitaries Infiltrate Urban 'Refuges,'" Inter-Press Service, June 26, 2006; Juan Forero, "Colombian Paramilitaries Adjust Attack Strategies," *New York Times*, January 22, 2001; Caleb Harris, "Paramilitaries Reemerge in Pockets of Colombia," *Christian Science Monitor*, March 12, 2007; Joshua Goodman, "Report: New Criminal Gangs in Colombia," AP News, August 16, 2007; Mayer Nudell, "Ex-paramilitaries Form Crime Gangs in Colombia," *Washington Post*, July 31, 2006; and International Crisis Group, *Colombia's New Armed Groups*.

50. See previous note.

51. International Crisis Group, *Colombia's New Armed Groups*, 2007.

52. Ibid.; and Author Interviews. Also see Ana Maria Bejarano and Eduardo Pizarro, "The Crisis of Democracy in Colombia: From 'Restricted' Democracy to 'Besieged' Democracy," unpublished manuscript in the author's possession, 2001; and Bejarano and Pizarro, "Colombia: A Failing State?" *ReVista: Harvard Review of Latin America* (Spring 2003): 1–6.

53. See previous note.

54. Jordan, *Drug Politics*, 158–70 and 193–94.

55. Author Interviews; Inter-American Development Bank, *Annual Report 1999* (Washington, D.C.: Inter-American Development Bank, 2000), 141; and data taken from Mauricio Rubio, "La justicia en una sociedad violenta," in *Reconocer la guerra para construir la paz*, ed. Maria Victoria Llorente and Malcom Deas (Bogota: Ediciones Uniandes CERED Editorial Norma, 1999), 215.

56. A recent example is Colombia's extradition of Carlos Maria Jimenez, one of the country's most feared paramilitary leaders, to the United States on May 7, 2008, to face drug trafficking charges. See "Colombian Warlord Pleads Not Guilty to Drug Trafficking," CNN News, May 7, 2008. Also see Frank Bajak, "Colombia Extradites 14 Jailed Warlords to US," AP Online, May 13, 2008.

57. Jordan, *Drug Politics*, 161.

58. Ibid.; and Author Interviews.

59. Daniel C. Esty, Jack Goldstone, Ted Robert Gurr, Barbara Harff, and Pamela T. Surko, "The State Failure Project: Early Warning Research for U.S. Foreign Policy Planning," in *Preventive Measures: Building Risk Assessment and Crisis Early Warning Systems*, ed. John L. Davies and Ted Robert Gurr (New York: Rowman and Littlefield, 1998), 27–38.

60. Chester A. Crocker, "Engaging Failed States," *Foreign Affairs* (September/October 2003): 32–44; Stephen D. Krasner and Carlos Pascual, "Addressing State Failure," *Foreign Affairs* (July/August 2005): 153–63.

61. Phil Williams, *From the New Middle Ages to a New Dark Age: The Decline of the State and U.S. Strategy* (Carlisle Barracks, Penn.: Strategic Studies Institute, 2008); and John Rapley, "The New Middle Ages," *Foreign Affairs* (May/June 2006): 93–103.

62. See previous note. Also see Author Interviews; Ivelaw L. Griffith, *Drugs and Security in the Caribbean: Sovereignty under Siege* (University Park: Pennsylvania State University Press, 1997); Rensselaer, *White Labyrinth;* and Belaunde, "Corrupción y discomposición."

63. See previous note.

64. Ambassador Myles R. Frechette, *In Search of the Endgame: A Long-Term Multilateral Strategy for Colombia* (Miami, Fla.: Dante B. Fascell North-South Center at the University of Miami, February 2003).

65. Ambassador Myles R. Frechette, "Colombia and the United States—The Partnership: But What Is the Endgame?" (Carlisle Barracks, Penn.: Strategic Studies Institute, 2006).

66. See the introduction to the present volume.

67. Author Interviews. Also see Max Manwaring, "U.S. Too Narrowly Focused on Drug War in Colombia," *Miami Herald,* August 15, 2001; and Ambassador Myles Frechette, "U.S. and Latin American Realities and Challenges," keynote address at "Forum on the U.S. and Latin America: Toward a New Relationship," University of Central Florida, Orlando, February 27, 2008.

68. "After Sureshot," *Economist,* May 31, 2008.

69. Sun Tzu, *The Art of War,* trans. Samuel B. Griffith (London: Oxford University Press, 1971), 73.

CHAPTER 4. HUGO CHAVEZ'S USE OF POPULAR MILITIAS AND OTHER INSTRUMENTS OF POWER

1. President Chavez used this language in a charge to the National Armed Forces (FAN) to develop a doctrine for fourth-generation war. It was made before an audience gathered in the Military Academy auditorium for the "1st Military Forum on Fourth Generation War and Asymmetric War" in Caracas, Venezuela, and was reported in *El Universal* on April 8, 2005. Additionally, in January 2005, General Melvin Lopez Hidalgo, secretary of the Venezuelan Defense Council, stated publicly that Venezuela was changing its security doctrine to better confront "la amenaza permanente de los Estados Unidos" (the permanent threat of the United States). Reported in *Panorama,* April 27, 2005.

2. Jean Jacques Rousseau wrote, "For whoever refuses to obey the general will and is unwilling to comply with the body politic, there is no other recourse than to force him to be free." See note 48, chapter 2. Also see J. L. Talmon, *The Origins of Totalitarian Democracy* (New York: Praeger, 1968).

3. Andrés Benavente Urbina and Julio Alberto Cirino, *La democracia defraudada* (Buenos Aires: Grito Sagrado, 2005); and Arturo Contreras Polgatti, *Conflicto y guerra en la post modernidad* (Santiago, Chile: Mago Editores, 2004). Also see note 1, this chapter.

4. See previous note.

5. Col. Thomas X. Hammes (USMC, ret.), "Fourth Generation Warfare," *Armed Forces Journal* (November 2004): 40–44.

6. Hubert Herring, *A History of Latin America* (New York: Alfred A. Knopf, 1972), 513–14; also see Winfield J. Burggraff, *The Venezuelan Armed Forces in Politics, 1935–1959* (Columbia: University of Missouri Press, 1972); and Frank Tannenbaum, *Ten Keys to Latin America* (New York: Alfred A. Knopf, 1962), 153–56.

7. See previous note.

8. See note 6, this chapter.

9. Vladimir Torres, *The Impact of "Populism" on Social, Political, and Economic Development in the Hemisphere*, FOCAL Policy Paper (Ottawa, Canada: FOCAL, 2006), 4.

10. Francisco Rojas Aravena, *El crimen organizado internacional: Una grave amenaza a la democracia en America Latina y el Caribe* (San Jose, Costa Rica: FLACSO, 2006); and Aravena, "Nuevo contexto de seguridad internacional: Nuevos desafios, nuevas opportunidades," in Aravena, ed., *La seguridad en America Latina pos 11 de Septiembre* (Santiago, Chile: FLACSO, 2003), 23–43. Also see "Democracy's Ten-Year Rut" (the Latinobarometro Poll), *Economist*, October 31, 2005.

11. See previous note. Also see Steve Ropp, *The Strategic Implications of the Rise of Populism in Europe and South America* (Carlisle Barracks, Penn.: Strategic Studies Institute, 2005).

12. The term "neopopulism" was coined to differentiate the contemporary populists from the traditional populists, such as Juan Peron and Getulio Vargas, and as a way of avoiding the left-right dichotomy. Neopopulism also goes further than traditional populism: whereas traditional populism was simply antiestablishment, neopopulism brings the entire policy into question and is thus antisystem. Nevertheless, neopopulism more often than not is portrayed as the antithesis of traditional politics (representative democracy). See Thomas Legler, *Bridging Divides, Breaking Impasses: Civil Society in the Promotion and Protection of Democracy in the Americas*, FOCAL Policy Paper (Ottawa: FOCAL, 2006).

13. Torres, *Impact of "Populism"*; and Ropp, *Strategic Implications*.

14. See previous note.

15. Jean Jacques Rousseau, *The Social Contract*, trans. G.D.H. Cole (1762; Chicago: Encyclopedia Britannica, 1952); John Locke, *Of Civil Government: Second Treatise of Civil Government* (1689; New York: Gateway, n.d.); Alexis de Tocqueville, *Democracy in America*, ed. J. Mayer and Max Lerner (New York: Harper

and Row, 1996), 213–26; and Jacques Maritain, *Man and the State* (Chicago: University of Chicago Press, 1951), 12–19.

16. Thus, some states became totalitarian democracies even before Georg Hegel began to write on the totalitarian state. See Maritain, *Man and the State,* 13–27 and 192.

17. For excellent discussions of general Latin American and specific Venezuelan corporate traditions, see Howard J. Wiarda, ed., *Authoritarianism and Corporatism in Latin America* (Gainesville: University Press of Florida, 2004); David J. Meyers, "Venezuela's *Punto Fijo* Party System," in Wiarda, *Authoritarianism and Corporatism,* 141–72; and John V. Lombardi, *Venezuela: The Search for Order, the Dream of Progress* (Oxford: Oxford University Press, 1982).

18. Rousseau, *Social Contract;* Wiarda, *Authoritarianism and Corporatism;* Steve Ellner, "Revolutionary and Non-revolutionary Paths of Radical Populism: Directions of the Chavez Movement in Venezuela," *Science and Society* (April 2005): 160–90; and Urbina and Cirino, *La democracia defraudada.*

19. Torres, *Impact of "Populism";* and Ropp, *Strategic Implications.* Also see note 17, this chapter.

20. Carlos Gueron, "Introduction," in *Venezuela in the Wake of Radical Reform,* ed. Joseph S. Tulchin (Boulder, Colo.: Lynne Rienner Publishers, 1993), 1–3.

21. Filipe Aguero and Jeffrey Stark, *Fault Lines of Democracy in Post-transition Latin America* (Miami, Fla.: North-South Center Press, 1998), 103–104, 109, 216.

22. "Special Report," *Economist,* October 27, 2005.

23. "Special Report: Hugo Chavez's Venezuela," *Economist,* May 14, 2005, pp. 23–24; Martin Edward "Mick" Anderson, "Country Report—Venezuela," *Countries at the Crossroads 2006* (Washington, D.C.: Freedom House, 2006), 591–610; and Carlos Basombrío Iglesias, "Venezuela: Politics in the Military, the Military in Politics," in Iglesias, "The Military and Politics in the Andean Region," *Inter-American Dialogue* (April 2006): 6–8; "The Chavez Machine Rolls On," *Economist,* December 2, 2006, pp. 41–42; Michael Shifter, "In Search of Hugo Chavez," *Foreign Affairs* (May/June 2006): 46; "Chavez Victorious," *Economist,* December 9, 2006; Michael Shifter, *Hugo Chavez: A Test for U.S. Policy* (Washington, D.C.: Inter-American Dialogue, 2007); and Juan Forero, "Venezuela Lets Councils Bloom," *Washington Post,* May 17, 2007.

24. See previous note; also see Author Interviews, note 2, chapter 2.

25. See notes 23 and 24, this chapter. Also see Stephen Johnson, "South America's Mad-TV: Hugo Chavez Makes Broadcasting a Battleground," *Heritage Foundation Policy Research and Analysis,* August 10, 2005; Ellner, "Revolutionary and Non-revolutionary Paths"; "New Regional Voice," Foreign Broadcast Information Service (FBIS), April 22, 2005; "Expanded Telesur News Coverage Furthers Anti-US Line," FBIS, December 22, 2005; "Perspective Audience," FBIS, August 5, 2006; and "Telesur's Deal with Al-Jazirah," FBIS, February 27, 2006.

26. See note 1, this chapter; and Norberto Ceresole, *Caudillo, Ejército, Pueblo* (Caracas: Analítica Editora, 1999). Also reported in *El Universal,* January 5, 2005; *La Voz,* April 3, 2005; and *El Universal,* April 8, 2005.

27. See previous note. Also see notes 22 and 23, this chapter.

28. Neopopulism is defined as antisystem, and populism is defined as anti-democracy. See Torres, *Impact of "Populism."*

29. See various essays by V. I. Lenin in *The Lenin Anthology,* ed. Robert C. Tucker (New York: W. W. Norton, 1975): "The Tasks of Russian Social-Democrats," 3–11; "Socialism and War," 183–95; "April Thesis," 295–300; "The State and Revolution," 311–98; "On Revolutionary Violence and Terror," 423–32; "Great Beginning," 478; "Report on War and Peace," 545; and "Tasks of the Youth Leagues," 661–74. Also, evidence of President Chavez's expanding horizons may be seen in numerous different activities. For example, see Fernando Baez, "On the Road with Bush and Chavez," *New York Times,* March 11, 2007; "Iran, Venezuela to Set Up HQ for Joint Cooperation," Iran Mania News, April 14, 2007; Steven Dudley, "Chavez in Search of Leverage," *Miami Herald,* April 28, 2007, p. 9A; Christopher Toothaker, "Venezuela Weapons Worry US, Colombia," Associated Press, May 16, 2008; and Simon Romero, "Venezuela," *New York Times,* February 24, 2007. Also see Max G. Manwaring, *Latin America's New Security Reality: Irregular Asymmetric Conflict and Hugo Chavez* (Carlisle Barracks, Penn.: Strategic Studies Institute, 2007), 32–36.

30. Abraham Guillen, *Philosophy of the Urban Guerrilla: The Revolutionary Writings of Abraham Guillen,* trans. and ed. Donald C. Hodges (New York: William Morrow, 1973), 231, 249, 253, 283.

31. Ibid., 230–49, 283, 299.

32. Ibid., 232, 251.

33. Ibid., 233, 279.

34. Ibid.

35. See note 1, this chapter.

36. "Discurso del General en Jefe Gustavo Reyes Rangel Briceño, on Assuming the Post of Ministro de Poder Popular para la Defensa," July 18, 2007; hereafter cited as Public Address of General Briceño.

37. Ibid.; also see note 13, this chapter.

38. Public Address of General Briceño.

39. Thomas X. Hammes, *The Sling and the Stone: On War in the 21st Century* (St. Paul, Minn.: Zenith Press, 2006). Also see SWORD Papers; Author Interviews.

40. See note 29, this chapter. Also, evidence of Venezuelan agitator activities may be seen in Oscar Castella and Nelly Luna, "Acusan de terrorismo a 24 vinculados con chavismo," March 14, 2008, www.hacer.org/current/Peru/02.php; Jose de Cordoba and Jay Solomon, "Chavez Aided Colombia Rebels, Captured Computer Files Show," *Wall Street Journal,* May 9, 2008; Juan Forero, "Venezuela Offered Aid to Colombian Rebels," *Washington Post,* May 15, 2008; and Simon

Romero, "Files Tying Venezuela to Rebels Not Altered, Report Says," *New York Times*, May 16, 2008.

41. See previous note.

42. See notes 1 and 23, this chapter; also see Qiao Liang and Wang Xiangsui, *Unrestricted Warfare* (Beijing: PLA Literature and Arts Publishing House, 1999).

43. See previous note.

44. Steven D. Krasner and Carlos Pascual, "Addressing State Failure," *Foreign Affairs* (July / August 2005): 153–55.

45. Ibid.

46. John T. Fishel and Max G. Manwaring, *Uncomfortable Wars Revisited* (Norman: University of Oklahoma Press, 2006); and Max G. Manwaring, *Insurgency, Terrorism, and Crime: Shadows from the Past and Portents for the Future* (Norman: University of Oklahoma Press, 2008).

47. Author Interviews.

48. Ibid.

49. Ibid.

50. This argument is strengthened as a result of a recent Colombian incursion into the sovereign territory of Ecuador. See Simon Romero, "Crisis at Colombia Border Spills into Diplomatic Realm," *New York Times*, March 4, 2008; and Simon Romero and James C. McKinley, Jr., "Crisis over Colombian Raid Ends in Handshakes," *New York Times*, March 8, 2008.

51. Rupert Smith, *The Utility of Force: The Art of War in the Modern World* (New York: Alfred A. Knopf, 2007), 3.

CHAPTER 5. DEFENSIVE JIHAD IN WESTERN EUROPE

1. See, as examples, Frank N. Trager and Philip S. Kronenberg, eds., *National Security and American Society* (Lawrence: University Press of Kansas, 1973); Sam C. Sarkesian, *U.S. National Security: Policymakers, Processes, and Politics* (Boulder, Colo.: Lynne Riener Publishers, 1989); and Amos A. Jordan, William J. Taylor, Jr., and Michael J. Mazarr, *American National Security*, 5th ed. (Baltimore, Md.: Johns Hopkins University Press, 1999). For a notable exception to this position, see Kimbra L. Fishel, "Challenging the Hegemon: Al Qaeda's Elevation of Asymmetric Insurgent Warfare onto the Global Arena," in *Networks, Terrorism and Global Insurgency*, ed. Robert J. Bunker (London: Routledge, 2005), 115–28.

2. See previous note, especially Fishel, "Challenging the Hegemon." Also see Osama Bin Laden, "A Letter to America," *Guardian*, November 24, 2002.

3. See previous note.

4. For primary source material on statements made by Al Qaeda, see http://usinfo.state.gov/topical/pol/terror/99129502.html. Also see Raymond Ibrahim, *The Al Qaeda Reader* (New York: Broadway Books, 2007); Gustavo de

Aristigui, *La Yihad en España: La obsession por reconquistar Al-Andalus*, 5th ed. (Madrid: La Esfera de los Libros, 2006). Also see Author Interviews in Madrid, Spain, July 5–8, 2006, and September 14–21, 2008, hereafter cited as Author Interviews, Spain.

5. Marc Sageman, *Leaderless Jihad: Terror Networks in the 21st Century* (Philadelphia: University of Pennsylvania Press, 2007).

6. Ibid. Also see Rupert Smith, *The Utility of Force: The Art of War in the Modern World* (New York: Alfred A. Knopf, 2007), 332–34; Author Interviews, Spain.

7. See previous note. Also, "compelling one to accede to one's will" is a classic definition of war. See Carl von Clausewitz, *On War*, ed. and trans. Michael Howard and Peter Paret (Princeton, N.J.: Princeton University Press, 1976), 75.

8. Fishel, "Challenging the Hegemon"; and Author Interviews, Spain.

9. V. I. Lenin, "Tasks of Russian Social-Democrats," in *The Lenin Anthology*, ed. Robert C. Tucker (New York: W. W. Norton, 1975), 8.

10. Al Qaeda's doctrine and strategy, as these might be applied by diverse Islamic groups, are not well understood; many analysts disagree about what the organization is, what the war-fighting doctrine might be, or what any kind of response ought to be.

11. Lenin, "The Revolutionary Party and Its Tactics," 8; and Author Interviews, Spain. Also see Walter Laqueur, "Postmodern Terrorism," *Foreign Affairs* (September/October 1996): 24–36; Qiao Liang and Wang Xiangsui, *Unrestricted Warfare* (Beijing: PLA Literature and Arts Publishing House, 1999); Frank Kitson, *Warfare as a Whole* (London: Faber and Faber, 1987); and Max G. Manwaring and John T. Fishel, "Insurgency and Counterinsurgency: Toward a New Analytical Approach," *Small Wars and Insurgencies* 3, no. 3 (Winter 1992): 272–310 (hereafter cited as SWORD Papers).

12. Daniel C. Esty, Jack Goldstone, Ted Robert Gurr, Barbara Harff, Pamela T. Surko, Alan N. Unger, and Robert S. Chen, "The State Failure Project: Early Warning Research for U.S. Foreign Policy Planning," in *Preventive Measures: Building Risk Assessment and Crisis Early Warning Systems*, ed. John L. Davies and Ted Robert Gurr (New York: Rowman and Littlefield, 1998), 27–38; Thomas F. Homer-Dixon, "On the Threshold: Environmental Changes as Causes of Acute Conflict," *International Security* (Fall 1991): 76–116; and Thomas F. Homer-Dixon, *Environment, Scarcity, and Violence* (Princeton, N.J.: Princeton University Press, 1999), 133–68. Also see Qiao and Wang, *Unrestricted Warfare*; and SWORD Papers.

13. Robert M. Cassidy, "Feeding Bread to Luddites: The Radical Fundamentalist Islamic Revolution in Guerrilla Warfare," *Small Wars and Insurgencies* (December 2005): 348; Peter L. Bergen, *Holy War, Inc.: Inside the Secret World of Osama bin Laden* (New York: Free Press, 2001); Paul Rich, "Al Qaeda and the Radical Islamic Challenge to Western Strategy," *Small Wars and Insurgencies* (Spring 2003): 45–46; and Thomas A. Marks, "Ideology of Insurgency: New

Ethnic Focus or Old Cold War Distortions?" *Small Wars and Insurgencies* (Spring 2004): 122–25. Also see Author Interviews, Spain.

14. See previous note. Also see Rohan Gunaretna, *Inside the al-Qai'da Global Network of Terror* (London: Hurst, 2002), 89.

15. Rich, "Al Qaeda," 47.

16. This document is entitled "Pledge of Death in God's Path." For primary source material on statements made by Al Qaeda, see note 4, this chapter. Also see Stephen Ulph, "Mujahideen Pledge Allegiance on the Web," *Terrorism Focus* 2, no. 22 (November 29, 2005).

17. See essays by V. I. Lenin in *The Lenin Anthology:* "Report on War and Peace," 545; and "Symptoms of a Revolutionary Situation," 275–76. Also see Mao Tse-Tung, *On Guerrilla Warfare,* edited by Samuel B. Griffith (1937 [1961]; reprint, Champaign: University of Illinois Press, 2000).

18. Fishel, "Challenging the Hegemon," 121. Also see Peter Bergen, "The Dense Web of Al Qaeda," *Washington Post,* December 25, 2003, p. A29. Bergen describes Al Qaeda and its supporters as a structure of concentric rings in which different kinds of operations may be conducted vertically and horizontally by different parts of different rings.

19. Michael Scheuer, "Al Qaeda's New Generation: Less Visible and More Lethal," *Terrorism Focus* 2, no. 18 (October 3, 2005); Thomas X. Hammes, *The Sling and the Stone: On War in the 21st Century* (St. Paul, Minn.: Zenith Press, 2006), 135.

20. See previous note; also see Gunaretna, *Inside the al-Qai'da Global Network,* 54.

21. See previous note; also see Cassidy, "Feeding Bread to Luddites," 338–49; Fishel, "Challenging the Hegemon," 121–25; Hammes, *Sling and the Stone,* 350; and Chris Heffelfinger, "Al Qaeda's Evolving Strategy Five Years after September 11," *Terrorism Focus* 3, no. 35 (September 12, 2006).

22. Scheuer, "Al Qaeda's New Generation."

23. Ibid.; also see Michael Moss and Souad Mekhennet, "Rising Leader for Next Phase of Al Qaeda's War," *New York Times,* April 4, 2008.

24. See previous note; also see Michael Scheuer, "Is Global Jihad a Fading Phenomenon?" *Terrorism Focus* 5, no. 13 (April 1, 2008).

25. Author Interviews, Spain.

26. See note 4, this chapter, regarding primary source material; also see Michael Scheuer, "Osama bin Laden: Taking Stock of the 'Zionist-Crusader War,'" *Terrorism Focus* 3, no. 16 (April 25, 2006).

27. Walter Laqueur, "Postmodern Terrorism," *Foreign Affairs* (September/ October 1996): 24–25.

28. Ibid.; and Michael Scheuer, "Al-Qaeda's Insurgency Doctrine: Aiming for a 'Long War,'" *Terrorism Focus* 3, no. 8 (February 28, 2006).

29. See previous note.

30. See note 28; also see Michael Scheuer, "Al-Zawahiri's September 11 Video Hits Main Themes of Al-Qaeda Doctrine," *Terrorism Focus* 3, no. 36 (September 19, 2006). Ayman al-Zawahiri is the deputy chief of Al Qaeda.

31. See note 4, this chapter.

32. Ibid.; also see Heffelfinger, "Al Qaeda's Evolving Strategy."

33. See previous note; also see Smith, *Utility of Force,* 332–34.

34. See previous note; also see Kathryn Haahr, "Italy's Underground Islamist Network," *Terrorism Monitor* 5, no. 16 (August 16, 2007).

35. See previous note.

36. Ibid.; also see note 4, this chapter.

37. Haahr, "Italy's Underground Islamist Network"; and Javier Jordan and Nicola Horsburg, "Mapping Jihadist Terrorism in Spain," *Studies in Conflict and Terrorism* 28, no. 3 (2005): 174–79.

38. V. I. Lenin, "The Tasks of Russian Social-Democrats," in *The Lenin Anthology,* 4.

39. Ibid., 4–5.

40. Ibid., 6–7. Also see pp. 3–11 and "The State and Revolution" in *The Lenin Anthology,* 324.

41. See previous note.

42. Ibid.

43. Author Interviews, Spain. Also see Jordan and Horsburg, "Mapping Jihadist Terrorism," 176–77, 187.

44. See previous note.

45. See note 43, this chapter.

46. See essays by V. I. Lenin in *The Lenin Anthology:* "Socialism and War," 183–95; "April Thesis," 295–300; "The State and Revolution," 311–98; "On Revolutionary Violence and Terror," 423–32; and "The Tasks of the Youth Leagues," 661–64.

47. Author Interviews, Spain.

48. A copy of the proceedings and charges against the twenty-nine accused can be found at http://www.elpais.es/static/especiales/2006/auto11M/elpais_auto.html?sumpag1. Also see "Madrid Bombing Suspect Denies Guilt," *USA Today,* May 15, 2007.

49. See previous note; also see Victoria Burnett, "Spain Arrests 16 North Africans Accused of Recruiting Militants," *New York Times,* May 29, 2007.

50. Author Interviews, Spain. Also see "The Madrid Train Bombings," in Lorenzo Vidino, *Al Qaeda in Europe* (Amherst, N.Y.: Prometheus Books, 2006), 291–335. For details regarding first-, second-, and third-generation gangs in the Americas, see Max G. Manwaring, *Street Gangs: The New Urban Insurgency* (Carlisle Barracks, Penn.: Strategic Studies Institute, 2005).

51. See notes 48, 49, and 50, this chapter.

52. Ibid.

53. Investigations in the United Kingdom regarding the bombings in London in 2005 yielded the information that there was a close relationship between that attack and the one in Madrid a year earlier—in particular, that Al Qaeda had been more involved in the Madrid bombings than had been originally reported by Spanish authorities. See House of Commons, "Report of the Official Account of the Bombings in London on 7th July 2005," May 2006, www.officialdocuments .co.uk/hc0506/hc10/1087/1087.asp.59. Also see Ludo Block, "Developing a New Counter-Terrorism Strategy in Europe," *Terrorism Monitor* 4, no. 21 (November 21, 2006); and "From Afghanistan to Iraq through Europe," in Vidino, *Al Qaeda in Europe,* 233–62. The Dutch have also looked carefully into jihadi activities in Europe. See Edwin Baker, *Jihadi Terrorists in Europe* (The Hague: Netherlands Institute of International Relations, 2006); and Ministry of the Interior and Kingdom Relations, *Violent Jihad in the Netherlands: Current Trends in the Islamist Terrorist Threat* (The Hague: Ministry of the Interior and Kingdom Relations, n.d.). Also see Kathryn Haahr, "GSPC in Italy: The Forward Base of Jihad in Europe," *Terrorism Monitor* 4, no. 3 (February 9, 2006).

54. "Britain's National Security Plans to Be Overhauled," *International Herald Tribune,* March 19, 2008; "Terror Trial Exposes Network of Terror Camps in Picturesque Rural England," *International Herald Tribune,* February 27, 2008; "Intelligence Chief Says 'Several Hundred' Extremists Living in Germany," *International Herald Tribune,* March 24, 2008; Thomas Renard, "German Intelligence Describes a 'New Quality' in Jihadi Threats," *Terrorism Focus* 5, no. 7 (February 20, 2008); Javier Jordan and Robert Wesley, "After 3/11: The Evolution of Jihadist Networks in Spain," *Terrorism Monitor* 4, no. 1 (January 12, 2006); "Terrorist Threat to UK—MI5 Chief's Full Speech," *Times Online,* November 11, 2006; and James Brandon, "The Pakistan Connection to the United Kingdom's Jihad Network," *Terrorism Monitor* 6, no. 4 (February 22, 2008).

55. Aristigui, *La Yihad en España,* 85, 131–32, 136–42, and 187; also see Author Interviews, Spain.

56. See "Terrorism: Al-Qaeda Leader Threatens France and Spain," Adnkronos News, September 22, 2008, www.adnkronos.com/IGN/ext/printNews Aki.php?lang=English.

57. Author Interviews, Spain. Also see Jordan and Wesley, "After 3/11." The term "3/11," in Spain, refers to the March attacks in Madrid. See Burnett, "Spain Arrests 16 North Africans"; Kathryn Haahr, "Catalonia: Europe's New Center of Global Jihad," *Terrorism Monitor* 5, no. 11 (June 7, 2007).

58. Author Interviews, Spain.

59. Ibid.; also see Steve Kingstone, "Spain's Radical Plan for Migrants," BBC News, September 3, 2008.

60. "Terrorist Threat to UK—MI5 Chief's Full Speech," *Times Online,* November 11, 2006.

61. "Britain's National Security Plans to Be Overhauled," *International Herald Tribune,* March 19, 2008.

62. Hayder Mill, "Tangled Webs: Terrorist and Organized Crime Groups," *Terrorism Monitor* 4, no. 1 (January 13, 2006); Kathryn Haahr, "GSPC Joins Al Qaeda and France Becomes Top Enemy," *Terrorism Focus* 3, no. 37 (September 26, 2006); and "Paris Court Convicts 7 Men Linked to Iraq Recruitment Cell," *International Herald Tribune,* May 14, 2008.

63. Author Interviews, Spain. Also see Haahr, "GSPC in Italy"; and Haahr, "Italy's Underground Islamist Network."

64. "Italian Troops to Patrol Cities," BBC News, August 1, 2008. Also see Christian Fraser, "Italy Crackdown on Foreign Crime," BBC News, August 1, 2008.

65. Aristigui, *La Yihad en España;* and Author Interviews, Spain.

66. Jane Barrett, "Court Finds 21 Guilty of Madrid Train Bombings," Reuters, May 27, 2008. Also see Jordan and Horsburg, "Mapping Jihadist Terrorism," 174–79.

67. See previous note; also see Author Interviews, Spain.

68. Michael Scheuer, "Al Qaeda Doctrine for International Political Warfare," *Terrorism Focus* 3, no. 42 (November 1, 2006); Scheuer, "Al Qaeda's Insurgency Doctrine"; and Renard, "German Intelligence."

69. Author Interviews, Spain.

70. Ibid.; also see Scheuer, "Al Qaeda Doctrine."

71. Craig Whitlock, "Al Qaeda Masters Terrorism on the Cheap," *Washington Post,* September 2, 2008.

72. Fishel, "Challenging the Hegemon," 115–28.

73. Clausewitz, *On War,* 596.

74. Gunaretna, *Inside the al-Qai'da Global Network,* 54, 89; Bergen, *Holy War, Inc.*

75. Giandominico Picco, "The Challenge of Strategic Terrorism," *Terrorism and Political Violence* 17 (2005): 13.

76. Ibid.

77. Jordan, Taylor, and Mazarr, *American National Security,* 3; Trager and Kronenberg, *National Security and American Society;* Lars Schoultz, *National Security and United States Policy toward Latin America* (Princeton, N.J.: Princeton University Press, 1987), 143–330.

78. See previous note.

79. See note 77, this chapter.

80. Lenin, "On Revolutionary Violence and Terror," 425.

81. Hammes, *Sling and the Stone.*

82. Lenin, "Socialism and War," 188.

83. Ibid.

84. Smith, *Utility of Force,* 375–77.

85. For early discussions of these phenomena, see Samuel Huntington, *The Clash of Civilizations and the Remaking of World Order* (New York: Simon and Schuster, 1996); and Robert D. Kaplan, *The Coming Anarchy* (New York: Random House, 2000). Also see David Easton, *A Framework for Political Analysis* (Englewood Cliffs, N.J.: Prentice-Hall, 1965).

86. Author Interviews, Spain.

87. The idea of wizard's chess is taken from J. K. Rowling, *Harry Potter and the Sorcerer's Stone* (New York: Arthur A. Levine Books, 1997), 282–84.

88. Col. Thomas X. Hammes (USMC, ret.), "Fourth Generation Warfare," *Armed Forces Journal* (November 2004): 40–44.

89. See note 87, this chapter.

90. Lenin, "Report on War and Peace," 549.

CHAPTER 6. THE NEIGHBORS DOWN THE ROAD AND ACROSS THE RIVER

1. Lincoln B. Krause, "The Guerrillas Next Door," *Low Intensity Conflict and Law Enforcement* (Spring 1999): 34–56. Also see José Luis Velasco, *Insurgency, Authoritarianism, and Drug Trafficking in Mexico's Democratization* (New York: Routledge, 2005); Max G. Manwaring, "Sovereignty under Siege: Gangs and Other Criminal Organizations in Central America and Mexico," in Manwaring, *Insurgency, Terrorism, and Crime* (Norman: University of Oklahoma Press, 2008), 104–28; Charles Gibson, *Spain in America* (New York: Harper and Row, 1966); and Hubert Herring, *A History of Latin America from the Beginnings to the Present* (New York: Knopf, 1968).

2. See Krause, "Guerrillas Next Door"; Velasco, *Insurgency, Authoritarianism.*

3. See note 1. Also see Mark Stevenson, "Commission Says Central American Mara Gangs Have Taken Root in Mexico," April 4, 2008; Alfredo Corchado and Laurence Iliff, "Ex-rivals Merge to 'Megacartel' Intensifies Brutality in Mexico," *Dallas News*, July 9, 2008; Ioan Grillo, "Behind Mexico's Wave of Beheadings," *Time*, January 22, 2009; Ioan Grillo, "Confessions of a Mexican Narco Foot-Soldier," *Time*, January 22, 2009; Robin Emmott, "Mexico's Gulf Cartel Undaunted by Military Assault," Reuters, January 22, 2009; and Tim Padgett, "The Killers Next Door," *Time*, January 22, 2009.

4. Private armies are not new; they have been operating at one level or another for centuries. John Sullivan cites data to the effect that "[s]everal hundred currently operate in over 100 nations, on six continents, generating over $100 billion in annual revenues." John P. Sullivan, "Terrorism, Crime, and Private Armies," *Low Intensity Conflict and Law Enforcement* (Winter 2002): 239–53.

5. James Rosenau, *Turbulence in World Politics* (Princeton, N.J.: Princeton University Press, 1990). Also, note that Mexico admits to 233 zones of impunity; see

Marc Lacey, "In Drug War, Mexico Fights Cartels and Itself," *New York Times*, March 30, 2009. Also see Peter W. Singer, "Peacekeepers, Inc.," *Policy Review*, no. 119 (June/July 2003).

6. See note 1, this chapter. Also informative was the author interview with the personal representative of the attorney general of Mexico in the United States, Dr. Manuel Suarez-Meir, in Washington, D.C., January 29, 2009.

7. Sullivan, "Terrorism," 244–49.

8. This term comes from the title of Krause's article cited in note 1, this chapter.

9. The methodology is taken from Robert K. Yin, *Case Study Research: Design and Methods*, 2nd ed. (Thousand Oaks, Calif.: Sage Publications, 1994), 1–10, 15, 31–32, 140, and 147.

10. Gibson, *Spain in America*; Herring, *History . . . from the Beginnings to the Present*; Thomas E. Skidmore and Peter H. Smith, *Modern Latin America* (New York: Oxford University Press, 1984); and Frank Tannenbaum, *Ten Keys to Latin America* (New York: Knopf, 1962). Also see George W. Grayson, "Los Zetas: The Ruthless Army Spawned by a Mexican Drug Cartel," Foreign Policy Research Institute, April 30, 2008; George W. Grayson, *Mexico's Struggle with "Drugs and Thugs,"* Foreign Policy Association Headline Series (Washington, D.C.: Foreign Policy Association, 2009); Colleen W. Cook, "Mexico's Drug Cartels," Congressional Research Service Report to Congress, February 25, 2008, Order Code RL34215, hereafter cited as *CRS Report*; Michael Petrou, "Mexico's Civil War," *Maclean's*, December 8, 2008; and Sullivan, "Terrorism," 239–53.

11. Robert E. Scott, *Mexican Government in Transition* (Urbana: University of Illinois Press, 1964); Roger D. Hanson, *The Politics of Mexican Development* (Baltimore, Md.: Johns Hopkins University Press, 1971); Martin C. Needler, *Mexican Politics: The Containment of Conflict* (New York: Dragon, 1982); and Daniel Levy and Gabriel Szekelup, *Mexico: Paradoxes of Stability and Change* (Boulder, Colo.: Westview Press, 1983).

12. See notes 10 and 11, this chapter.

13. Tannenbaum, *Ten Keys to Latin America*.

14. Ibid., and note 11, this chapter.

15. David C. Jordan, *Drug Politics* (Norman: University of Oklahoma Press, 1999), 19, 142–57.

16. Sullivan, "Terrorism."

17. Jordan, *Drug Politics*, 19.

18. Ibid. Also see Mark Stevenson, "Mexican Singer Slain in Hospital while Recovering from Gunshot Wounds," December 4, 2007; Ana Arana, "How the Street Gangs Took Control of Central America," *Foreign Affairs* (May/June 2005): 98–110; and John Sullivan, "Maras Morphing: Revisiting Third Generation Gangs," *Global Crime* (August–November 2006): 488–90.

19. Jordan, *Drug Politics*, 142–57.

20. Sullivan, "Terrorism," 239–53. Also see Brian Jenkins, "Redefining the Enemy: The World Has Changed, but Our Mindset Has Not," *Rand Review* (Spring 2004).

21. Jordan, *Drug Politics*, 193–94.

22. Ibid., 152. Also see Grayson, *Mexico's Struggle*; "Sinaloa Drug Cartel Said to Infiltrate Executive Branch," *Economic News and Analysis on Mexico*, January 23, 2009, www.thefreelibrary.com; Jane Bussey, "Organized Crime Takes Control in Parts of Mexico," McClatchy Washington Bureau, September 20, 2008; and "Reports: Cancun Police Chief Questioned in General's Killing," CNN News, March 17, 2009.

23. Phil Williams, *From the New Middle Ages to a New Dark Age: The Decline of the State and U.S. Strategy* (Carlisle Barracks, Penn.: Strategic Studies Institute, 2008).

24. Sullivan, "Terrorism," 239.

25. Chester A. Crocker, "Engaging Failed States," *Foreign Affairs* (September/October 2003): 32–44; Steven D. Krasner and Carlos Pascual, "Addressing State Failure," *Foreign Affairs* (July/August 2005): 153–55.

26. *CRS Report*. Also see "Central America and Mexico Gang Assessment," U.S. Agency for International Development, Bureau for Latin America and Caribbean Affairs, April 2006, hereafter cited as AID Paper.

27. Rensselaer W. Lee III, *The White Labyrinth* (New Brunswick, N.J.: Transaction, 1990). Also see Max G. Manwaring, *Street Gangs: The New Urban Insurgency* (Carlisle Barracks, Penn.: Strategic Studies Institute, 2005), 24.

28. See note 26, this chapter. Also see Mark Stevenson, "Mexico: Drug Gangs Using Terror Tactics," *Miami Herald,* May 17, 2007.

29. See previous note. Also see Kevin G. Hall, "Mexican Drug War Getting Bloodier," *Miami Herald,* March 21, 2007; and AID Paper.

30. See note 28, this chapter. Also see statement of the assistant director of the Criminal Investigation Division, Federal Bureau of Investigation, Chris Swecker, before the U.S. House of Representatives Committee on Judiciary, November 17, 2005, www.fbi.gov/congress05/swecker111705.html; "President Felipe Calderon Launches Ambitious Campaign against Drug cartels," *Economic News and Analysis on Mexico*, January 24, 2007; and Oscar Becerra, "A to Z of Crime: Mexico's Zetas Expand Operations," *Jane's Intelligence Review,* January 30, 2009.

31. See note 29, this chapter. Also see Grayson, "Mexico and the Drug Cartels"; and notes 3, 10, 22, and 24, this chapter.

32. See note 30, this chapter. Also see Williams, *From the New Middle Ages*.

33. Steven Metz and Raymond Millen, *Future Wars/Future Battlespace* (Carlisle Barracks, Penn.: Strategic Studies Institute, 2003), ix, 15–17.

34. Paul E. Smith, *On Political War* (Washington, D.C.: National Defense University Press, 1989), 3. Also see Carl von Clausewitz, *On War,* trans. and ed.

Michael Howard and Peter Paret (New Brunswick, N.J.: Rutgers University Press, 1976), 75.

35. For an interesting discussion of this issue, see Qiao Liang and Wang Xiangsui, *Unrestricted Warfare* (Beijing: PLA Literature and Arts Publishing House, 1999), 109.

36. Ibid. Also see Jorge Verstrynge Rojas, *La guerra asimetrica y el Islam revolucionario* (Madrid: El Viejo Topo, 2005).

37. Frank Kitson, *Warfare as a Whole* (London: Faber and Faber, 1987). Also see Rupert Smith, *The Utility of Force: The Art of War in the Modern World* (New York: Alfred A. Knopf, 2007).

38. Carlos Marighella, *The Manual of the Urban Guerrilla* (Chapel Hill, N.C.: Documentary Publications, 1985), 84.

39. Ibid.

40. *CRS Report*, 4–5. Also see "Mexico's Civil War," *Maclean's*, December 8, 2008, 24–25; Grayson, "Los Zetas"; and Grayson, *Mexico's Struggles*.

41. Subdued debate regarding whether Mexico was or is moving toward failed state status was enlivened both in Mexico and in the United States by General (Retired) Barry R. McCaffrey's presentation to Roger Rufe, entitled "A Strategic and Operational Assessment of Drugs and Crime in Mexico," dated March 16, 2009. See http://www.gather.com/viewArticle.action?article Id=281474977632267. Also note José Velasco's statement that Mexico's democracy is "partial, weak, contradictory, and superficial"; Velasco, *Insurgency*, 2.

42. Grayson, "Los Zetas."

43. *CRS Report*, 11. Also see Martin Morita, "Desaten carteles guerra en el sureste," *Reforma*, July 27, 2006.

44. Marighella, *Manual of the Urban Guerrilla*. Also see Grayson, "Los Zetas." In response to Gulf Cartel initiatives, the rival Sinaloa Cartel has created its own enforcer gangs. The Negros and the Polones are less sophisticated and effective than the Zetas, but they appear to have little problem confronting local police and—of course—unprotected civilians. See Alfredo Corchado, "Cartel's Enforcers Outpower Their Boss," *Dallas Morning News*, June 11, 2007.

45. See note 43, this chapter. Benetez is quoted in the Corchado article in the preceding note.

46. AID Paper.

47. Max G. Manwaring, "La sobenia bajo asedio: Las Pandillas y otras organizaciones criminales en Centroamerica y en Mexico," *Air and Space Power Journal* (2nd trimester 2008): 25–41.

48. Alejanddro Suverza, "Los Zetas, una pasadilla para el cartel de Golfo," *El Universal*, January 12, 2008; Oscar Becerra, "A to Z of Crime: Mexico's Zetas Expand Operations," *Jane's Intelligence Review*, January 30, 2009; Grayson, "Los Zetas"; and Grayson, *Mexico's Struggles*.

49. See previous note.

50. *Economist*, March 7, 2009, pp. 30–33; and Marc Lacey, "With Deadly Persistence, Mexican Drug Cartels Get Their Way," *New York Times*, March 1, 2009, pp. 1, 9.

51. Becerra, "A to Z of Crime," 1–9; and Grayson, "Los Zetas," 2.

52. Williams, *From the New Middle Ages;* and Phil Williams, "Mexican Futures," unpublished monograph, n.d.

53. See note 51, this chapter.

54. John Sullivan and Robert J. Bunker, "Drug Cartels, Street Gangs, and Warlords," in *Nonstate Threats and Future Wars*, ed. Robert J. Bunker (London: Frank Cass, 2003), 45–53.

55. Robert J. Bunker and John Sullivan, "Cartel Evolution: Potentials and Consequences," *Transnational Organized Crime* (Summer 1998): 55–74.

56. Sullivan, "Maras Morphing," 501.

57. Peter Lupsha, "Grey Area Phenomenon: New Threats and Policy Dilemmas," unpublished paper presented at the "High Intensity Crime/Low Intensity Conflict" Conference, Chicago, Illinois, September 27–30, 1992, pp. 22–23.

58. Guy Lawson, "The War Next Door," *Rolling Stone* (November 13, 2008): 74–111.

59. Ibid., 76.

60. Ibid., 108.

61. Mark Stevenson, "Top Mexico Cops Charged with Favoring Drug Cartel," Associated Press, January 24, 2009.

62. Lawson, "War Next Door," 78.

63. Ibid.

64. Ibid., 81.

65. Ibid.

66. Ibid.

67. Ibid.

68. See, as an example, Clausewitz, *On War*, 75.

69. Sun Tzu, *The Art of War*, trans. Samuel B. Griffiths (London: Oxford University Press, 1971), 63.

CHAPTER 7. SOME FINAL THOUGHTS

1. Jorge Verstrynge Rojas, *La guerra periferica y el Islam revolucionario: Origines, reglas, y ética de la guerra asimétrica* (Madrid: El Viejo Topo, 2005), 7.

2. Ibid. Also see Qiao Liang and Wang Xiangsui, *Unrestricted Warfare* (Beijing: PLA Literature and Arts Publishing House, 1999), 129–38; and Rupert Smith, *The Utility of Force: The Art of War in the Modern World* (New York: Alfred A. Knopf, 2007), 3, 5–28.

3. See previous note. Also see Sun Tzu, *The Art of War*, trans. Samuel B. Griffith (London: Oxford University Press, 1963); B. H. Liddell-Hart, *Strategy*, 2nd ed. (New York: Praeger, 1954); John Holloway, *Cambiar el mundo sin tomar al poder: El significado de la revolucion hoy* (Buenos Aires: Universidad Autonoma del Pueblo, 2002); and Thomas X. Hammes, *The Sling and the Stone: On War in the 21st Century* (St. Paul, Minn.: Zenith Press, 2006).

4. See previous note.

5. See note 3, this chapter. For additional examples, see Max G. Manwaring and John T. Fishel, "Insurgency and Counter-Insurgency: Toward a New Analytical Approach," *Small Wars and Insurgencies* (Winter 1992): 272–310. Also see John T. Fishel and Max G. Manwaring, "The SWORD Model of Counterinsurgency: A Summary and Update," *Small Wars Journal* (December 20, 2008).

6. David C. Miller, Jr., "Back to the Future: Structuring Foreign Policy in the Post–Cold War World," in Max G. Manwaring and William J. Olson, eds., *Managing Contemporary Conflict: Pillars of Success* (Boulder, Colo.: Westview Press, 1996), 13–28.

7. Ibid., 3–28.

8. See notes 1–5, this chapter.

9. Carl von Clausewitz, *On War*, trans. Michael Howard and Peter Paret (Princeton, N.J.: Princeton University Press, 1976). Also see Michael Howard, *The Causes of Wars and Other Essays* (Cambridge, Mass.: Harvard University Press, 1983), 103–104, 109.

10. See notes 3, 5, 6, and 9, this chapter.

11. See notes 1, 2, and 3, this chapter. Also see Niccolò Machiavelli, *The Art of War* (New York: Da Capo Press, 1965); and essays by V. I. Lenin in *The Lenin Anthology*, ed. Robert C. Tucker (New York: W. W. Norton, 1975): "The Tasks of Russian Social-Democrats," 3–11; and "What Is to Be Done?" 12–114.

12. Qiao and Wang, *Unrestricted Warfare*, 133, 138, and 145. These authors also remind us, "If too many accidents demonstrate the same phenomenon, can you still calmly view them as accidents? No, at this moment, you have to admit that there is a rule there" (p. 133).

13. For the methodology, see Robert K. Yin, *Case Study Research: Design and Methods*, 2nd ed. (Thousand Oaks, Calif.: Sage Publications, 1994), 31–46.

14. Jacques Maritain, *Man and the State* (Chicago: University of Chicago Press, 1963), 19.

15. Jose Maria Aznar, *Latin America: An Agenda for Freedom*, ed. Miguel Angel Cortes (Madrid: FAES, 2007); and Arturo Contreras Polgatti, *Estrategia: La viejas y las nuevas amenazas* (Santiago, Chile: Mago Editores, 2008).

16. See previous note. Also see, as examples of this discussion, John Locke, *Of Civil Government* (Chicago: Gateway, n.d.); Jean-Jacques Rousseau, *The Social Contract*, trans. Charles Frankel (New York: Hafner Publishing Company, 1951); Leo Strauss and Joseph Cropsey, *History of Political Philosophy*, 2nd ed. (Chicago:

University of Chicago Press, 1972); and J. L. Talmon, *The Origins of Totalitarian Democracy* (New York: Praeger, 1960).

17. Manwaring and Fishel, "Insurgency and Counter-Insurgency."

18. See note 11, this chapter.

19. See note 12, this chapter. Also see Max G. Manwaring and Courtney E. Prisk, "The Umbrella of Legitimacy," in *Gray Area Phenomena: Confronting the New World Disorder*, ed. Max Manwaring (Boulder, Colo.: Westview Press, 1993), 77–91; and Edwin G. Corr and Max G. Manwaring, "The Central Political Challenge in the Global Security Environment: Governance and Legitimacy," in *The Search for Security: A U.S. Grand Strategy for the Twenty-first Century*, ed. Max G. Manwaring, Edwin G. Corr, and Robert H. Dorff (Westport, Conn.: Greenwood, 2003), 46–61.

20. See previous note and notes 1 and 2, this chapter. Also see Thomas A. Marks, "Ideology of Insurgency: New Ethnic Focus or Old Cold War Distortions?" *Small Wars and Insurgencies* (Spring 2004): 107–28; and Marks, "Urban Insurgency," *Small Wars and Insurgencies* (Autumn 2003): 100–157.

21. Sun Tzu, *Art of War*, 88.

22. J. Bowyer Bell, *Dragonwars* (New Brunswick, N.J.: Transaction Publishers, 1999), 417–18.

23. Hugh Thomas, *Armed Truce* (New York: Atheneum, 1987), 549–50.

24. Frank Kitson, *Warfare as a Whole* (London: Faber and Faber, 1987).

25. Colin S. Gray, "Deterrence and the Nature of Strategy," in *Deterrence in the Twenty-first Century*, ed. Max G. Manwaring (London: Frank Cass, 2001), 17–26.

26. Ibid. Also see Edwin G. Corr and Max G. Manwaring, "The Challenge of Preventive Diplomacy and Deterrence in the Global Security Environment," in Manwaring, *Deterrence in the Twenty-first Century*, 124–31.

27. Smith, *Utility of Force.*

28. Qiao and Wang, *Unrestricted Warfare*, 41.

29. Interview with Gen. Anthony Zinni (USMC, ret.), in Washington, D.C., June 1999.

30. See essays by V. I. Lenin in *The Lenin Anthology*: "Tasks of Russian Social-Democrats," 3–11; "The State and Revolution," 324; and "Communism and the New Economic Policy," 533.

31. Qaio and Wang, *Unrestricted Warfare*, 123–57.

32. Ibid. Also see Kitson, *Warfare as a Whole*, 35, 69, 123–24, 154.

33. See previous note.

34. Ibid.; also see Howard, *Causes of Wars*, 109–10.

35. See previous note.

36. Author interviews with Lt. Gen. William G. Carter III (USA, ret.), on November 30, 1998, and March 2, 1999, in Washington, D.C.

37. V. I. Lenin, "The Chief Task of Our Day," in *The Lenin Anthology*, 433–37.

38. Niccolò Machiavelli, *The Art of War* (New York: Da Capo Press, 1965), lxxxviii, 12.

39. Miller, "Back to the Future," 13–28.

40. Eugene V. Rostow, *Toward Managed Peace: The National Security Interests of the United States, 1759 to the Present* (New Haven, Conn.: Yale University Press, 1993), 4.

41. Leslie H. Gelb, "Quelling the Teacup Wars," *Foreign Affairs* (November/December 1994): 5.

42. Miller, "Back to the Future."

43. Albert Camus, *The Rebel* (New York: Alfred A. Knopf, 1956), 302.

44. Sun Tzu, *Art of War*, 63.

45. Qaio and Wang, *Unrestricted Warfare*, 133, 138, 145.

46. V. I. Lenin, "Report on War and Peace," in *The Lenin Anthology*, 549.

AFTERWORD

1. See John T. Fishel and Max G. Manwaring, *Uncomfortable Wars Revisited* (Norman: University of Oklahoma Press, 2006). See especially the foreword, by Edwin G. Corr. The term "Max Factors" was coined by *New York Times* military affairs correspondent Richard Halloran in a 1986 article.

2. Victor Davis Hanson, *Carnage and Culture* (New York: Anchor Books, 2002), 33.

3. Available at http://about.com/library/bl/bl/text_plutarch_caesar_pirates .htm.

4. Ibid.

5. This tale was told to me by two of my students at the U.S. Army Command and General Staff College at Fort Leavenworth, Kansas. One was the officer of the deck on the sub; the other had been a watch officer at Pacific Command (PACOM) and had received the radio call reporting the attack.

6. Julius Caesar, *The Gallic War*, trans. Carolyn Hammond (Oxford: Oxford University Press, 1996), 35.

7. Rudyard Kipling, *The Works of Rudyard Kipling* (Ware, England: Wordsworth Editions, 1994), 234.

8. David Kilcullen, *The Accidental Guerrilla* (Oxford: Oxford University Press, 2009), xiv.

9. Anthony Everitt, *Cicero: The Life and Times of Rome's Greatest Politician* (New York: Random House, 2003), 187.

10. Ibid., 315–18.

11. Josephus, *The Jewish War*, trans. G. A. Williamson (London: Penguin, 1981).

12. Ibid., esp. 240–50.

13. Ibid., 461–62.

14. David O. Stewart, *Impeached* (New York: Simon and Schuster, 2009), 31–32.

15. Daniel Walker, "A Summary," in *Rights in Conflict*, a report submitted to the National Commission on the Causes and Prevention of Violence (1968).

16. Quoted in Will Durant, *The Story of Philosophy*, 2nd ed. (1927; reprint, New York: Simon and Schuster, 2009), 168.

17. See, for example, Max G. Manwaring and John T. Fishel, "Insurgency and Counter-Insurgency: Toward a New Analytical Approach," *Small Wars and Insurgency* 3, no. 3 (Winter 1972): 272–310; Max G. Manwaring, ed., *Gray Area Phenomena: Confronting the New World Disorder* (Boulder, Colo.: Westview Press, 1993); John T. Fishel, ed., *"The Savage Wars of Peace": Toward a New Paradigm of Peace Operations* (Boulder, Colo.: Westview Press, 1998); and Max G. Manwaring, *Insurgency, Terrorism and Crime: Shadows from the Past and Portents for the Future* (Norman: University of Oklahoma Press, 2008).

18. The principal variables of the dimension "actions versus subversion" are intelligence, psychological operations, and population and resource control.

19. Peter Hopkirk, *The Great Game* (New York: Kodansha International, 1992), 401.

20. See note 18: these are the principal variables making up the dimension "actions versus subversion."

21. See Gary C. Schroen, *First In: An Insider's Account of How the CIA Spearheaded the War on Terror in Afghanistan* (New York: Ballantine Books, 2005); and Gary Berntsen, with Ralph Pezzullo, *Jawbreaker: The Attack on Bin Laden and Al-Qaeda, a Personal Account of the CIA's Key Field Commander* (New York: Crown, 2005).

22. Quoted by John Nagl, *Learning to Eat Soup with a Knife: Counterinsurgency Lessons from Malaya and Vietnam* (Chicago: University of Chicago Press, 2005).

23. Fishel and Manwaring, *Insurgency and Counter-Insurgency*, 204–29.

24. Carl von Clausewitz, *On War*, edited and translated by Michael Howard and Peter Paret (1832; reprint, Princeton, N.J.: Princeton University Press, 1976). Two points must be made here. First, the German word *politika* translates into English as both "politics" and "policy," hence the quote is rendered both ways depending on context. Second, it is the one point on which Clausewitz is entirely consistent throughout all eight books of his work.

BIBLIOGRAPHY

Aguero, Filipe, and Jeffrey Stark. *Fault Lines of Democracy in Post-transition Latin America*. Miami, Fla.: North-South Center Press, 1998.

Alcañiz, Isabella, and Melissa Scheier. "New Social Movements with Old Party Politics: The MTL Piqueteros and the Communist Party in Argentina." *Latin American Perspectives* 34, no. 2 (2007): 157–71.

Anderson, Martin Edward ["Mick"]. *Countries at the Crossroads 2006*. Washington, D.C.: Freedom House, 2006.

Arana, Ana. "How the Street Gangs Took Control of Central America." *Foreign Affairs* (May–June 2005): 98–110.

Aristigui, Gustavo de. *La Yihad en España: La obsession por reconquistar Al-Andalus*. 5th ed. Madrid: La Esfera de los Libros, 2006.

Auyero, Javier. *Poor People's Politics: Peronist Survival Networks and the Legacy of Evita*. Durham, N.C.: Duke University Press, 2001.

———. "When Everyday Life, Routine Politics, and Protest Meet." *Theory and Society*, special issue (June–August 2004): 417–41.

Aznar, Jose Maria. *Latin America: An Agenda for Freedom*. Edited by Miguel Angel Cortes. Madrid: FAES (Foundation for Social Analysis and Studies), 2007.

Baker, Edwin. *Jihadi Terrorists in Europe*. The Hague: Netherlands Institute of International Relations, 2006.

Basombrío Iglesias, Carlos. "The Military and Politics in the Andean Region." *Inter-American Dialogue* (April 2006): 1, 3–12.

Becerra, Oscar. "A to Z of Crime: Mexico's Zetas Expand Operations." *Jane's Intelligence Review*, January 30, 2009.

Beckett, Ian F. W. "The Future of Insurgency." *Small Wars and Insurgencies* (March 2005): 22–36.

Bejarano, Ana Maria, and Eduardo Pizarro. "Colombia: A Failing State?" *ReVista: Harvard Review of Latin America* (Spring 2003): 1–6.

219

Belaunde, Luis Bustamente. "Corrupción y discomposición del estado." In *Pasta básica de cocaina, abuso de drogas,* edited by Federico R. León and Ramiro Castro de la Mata, 301–21. Lima, Peru: Centro de Información y Educación para la Prevención de Abuso de Drogas, 1990.

Bell, J. Bowyer. *Dragonwars.* New Brunswick, N.J.: Transaction Publishers, 1999.

Bergen, Peter L. *Holy War, Inc.: Inside the Secret World of Osama bin Laden.* New York: Free Press, 2001.

Berntsen, Gary, with Ralph Pezzullo. *Jawbreaker: The Attack on Bin Laden and Al-Qaeda, a Personal Account of the CIA's Key Field Commander.* New York: Crown, 2005.

Biddle, Stephen, and Jeffrey A. Friedman. *The 2006 Lebanon Campaign.* Carlisle Barracks, Penn.: Strategic Studies Institute, 2008.

Blank, Steven J. "Class War on a Global Scale: The Leninist Culture of Political Conflict." In Blank, et al., *Conflict, Culture, and History: Regional Dimensions,* 1–55. Maxwell Air Force Base, Ala.: Air University Press, 1993.

———. "Web War I: Is Europe's First Information War a New Kind of War." *Comparative Strategy* 27, no. 3 (2008): 227–47.

Block, Ludo. "Devising a New Counter-Terrorism Strategy in Europe." *Terrorism Monitor* 4, no. 21 (November 21, 2006).

Bozeman, Adda B. "War and the Clash of Ideas." *Orbis* (Spring 1976): 61–102.

Brandon, James. "The Pakistan Connection to the United Kingdom's Jihad Network." *Terrorism Monitor* 6, no. 4 (February 22, 2008).

Bull, Hedley. *The Anarchical Society.* New York: Columbia University Press, 1977.

Bunker, Robert J., and John P. Sullivan. "Cartel Evolution: Potentials and Consequences." *Transnational Organized Crime* (Summer 1998): 55–74.

Burggraff, Winfield J. *The Venezuelan Armed Forces in Politics, 1935–1959.* Columbia: University of Missouri Press, 1972.

Bushnell, David. "Politics and Violence in Nineteenth-Century Colombia." In *Violence in Colombia: The Contemporary Crisis in Historical Perspective,* edited by Charles Bergquist, Ricardo Penaranda, and Gonzalo Sanchez, 11–30. Wilmington, Del.: SR Books, 1992.

Calvo, Ernest F., and Maria Victoria Murillo. "Who Delivers? Partisan Clientelism in the Argentine Electoral Market." *American Journal of Political Science* 48, no. 4 (October 2004): 742–57.

Camus, Albert. *The Rebel.* New York: Alfred A. Knopf, 1956.

Cassidy, Robert M. "Feeding Bread to Luddites: The Radical Fundamentalist Islamic Revolution in Guerrilla Warfare." *Small Wars and Insurgencies* (December 2005): 334–59.

Ceresole, Norberto. *Caudillo, Ejército, Pueblo.* Caracas: Analítica Editora, 1999.

Cerny, Philip. "Neomedievalism, Civil War, and the New Security Dilemma: Globalization as Durable Disorder." *Civil Wars* 1, no. 1 (Spring 1998): 36–64.

Clausewitz, Carl von. *On War*. 1832. Edited and translated by Michael Howard and Peter Paret. Princeton, N.J.: Princeton University Press, 1976.

Cohen, Eliot, Lieutenant Colonel Conrad Crane (U.S. Army, ret.), Lieutenant Colonel Jan Horvath (U.S. Army), and Lieutenant Colonel John Nagl (U.S. Army), "Principles, Imperatives, and Paradoxes of Counterinsurgency," *Military Review* (March–April 2008): 49–53.

Contreras Polgatti, Arturo. *Conflicto y guerra en la post modernidad*. Santiago, Chile: Mago Editores, 2004.

———. *Estrategia: La viejas y las nuevas amenazas*. Santiago, Chile: Mago Editores, 2008.

Corr, Edwin G., and Max G. Manwaring. "The Challenge of Preventive Diplomacy and Deterrence in the Global Security Environment." In *Deterrence in the Twenty-first Century*, edited by Max G. Manwaring, 124–31. London: Frank Cass, 2001.

Crenshaw, Martha, ed. *Terrorism in Context*. University Park: Pennsylvania State University Press, 1995.

Crocker, Chester A. "Engaging Failed States." *Foreign Affairs* (September–October 2003): 32–44.

Cronin, Audry Kurth. "Foreign Terrorist Organizations." CRS Report for Congress. February 6, 2004.

Dahl, Robert A. *Modern Political Analysis*. Englewood Cliffs, N.J.: Prentice-Hall, 1976.

———. *On Democracy*. New Haven, Conn.: Yale University Press, 1998.

David, Steven R. "Saving America from the Coming Civil Wars." *Foreign Affairs* (January–February 1999): 103–116.

Delamata, Gabriela. *Los barrios desbordades, las organicaciones de desocopados del Gran Buenos Aires*. Buenos Aires: Eudeba Libros del Rojas, 2004.

———. *Reporte sobre Plan Jefe y Jefas*. Buenos Aires: Centro de Estudies Legals y Sociales (CELS), 2003.

Dinerstein, Ana C. "Power or Counter-power? The Dilemma of the Piquetero Movement in Argentina Post-crisis." *Capital and Class* no. 81 (Autumn 2003): 1–8.

———. "Roadblocks in Argentina: Against the Violence of Stability." *Capital and Class* no. 74 (Summer 2001): 1–7.

Durant, Will. *The Story of Philosophy*. 1927. 2nd ed. Reprint, New York: Simon and Schuster, 2009.

Easton, David. *A Framework for Political Analysis*. Englewood Cliffs, N.J.: Prentice-Hall, 1965.

———. *The Political System: An Inquiry into the State of Political Science*. 3rd ed. Chicago: University of Chicago Press, 1981.

Ellner, Steve. "Revolutionary and Non-revolutionary Paths of Radical Populism: Directions of the Chavez Movement in Venezuela." *Science and Society*
(April 2005): 160–90.

El pais que proponemos construer. Bogota: Editorial La Oveja Negra, 2001.

Esty, Daniel C., Jack Goldstone, Ted Robert Gurr, Barbara Harff, and Pamela T.
Surko. "The State Failure Project: Early Warning Research for U.S. Foreign
Policy Planning." In *Preventive Measures: Building Risk Assessment and Crisis
Early Warning Systems,* edited by John L. Davies and Ted Robert Gurr, 27–38.
New York: Rowman and Littlefield, 1998.

Everitt, Anthony. *Cicero: The Life and Times of Rome's Greatest Politician.* New
York: Random House, 2003.

Fishel, John T., ed. *"The Savage Wars of Peace": Toward a New Paradigm of Peace
Operations.* Boulder, Colo.: Westview Press, 1998.

Fishel, John T., and Max G. Manwaring. "The SWORD Model of Counterinsurgency: A Summary and Update." *Small Wars Journal* (December 20, 2008):
n.p.

———. *Uncomfortable Wars Revisited.* Norman: University of Oklahoma Press,
2006.

Fishel, Kimbra L. "Challenging the Hegemon: Al Qaeda's Elevation of Asymmetric Insurgent Warfare onto the Global Arena." In *Networks, Terrorism and
Global Insurgency,* edited by Robert J. Bunker, 115–28. London: Routledge,
2005.

Fluherty, Vernon Lee. *Dance of the Millions: Military Rule and the Social Revolution in Colombia, 1930–1956.* Pittsburgh: University of Pittsburgh Press, 1957.

Frechette, Myles R. "Colombia and the United States—The Partnership: But
What Is the Endgame?" Carlisle Barracks, Penn.: Strategic Studies Institute,
2006.

———. *In Search of the Endgame: A Long-Term Multilateral Strategy for Colombia.*
Miami, Fla.: Dante B. Fascell North-South Center at the University of Miami,
February 2003.

Friedrichs, Jorge. "The Meaning of the New Medievalism." *European Journal of
International Relations* 7, no. 4 (2001): 475–502.

Gelb, Leslie H. "Quelling the Teacup Wars." *Foreign Affairs* (November–
December 1994): 5.

Giap, Nguyen. *Peoples' War, Peoples' Army.* New York: Frederick A. Praeger,
1962.

Gibson, Charles. *Spain in America.* New York: Harper and Row, 1966.

Gillespie, Richard. "Political Violence in Argentina: Guerrillas, Terrorists, and
Carapintadas." In *Terrorism in Context,* edited by Martha Crenshaw, 211–48.
University Park: Pennsylvania State University Press, 1995.

Gini, Guillermo E. "Piqueteros: De la protesta social a la accion politica."
Estrategia, CIFE (September 2004): 60–66.

Gray, Colin S. "Deterrence and the Nature of Strategy." In *Deterrence in the Twenty-first Century,* edited by Max G. Manwaring, 17–26. London: Frank Cass, 2001.

Greenlee, Todd. *Crossroads of Intervention: Insurgency and Counterinsurgency Lessons from Central America.* Westport, Conn.: Praeger Security International, 2008.

Griffith, Ivelaw L. *Drugs and Security in the Caribbean: Sovereignty under Siege.* University Park: Pennsylvania State University Press, 1997.

Grynkewich, Alexus G. "Welfare as Warfare: How Violent Non-state Groups Use Social Services to Attack the State." *Studies in Conflict and Terrorism* 31 (2008): 350–70.

Gueron, Carlos. "Introduction." In *Venezuela in the Wake of Radical Reform,* edited by Joseph S. Tulchin, 1–3. Boulder, Colo.: Lynne Rienner Publishers, 1993.

Guillen, Abraham. *Philosophy of the Urban Guerrilla: The Revolutionary Writings of Abraham Guillen.* Translated and edited by Donald C. Hodges. New York: William Morrow, 1973.

Gunaretna, Rohan. *Inside the al-Qai'da Global Network of Terror.* London: Hurst, 2002.

Haahr, Kathryn. "Catalonia: Europe's New Center of Global Jihad," *Terrorism Monitor* 5, no. 11 (June 7, 2007).

———. "GSPC in Italy: The Forward Base of Jihad in Europe." *Terrorism Monitor* 4, no. 3 (February 9, 2006).

———. "GSPC Joins Al Qaeda and France Becomes Top Enemy." *Terrorism Focus* 3, no. 37 (September 26, 2006).

———. "Italy's Underground Islamist Network." *Terrorism Monitor* 5, no. 16 (August 16, 2007).

HACER. *Evolucion de la delincuencia terorista en la Argentina.* Madrid: HACER, n.d.

Hammes, Thomas X. "Fourth Generation Warfare." *Armed Forces Journal* (November 2004): 40–44.

———. *The Sling and the Stone: On War in the 21st Century.* St. Paul, Minn.: Zenith Press, 2006.

Hanson, Roger D. *The Politics of Mexican Development.* Baltimore, Md.: Johns Hopkins University Press, 1971.

Hanson, Victor Davis. *Carnage and Culture.* New York: Anchor Books, 2002.

Heffelfinger, Chris. "Al Qaeda's Evolving Strategy Five Years after September 11." *Terrorism Focus* 3, no. 35 (September 12, 2006).

Herring, Hubert. *A History of Latin America.* New York: Alfred A. Knopf, 1972.

———. *A History of Latin America from the Beginnings to the Present.* New York: Knopf, 1968.

Holloway, John. *Cambiar el mundo sin tomar al poder: El significado de la revolucion hoy.* Buenos Aires: Universidad Autonoma del Pueblo, 2002.

Homer-Dixon, Thomas F. *Environment, Scarcity, and Violence.* Princeton, N.J.: Princeton University Press, 1999.

———. "On the Threshold: Environmental Changes as Causes of Acute Conflict." *International Security* (Fall 1991): 76–116.

Hopkirk, Peter. *The Great Game.* New York: Kodansha International, 1992.

Horowitz, Joel. "Populism and Its Legacies in Argentina." In *Populism in Latin America,* edited by Michael L. Conniff, 22–42. Tuscaloosa: University of Alabama Press, 1999.

Howard, Michael. *The Causes of Wars and Other Essays.* Cambridge, Mass.: Harvard University Press, 1983.

Huntington, Samuel P. *The Clash of Civilizations and the Remaking of World Order.* New York: Simon and Schuster, 1996.

Ibrahim, Raymond. *The Al Qaeda Reader.* New York: Broadway Books, 2007.

Inter-American Development Bank. *Annual Report 1999.* Washington, D.C.: Inter-American Development Bank, 2000.

International Crisis Group. *Colombia's New Armed Groups.* Latin America Report no. 20. Bogota/Brussels: International Crisis Group, May 10, 2007.

Jenkins, Brian. "Redefining the Enemy: The World Has Changed, but Our Mindset Has Not." *Rand Review* (Spring 2004).

Jones, Robert A. *The Soviet Concept of Limited Sovereignty from Lenin to Gorbachev.* New York: St. Martin's Press, 1990.

Jordan, Amos A., William J. Taylor, Jr., and Michael J. Mazarr. *American National Security.* 5th ed. Baltimore, Md.: Johns Hopkins University Press, 1999.

Jordan, David C. *Drug Politics: Dirty Money and Democracies.* Norman: University of Oklahoma Press, 1999.

Jordan, Javier, and Nicola Horsburg. "Mapping Jihadist Terrorism in Spain." *Studies in Conflict and Terrorism* 28, no. 3 (2005): 169–91.

Jordan, Javier, and Robert Wesley. "After 3/11: The Evolution of Jihadist Networks in Spain." *Terrorism Monitor* 4, no. 1 (January 12, 2006).

Josephus. *The Jewish War.* Translated by G. A. Williamson. London: Penguin, 1981.

Judt, Tony. *Postwar: A History of Europe since 1945.* New York: Penguin Press, 2005.

Julius Caesar. *The Gallic War.* Translated by Carolyn Hammond. Oxford: Oxford University Press, 1996.

Kaplan, Robert D. *The Coming Anarchy.* New York: Random House, 2000.

Kilcullen, David. *The Accidental Guerrilla.* Oxford: Oxford University Press, 2009.

Kipling, Rudyard. *The Works of Rudyard Kipling.* Ware, England: Wordsworth Editions, 1994.

Kitson, Frank. *Warfare as a Whole.* London: Faber and Faber, 1987.

Krasner, Steven D. "Abiding Sovereignty." *International Political Science Review* 22, no. 3 (2001): 229–52.

Krasner, Steven D., and Carlos Pascual. "Addressing State Failure." *Foreign Affairs* (July–August 2005): 153–63.

Krause, Lincoln B. "The Guerrillas Next Door." *Low Intensity Conflict and Law Enforcement* (Spring 1999): 34–56.

Laqueur, Walter. "Postmodern Terrorism." *Foreign Affairs* (September–October 1996): 24–36.

Laurent, Gregory, and Baudin O'Hayon. *Big Men, Godfathers, and Zealots: Challenges to the State in the New Middle Ages.* Pittsburgh: University of Pittsburgh Dissertations and Theses, 2003.

Lawson, Guy. "The War Next Door." *Rolling Stone* (November 13, 2008): 74–111.

Le Carré, John. *The Constant Gardener.* New York: Scribner, 2001.

Lee, Rensselaer W., III. *The White Labyrinth.* New Brunswick, N.J.: Transaction, 1990.

Leech, Garry M. "An Interview with FARC Commander Simon Trinidad," *NACLA Report on the Americas* 34, no. 2 (September–October 2000).

Legler, Thomas. "Bridging Divides, Breaking Impasses: Civil Society in the Promotion and Protection of Democracy in the Americas." FOCAL Policy Paper. Ottawa: FOCAL, 2006.

Lenin, V[ladimir]. I[lyich]. *The Lenin Anthology.* Edited by Robert C. Tucker. New York: W. W. Norton, 1975.

Levitsky, Steven. "From Labor Politics to Machine Politics: The Transformation of Party-Union Linkages in Argentine Peronism." *Latin American Research Review* 38, no. 3 (2003): 3–36.

Levy, Daniel, and Gabriel Szekelup. *Mexico: Paradoxes of Stability and Change.* Boulder, Colo.: Westview Press, 1983.

Liddell-Hart, B. H. *Strategy.* 2nd ed. New York: Praeger, 1954.

Locke, John. *Of Civil Government: Second Treatise of Civil Government.* 1689. New York: Gateway, n.d.

Lombardi, John V. *Venezuela: The Search for Order, the Dream of Progress.* Oxford: Oxford University Press, 1982.

Lozano, Claudio. "Acerca del programa nacional para jefes y jefas de hogar sin empleo." Central de los Trabajadores Argentina, Instituto de Estudios y Formación.

Lupsha, Peter A. "The Role of Drugs and Drug Trafficking in the Invisible Wars." In *International Terrorism: Operational Issues,* edited by Richard H. Ward and H. E. Smith, 177–90. Chicago: Office of International Criminal Justice, University of Illinois at Chicago, 1988.

———. "Towards an Etiology of Drug Trafficking and Insurgent Relations: The Phenomenon of Narcoterrorism." *International Journal of Comparative and Allied Criminal Justice* 13, no. 2 (Fall 1989): 60–74.

Machiavelli, Niccolò. *The Art of War*. 1521. New York: DaCapo Press, 1965.

———. *The Prince and the Discourses*. New York: Random House, Modern Library, 1950.

Manwaring, Max G. *A Contemporary Challenge to State Sovereignty: Gangs and Other Illicit Transnational Criminal Organizations in Central America, El Salvador, Mexico, Jamaica, and Brazil*. Carlisle Barracks, Penn.: Strategic Studies Institute, 2007.

———, ed. *Gray Area Phenomena: Confronting the New World Disorder*. Boulder, Colo.: Westview Press, 1993.

———. *Insurgency, Terrorism, and Crime: Shadows from the Past and Portents for the Future*. Norman: University of Oklahoma Press, 2008.

———. *Latin America's New Security Reality: Irregular Asymmetric Conflict and Hugo Chavez*. Carlisle Barracks, Penn.: Strategic Studies Institute, 2007.

———. "La sobenia bajo asedio: Las Pandillas y otras organizaciones criminales en Centroamerica y en Mexico," *Air and Space Power Journal* (2nd trimester 2008): 25–41.

———. *Street Gangs: The New Urban Insurgency*. Carlisle Barracks, Penn.: Strategic Studies Institute, 2005.

Manwaring, Max G., and Edwin G. Corr. "The Central Political Challenge in the Global Security Environment: Governance and Legitimacy." In *The Search for Security: A U.S. Grand Strategy for the Twenty-first Century*, edited by Max G. Manwaring, Edwin G. Corr, and Robert H. Dorff, 46–61. Westport, Conn.: Greenwood, 2003.

Manwaring, Max G., and John T. Fishel. "Insurgency and Counter-Insurgency: Toward a New Analytical Approach." *Small Wars and Insurgencies* 3, no. 3 (Winter 1992): 272–310.

Manwaring, Max G., and William J. Olson, eds. *Managing Contemporary Conflict: Pillars of Success*. Boulder, Colo.: Westview Press, 1996.

Manwaring, Max G., and Courtney E. Prisk. "The Umbrella of Legitimacy." In *Gray Area Phenomena: Confronting the New World Disorder*, ed. Max Manwaring, 77–91. Boulder, Colo.: Westview Press, 1993.

Mao Tse-Tung. *On Guerrilla Warfare*. 1937 (1961). Edited by Samuel B. Griffith. Reprint, Champaign: University of Illinois Press, 2000.

Marighella, Carlos. *The Manual of the Urban Guerrilla*. Chapel Hill, N.C.: Documentary Publications, 1985.

Maritain, Jacques. *Man and the State*. Chicago: University of Chicago Press, 1951.

Marks, Thomas A. *Colombian Army Adaptation to FARC Insurgency*. Carlisle Barracks, Penn.: Strategic Studies Institute, 2002.

———. "Ideology of Insurgency: New Ethnic Focus or Old Cold War Distortions?" *Small Wars and Insurgencies* (Spring 2004): 107–28.

———. *Maoist Insurgency since Vietnam*. London: Frank Cass, 1996.

———. *Sustainability of Colombian Military/Strategic Support for "Democratic Security."* Carlisle Barracks, Penn.: Strategic Studies Institute, 2005.

———. "Urban Insurgency." *Small Wars and Insurgencies* (Autumn 2003): 100–157.

Matthews, Matt M. *We Were Caught Unprepared: The 2006 Hezbollah-Israeli War.* Occasional Paper 26. Ft. Leavenworth, Kans.: U.S. Army Combined Arms Center Combat Studies Institute Press, 2008.

McAdams, Doug, Sidney Tarrow, and Charles Tilly. *The Dynamics of Contention.* Cambridge: Cambridge University Press, 2001.

Metz, Steven, and Douglas V. Johnson II. *Asymmetry and U.S. Military Strategy: Definition, Background, and Strategic Concepts.* Carlisle Barracks, Penn.: Strategic Studies Institute, 2001.

Metz, Steven, and Raymond Millen. *Future Wars/Future Battlespace: The Strategic Role of American Landpower.* Carlisle Barracks, Penn.: Strategic Studies Institute, 2003.

Meyers, David J. "Venezuela's *Punto Fijo* Party System." In *Authoritarianism and Corporatism in Latin America,* edited by Howard J. Wiarda, 141–72. Gainesville: University Press of Florida, 2004.

Mill, Hayder. "Tangled Webs: Terrorist and Organized Crime Groups." *Terrorism Monitor* 4, no. 1 (January 13, 2006).

Miller, David C. "Back to the Future: Restructuring Foreign Policy in a Post–Cold War World." In *Managing Contemporary Conflict: Pillars of Success,* edited by Max G. Manwaring and William J. Olson, 13–28. Boulder, Colo.: Westview Press, 1996.

Ministry of the Interior and Kingdom Relations. *Violent Jihad in the Netherlands: Current Trends in the Islamist Terrorist Threat.* The Hague: Ministry of the Interior and Kingdom Relations, n.d.

Molano, Alfred. "The Evolution of the FARC: A Guerrilla Group's Long History." *NACLA Report on the Americas* 34, no. 2 (September–October 2000).

Moyano, Maria Jose. *Argentina's Lost Patrol: Armed Struggle, 1969–1979.* New Haven, Conn.: Yale University Press, 1995.

Nagl, John. *Learning to Eat Soup with a Knife: Counterinsurgency Lessons from Malaya and Vietnam.* Chicago: University of Chicago Press, 2005.

Naím, Moisés. "From Normalcy to Lunacy." *Foreign Policy,* no. 141 (March–April 2004): 104–103.

Needler, Martin C. *Mexican Politics: The Containment of Conflict.* New York: Dragon, 1982.

Norton, Richard Augustus. *Hezbollah: A Short History.* Princeton, N.J.: Princeton University Press, 2007.

O'Donnell, Guillermo A. *Modernization and Bureaucratic Authoritarianism.* Berkeley: University of California Press, 1979.

Olson, William J. "International Organized Crime: The Silent Threat to Sovereignty." *Fletcher Forum* (Summer–Fall 1997): 65–80.

Peters, Ralph. "Constant Conflict." *Parameters* (Summer 1997): 10.

———. "The Culture of Future Conflict." *Parameters* (Winter 1995–96): 18–27.

Picco, Giandominico. "The Challenge of Strategic Terrorism." *Terrorism and Political Violence* 17 (2005): 11–16.

Porch, Douglas. "Uribe's Second Mandate, the War, and the Implications for Civil-Military Relations in Colombia." *Strategic Insights* 5, no. 2 (February 2006).

Porch, Douglas, and Maria Jose Rasmussen. "Demobilization of Paramilitaries in Colombia: Transformation or Transition?" *Studies in Conflict and Terrorism* 31, no. 6 (2008): 520–40.

Qiao Liang and Wang Xiangsui. *Unrestricted Warfare*. Beijing: PLA Literature and Arts Publishing House, 1999.

Rabassa, Angel, and Peter Chalk. *Colombian Labyrinth*. Santa Monica, Calif.: RAND, 2001.

Rapley, John. "The New Middle Ages." *Foreign Affairs* (May–June 2006): 93–103.

Renard, Thomas. "German Intelligence Describes a 'New Quality' in Jihadi Threats." *Terrorism Focus* 5, no. 7 (February 20, 2008).

Restrepo, Luis Alberto. "The Crisis of the Current Political Regime and Its Possible Outcomes." In *Violence in Colombia: The Contemporary Crisis in Historical Perspective*, edited by Charles Bergquist, Ricardo Penaranda, and Gonzalo Sanchez, 273–92. Wilmington, Del.: SR Books, 1992.

Rich, Paul. "Al Qaeda and the Radical Islamic Challenge to Western Strategy." *Small Wars and Insurgencies* (Spring 2003), 45–46.

Robinson, Linda. *Tell Me How All This Ends: General David Petraeus and the Search for a Way Out of Iraq*. New York: Public Affairs, 2008.

Rojas Aravena, Francisco. *El crimen organizado internacional: Una grave amenaza a la democracia en America Latina y el Caribe*. San Jose, Costa Rica: FLACSO, 2006.

———. "Nuevo contexto de seguridad internacional: Nuevos desafios, nuevas oportunidades." In *La seguridad en America Latina pos 11 Septiembre*, edited by Francisco Rojas Aravena, 23–43. Santiago, Chile: FLACSO, 2003.

Ropp, Steve. *The Strategic Implications of the Rise of Populism in Europe and South America*. Carlisle Barracks, Penn.: Strategic Studies Institute, 2005.

Rosenau, James. *Turbulence in World Politics*. Princeton, N.J.: Princeton University Press, 1990.

Rostow, Eugene V. *Toward Managed Peace: The National Security Interests of the United States, 1759 to the Present*. New Haven, Conn.: Yale University Press, 1993.

Rousseau, Jean-Jacques. *The Social Contract*. 1762. Translated by G.D.H. Cole. Chicago: Encyclopedia Britannica, 1952.

―――. *The Social Contract*. Translated by Charles Frankel. New York: Hafner Publishing Company, 1947.

Rowling, J. K. *Harry Potter and the Sorcerer's Stone*. New York: Arthur A. Levine Books, 1997.

Rubio, Mauricio. "La justicia en una sociedad violenta." In *Reconocer la guerra para construir la paz*, edited by Maria Victoria Llorente and Malcom Deas, 201–235. Bogota: Ediciones Uniandes CERED Editorial Norma, 1999.

Sageman, Marc. *Leaderless Jihad: Terror Networks in the 21st Century*. Philadelphia: University of Pennsylvania Press, 2007.

Salvachea, Ramiro. "Clientelism in Argentina: Piqueteros and Relief Payment Plans for the Unemployed—Misunderstanding the Role of Civil Society." *Texas International Law Journal* 43 (Spring 2008): 295.

Samii, Abas William. "A Stable Structure on Shifting Sands: Assessing the Hezbollah-Iran-Syria Relationship." *Middle East Journal* 62, no. 1 (Winter 2008): 32–53.

Sanchez Ceren, Salvador. *Con suenos se escribe la vida: Autobiografía de un revolucionario salvadoreño*. Mexico City: Ocean Press and Ocean Sur, 2008.

Sarkesian, Sam C. *U.S. National Security: Policymakers, Processes, and Politics*. Boulder, Colo.: Lynne Riener Publishers, 1989.

Scheuer, Michael. "Al Qaeda Doctrine for International Political Warfare." *Terrorism Focus* 3, no. 42 (November 1, 2006).

―――. "Al-Qaeda's Insurgency Doctrine: Aiming for a 'Long War.'" *Terrorism Focus* 3, no. 8 (February 28, 2006).

―――. "Al Qaeda's New Generation: Less Visible and More Lethal." *Terrorism Focus* 2, no. 18 (October 3, 2005).

―――. "Al-Zawahiri's September 11 Video Hits Main Themes of Al-Qaeda Doctrine." *Terrorism Focus* 3, no. 36 (September 19, 2006).

―――. "Is Global Jihad a Fading Phenomenon?" *Terrorism Focus* 5, no. 13 (April 1, 2008).

―――. "Osama bin Laden: Taking Stock of the 'Zionist-Crusader War.'" *Terrorism Focus* 3, no. 16 (April 25, 2006).

Schoultz, Lars. *National Security and United States Policy toward Latin America*. Princeton, N.J.: Princeton University Press, 1987.

Schroen, Gary C. *First In: An Insider's Account of How the CIA Spearheaded the War on Terror in Afghanistan*. New York: Ballantine Books, 2005.

Scott, Robert E. *Mexican Government in Transition*. Urbana: University of Illinois Press, 1964.

Sharp, Jeremy M., coord. "Lebanon: The Israel-Hamas-Hezbollah Conflict." CRS Report for Congress. September 15, 2006.

Shifter, Michael. *Hugo Chavez: A Test for U.S. Policy*. Washington, D.C.: Inter-American Dialogue, 2007.

―――. "In Search of Hugo Chavez." *Foreign Affairs* (May–June 2006): 46.

Singer, Peter W. "Peacekeepers, Inc." *Policy Review,* no. 119 (June–July 2003).

Skidmore, Thomas E., and Peter H. Smith. *Modern Latin America.* New York: Oxford University Press, 1984.

Smith, Paul E. *On Political War.* Washington, D.C.: National Defense University Press, 1989.

Smith, Rupert. *The Utility of Force: The Art of War in the Modern World.* New York: Alfred A. Knopf, 2007.

Spencer, David. *Colombia's Paramilitaries: Criminals or Political Force?* Carlisle Barracks, Penn.: Strategic Studies Institute, 2001.

Stewart, David O. *Impeached.* New York: Simon and Schuster, 2009.

Strauss, Leo, and Joseph Cropsey. *History of Political Philosophy.* 2nd ed. Chicago: University of Chicago Press, 1972.

Sullivan, John P. "Maras Morphing: Revisiting Third Generation Gangs." *Global Crime* (August–November 2006): 488–90.

———. "Terrorism, Crime, and Private Armies." *Low Intensity Conflict and Law Enforcement* (Winter 2002): 239–53.

Sullivan, John P., and Robert J. Bunker. "Drug Cartels, Street Gangs, and Warlords." In *Nonstate Threats and Future Wars,* edited by Robert J. Bunker, 40–53. London: Frank Cass, 2003.

Sun Tzu. *The Art of War.* Translated by Samuel B. Griffith. Oxford: Oxford University Press, 1971.

Talmon, J. L. *The Origins of Totalitarian Democracy.* New York: Praeger, 1968.

Tannenbaum, Frank. *Ten Keys to Latin America.* New York: Alfred A. Knopf, 1962.

Thomas, Hugh. *Armed Truce.* New York: Atheneum, 1987.

Tocqueville, Alexis de. *Democracy in America.* Edited by J. Mayer and Max Lerner. New York: Harper and Row, 1996.

Torres, Vladimir. *The Impact of "Populism" on Social, Political, and Economic Development in the Hemisphere.* FOCAL Policy Paper. Ottawa: FOCAL (Canadian Foundation for the Americas), 2006.

Trager, Frank N., and Philip S. Kronenberg, eds. *National Security and American Society.* Lawrence: University Press of Kansas, 1973.

Ulph, Stephen. "Mujahideen Pledge Allegiance on the Web." *Terrorism Focus* 2, no. 22 (November 29, 2005).

Urbina, Andrés Benavente, and Julio Alberto Cirino. *La democracia defraudada [Democracy Defrauded].* Buenos Aires: Grito Sagrado, 2005.

U.S. Army and U.S. Marine Corps, with forewords by General David M. Petraeus and Lieutenant General James F. Amos and by Lieutenant Colonel John A. Nagle, and with an introduction by Sarah Sewall. *The U.S. Army–Marine Corps Counterinsurgency Field Manual.* Chicago: University of Chicago Press, 2007. Originally published as U.S. Army Field Manual 3-24 and

Marine Corps Warfighting Publication No. 3-335 (both issued December 15, 2006).

Vargas Llosa, Alvaro. "The Return of the Idiot." *Foreign Policy*, no. 160 (May–June 2007): 54–61.

Velasco, José Luis. *Insurgency, Authoritarianism, and Drug Trafficking in Mexico's Democratization*. New York: Routledge, 2005.

Verstrynge Rojas, Jorge. *La guerra periférica y el Islam revolucionario: Origines, reglas, y ética de la guerra asimétrica [Peripheral. Indirect) War and Revolutionary Islam: Origins, Regulations, and Ethics of Asymmetric War]*. Special Edition for the Army of the Bolivarian Republic of Venezuela, IDRFAN, Enlace Circular Militar. Madrid: El Viejo Topo, 2005.

Vidino, Lorenzo. *Al Qaeda in Europe*. Amherst, N.Y.: Prometheus Books, 2006.

Vinci, Anthony. "The Strategic Use of Fear by the Lord's Resistance Army." *Small Wars and Insurgencies* 16 (December 2005): 360–81.

Walker, Daniel. "A Summary." In *Rights in Conflict*, a report submitted to the National Commission on the Causes and Prevention of Violence. 1968.

Wiarda, Howard J., ed. *Authoritarianism and Corporatism in Latin America*. Gainesville: University Press of Florida, 2004.

Williams, Phil. *From the New Middle Ages to a New Dark Age: The Decline of the State and U.S. Strategy*. Carlisle Barracks, Penn.: Strategic Studies Institute, 2008.

Winograd Committee. "Winograd Committee Final Report." Israel Ministry of Foreign Affairs. January 30, 2008.

Wolff, Jonas. "(De-)Mobilizing the Marginalised: A Comparison of the Argentine Piqueteros and Ecuador's Indigenous Movement." *Journal of Latin American Studies* 39, no. 1 (2007): 1–29.

Yin, Robert K. *Case Study Research: Design and Methods*. 2nd ed. Thousand Oaks, Calif.: Sage Publications, 1994.

Zambelis, Chris. "Hezbollah Reacts to Israel's Winograd Report." *Terrorism Focus* 4, no. 13 (May 8, 2007).

Zibechi, Raúl. *Genealogia de la revuelta, Argentina: La sociedad en movimento*. Buenos Aires: Letra Libre and Nordan Comunidad, 2003.

INDEX

CPSIA information can be obtained
at www.ICGtesting.com
Printed in the USA
LVHW041943140122
708423LV00017B/685/J

9 780806 141466